盛唐卷

敦煌服饰文化图典

（下册）

刘元风　赵声良　主编

中国敦煌历代服饰图典

『十四五』国家重点图书

The Illustration of China Dunhuang Costumes in History

The 14th Five-Year Plan of National Important Books

The Illustration of Dunhuang Costume Culture

The High Tang Dynasty

Volume Two

Editors-in-Chief
Liu Yuanfeng
Zhao Shengliang

国家出版基金项目
NATIONAL PUBLICATION FOUNDATION

中国纺织出版社有限公司

·北京·

内 容 提 要

丛书选择敦煌历代壁画（尊像画、故事画、经变画、史迹画、供养人像等）和彩塑中的典型人物形象，包括佛国世界中的佛陀、菩萨、弟子、天王、飞天、伎乐人，以及世俗世界中的国王、王后、贵族、平民等，对其反映的服饰造型和图案进行整理绘制，并对其文化内涵进行理论研究。

书中每一单元的内容包括敦煌典型洞窟的壁画或彩塑原版图片、根据此图像整理绘制的服饰效果图和重点图案细节图，以及重要图像的服饰复原图。书中还收录了与主题相关的学术论文，并对图像的历史背景、服饰特征、艺术风格等进行了深入研究和说明。

本书适合院校师生、科研人员、设计师和敦煌文化艺术爱好者学习借鉴，同时具有一定的典藏价值。

图书在版编目（CIP）数据

敦煌服饰文化图典. 盛唐卷. 下册 / 刘元风、赵声良主编 . -- 北京：中国纺织出版社有限公司，2023.8
中国敦煌历代服饰图典　"十四五"国家重点图书
ISBN 978-7-5229-0623-2

Ⅰ . ①敦⋯　Ⅱ . ①刘⋯　②赵⋯　Ⅲ . ①敦煌学—服饰文化—中国—唐代—图集　Ⅳ . ① K878.45

中国国家版本馆 CIP 数据核字（2023）第 094161 号

DUNHUANG FUSHI WENHUA TUDIAN
SHENGTANGJUAN XIACE

策划编辑：董清松　孙成成　　　责任编辑：孙成成
责任校对：王花妮　　　　　　　责任印制：王艳丽

中国纺织出版社有限公司出版发行
地址：北京市朝阳区百子湾东里A407号楼　邮政编码：100124
销售电话：010—67004422　传真：010—87155801
http://www.c-textilep.com
中国纺织出版社天猫旗舰店
官方微博 http://weibo.com/2119887771
北京雅昌艺术印刷有限公司印刷　各地新华书店经销
2023年8月第1版第1次印刷
开本：635×965　1/8　印张：40
字数：524千字　定价：598.00元　印数：1—1000册

中国纺织出版社有限公司
官方微博

中国纺织出版社有限公司
官方微信

序

　　象征着中西方文化交流和友好往来的"丝绸之路"，是古代人民用巨大的智慧创造出来的一条光彩夺目的美丽缎带，而敦煌莫高窟则是镶嵌在这条缎带上的一颗闪闪发光的明珠。在延续一千多年的敦煌石窟艺术中，各个历史时期的彩塑、壁画人物的服装和服饰图案非常丰富精彩，是我们取之不尽、用之不竭的艺术源泉。

　　我有幸自小跟随父亲常书鸿在敦煌学习壁画临摹，后来又因梁思成、林徽因两位先生走上了工艺美术的人生道路。父亲曾经提醒我："不要忘记你是敦煌人……也是应该把敦煌的东西渗透一下的时候了！"多年来，我一直盼望对包括服饰图案在内的敦煌图案进行全面系统的研究。1959年，我和李绵璐、黄能馥两位老师曾去敦煌石窟专门收集整理服饰图案，这些原稿在20世纪80年代首先由香港万里书店出版为《敦煌历代服饰图案》一书。书中的图案部位示意图，是当时刚留校不久的刘元风老师和他的同学赵茂生老师帮忙绘制的。20世纪90年代，我又带领我的研究生团队对敦煌图案进行了分类整理，相继出版了《中国敦煌历代装饰图案》和《中国敦煌历代装饰图案（续编）》，完成了我的部分心愿。

　　2018年6月，敦煌服饰文化研究暨创新设计中心在北京服装学院正式挂牌成立。中心有两个主要任务：一是把敦煌服饰文化艺术作为专题进行深入化和系统性研究，二是根据研究成果和体会进行创新性设计运用，涵盖了继承与发展的永恒主题。围绕着这两个主要任务，中心举办并展开了学术论坛、科研项目、人才培养、设计展演等一系列具有学术高度且富有社会影响力的活动，获得了院校、科研院所及行业的广泛好评。

　　此次由北京服装学院和敦煌研究院两家单位合作推出的"中国敦煌历代服饰图典"系列丛书，集中了各自在敦煌学和服饰文化研究方面的专长和优势，在理论和实践两个方面进行继承和创新。一方面，以历史时代的划分进行敦煌石窟历史背景和服饰文化的理论阐述；另一方面，基于理论研究展开敦煌石窟壁画和彩塑服饰的艺术实践。丛书不仅以整理临摹的方式将壁画、彩塑的整体服饰效果和局部图案进行整理绘制，同时也在尊重服饰历史和工艺规律的基础上，将壁画和彩塑中的人物服饰形象进行艺术再现，使之更加直观生动和贴近时代。

　　对敦煌历代服饰文化的研究和继承工作，还仅仅是一个开始，绝不是结束。我希望更多的年轻学者、设计师、艺术家、学子们，能够继续前行，继续努力，做出更多的成绩，为弘扬我们引以为豪的敦煌艺术贡献自己的力量！

原中央工艺美术学院（现清华大学美术学院）院长

2020年9月

Preface

The Silk Road, which symbolizes the cultural exchange and friendship between China and the West, is a dazzling and beautiful ribbon created by the ancient people with their great wisdom. Mogao Grottoes is a shining pearl inlaid in this ribbon. It has lasted more than one thousand years, and the costumes and patterns on costumes of painted sculptures and mural figures in various historical periods are very rich and wonderful, which are our inexhaustible artistic source.

I was very lucky to learn mural copying at Dunhuang with my father Chang Shuhong when I was a child. Later, I took the road of arts and crafts because of Mr. Liang Sicheng and Mrs. Lin Huiyin. My father once reminded me: "Don't forget that you are from Dunhuang, you should study Dunhuang deeper..." For many years, I have been looking forward to a comprehensive and systematic study of Dunhuang patterns, including clothing patterns. In 1959, two scholars, Mr. Li Mianlu and Mr. Huang Nengfu and me went to Dunhuang Grottoes to collect and arrange clothing patterns. In the 1980s, these manuscripts were first published by Hong Kong Wanli Bookstore as the book *Costume Patterns from Dunhuang Frescoes*. The sketch illustration in the book was drawn by Mr. Liu Yuanfeng and his classmate Mr. Zhao Maosheng. In the 1990s, I led my postgraduate team to sort out Dunhuang patterns, and successively published the books *Decorative Designs from China Dunhuang Murals* and *Decorative Designs from China Dunhuang Murals* (*continued*), which fulfilled part of my wish.

In June 2018, Dunhuang Costume Culture Research and Innovation Design Center was officially established in Beijing Institute of Fashion Technology. The center has two main tasks: one is to take Dunhuang costume culture and art as a special topic for in-depth and systematic research; the other is to carry out innovative design and application according to the research results and experience, covering the eternal theme of inheritance and development. Around these two main tasks, the center has held and launched a series of activities with academic height and social influence, such as academic forum, scientific research project, talent training, design exhibition and so on, which has been widely praised by colleges, research institutes and the industry.

The Illustration of China Dunhuang Costumes in History jointly launched by Beijing Institute of Fashion Technology and Dunhuang Research Academy focus on their respective expertise and advantages in Dunhuang study and clothing culture research, inherits and innovates in theory and practice. On the one hand, the historical background and costume culture of Dunhuang Grottoes are expounded theoretically according to the division of historical times. On the other hand, the art practice of Dunhuang Grottoes murals and painted sculptures costumes are carried out based on theoretical research. The series not only arrange and draw the overall clothing effect and patterns of murals and painted sculptures in the way of sorting and copying, but also on the basis of respecting the clothing history and technological rules. The series also make artistic reproduction of the characters' clothing images in the murals and painted sculptures, so as to make them more intuitive, dynamic and close to the times.

This research and inheritance work of Dunhuang costume culture is just a beginning, by no means the end. I hope that more young scholars, designers, artists and students could continue moving forward, working hard and making more achievements to contribute the promotion of Dunhuang art which we are proud of !

Chang Shana

Former president of Central Academy of Arts and Crafts

(now Academy of Fine Arts, Tsinghua University)

September 2020

目录

敦煌莫高窟盛唐菩萨像服饰的造型特征

刘元风　常　青

盛唐时期（705—781年），敦煌处于唐王朝的直接管辖之下，社会稳定，政治、经济空前开放与繁荣，为敦煌的艺术发展创造了良好的机遇，加之丝绸之路的繁盛，使盛唐时期的敦煌石窟艺术无论是壁画还是彩塑水准都运到了前所未有的高度，形成了敦煌所特有的民族风格与时代特色。

敦煌盛唐壁画及彩塑中遗存大量菩萨图像，历史悠久、数量庞大且序列完整，形态变化丰富，多数菩萨的服饰形制及图案、色彩保存完好。从中展现出大唐文化背景下独特的审美观念及时代特征，对探究多元文化及多民族文化的交融互动具有重要价值。

一、敦煌盛唐菩萨像概况

菩萨，具名菩提萨埵（Bodhisattva），旧释为大道心众生、道众生等，新释为大觉有情、觉有情等。谓是求道之大心人，故曰道心众生，求道求大觉之人，故曰道众生，大觉有情❶。"凡修持大乘六度，求无上菩提，利益众生，于未来成就佛果的修行者都可以称为菩萨❷。"

1. 敦煌盛唐菩萨像的基本分类

敦煌盛唐洞窟中所见菩萨像基本分为两类：一类是佛经中有记载、有名号的菩萨画像，如观世音菩萨、大势至菩萨、文殊菩萨、普贤菩萨、地藏菩萨等；另一类是佛像旁听法的胁侍菩萨、听法菩萨等供养类菩萨像，通常无具体名号及题记。

2. 敦煌盛唐菩萨像的表现形式

敦煌盛唐洞窟中的菩萨像表现形式分为两种：一种是彩塑菩萨像，另一种是壁画菩萨像。彩塑菩萨像通常位于主室龛为、外两侧，或站，或半跏坐，又或胡跪，为主尊佛像的胁侍菩萨。壁画菩萨像的呈现方式较为丰富。

首先，在洞窟壁画相对独立的壁面中处于主体位置的菩萨像。其中最为显著的是位于洞窟主室西壁龛外两侧的单尊菩萨像，盛唐时期立姿单尊菩萨像出现的概率较前期相对普遍，加之位置显眼，形象突出，服饰绘制也更加精美绝伦。另外，敦煌盛唐壁画中的文殊菩萨像与普贤菩萨像也常见以主尊形象表现，不仅有尊像式的文殊、普贤菩萨像，更多的是在文殊变和普贤变中，均以对称形式出现，形象表现为文殊菩萨驾狮子、普贤菩萨乘白象。除此之外，也有单独表现在维摩诘经变"问疾品"中的文殊菩萨像。

其次，在洞窟壁画中属于主尊胁侍及其他听法的众菩萨像，主要包括经变画及说法图中的众菩萨。目前，学术界约定俗成的经变，是专指将某一部佛经的主要内容或几部相关的佛经组成首尾完整、主次分明的大幅壁画❸。敦煌盛唐时期，由于净土宗的发展，经变画达到鼎盛，通常由主尊佛像及胁侍菩萨与

---

❶ 丁福保. 佛学大辞典（全2册）[M]. 上海：上海书店出版社，2015：2115.
❷ 罗华庆. 敦煌石窟全集·尊像画卷 [M]. 香港：商务印书馆（香港）有限公司，2002：96.
❸ 施萍婷. 敦煌石窟全集·阿弥陀经画卷 [M]. 香港：商务印书馆（香港）有限公司，2002：5.

供养菩萨以及听法信众组成，场面宏大，其中的菩萨像大多无榜题，或站或坐，组合数量及形式较多。由于经变画的发展，敦煌盛唐时期的说法图数量相对减少，题材主要包括释迦佛说法图、阿弥陀佛说法图、药师佛说法图、弥勒佛说法图等，常见的组合形式为一佛二弟子与二菩萨，也有一佛二弟子与四菩萨或有一佛二弟子与六菩萨，甚至有一佛二弟子与十菩萨等。

另外，还有因特定故事情节而出现的菩萨像。例如，"维摩诘经·香积佛品"中出现的化菩萨，通常以胡跪或侧身而立、双手捧钵、敬献香饭的形象出现。

二、敦煌盛唐菩萨像服饰造型特征

伴随丝绸之路的繁盛及唐代纺织技艺的发达，敦煌盛唐菩萨像服饰呈现出与隋、初唐时期相比更加精美的状态。其造型比例生动逼真，款式变化丰富多样，纹样与色彩也更加繁复华美，表现出与盛唐世俗服饰一脉相承的富丽景象。

1. 比例协调与曲线之美

敦煌盛唐时期的菩萨像与早期菩萨像已有诸多不同，最明显的区别在于身体形态的变化。

首先，就身体的比例来看，敦煌早期石窟中菩萨像的头部较大，头身不完全合乎比例，这一特征在隋代塑像中变得更为突出。为了给信众在供养时营造一种高大威严的感觉，隋代菩萨像普遍头部偏大，肩部较宽，上半身占比较大；至初唐时期，菩萨像已逐步呈现为与真人近似的身体比例；敦煌盛唐菩萨像的头身比例更加写实，也更加注重对人体生理构造的诠释，基本与真人无二，甚至更加匀称、修长。

其次，对肢体动态的表达方面，相较于敦煌早期端庄肃立、姿势单一、变化较少，表现手法较为朴实的菩萨像，盛唐菩萨像造型强化其写实性，肌肉感与关节动态更加自然真实，追求健康与健美，身体姿态越发多变，或身体前倾，或扭腰出胯，呈现出婀娜多姿的曲线之美。

最后，对菩萨神态的刻画方面，敦煌盛唐菩萨像与早期菩萨形象多夸张与想象的表现有较大区别，神态刻画更加细腻，神采栩栩如生，肌肤生动逼真，面相丰腴、慈祥柔美，女性化程度也越加明显。这一变化体现出儒家文化影响下的中国社会对女性柔美、慈爱等民族文化特性的崇尚。

其中较有代表性的为莫高窟盛唐第45窟主室西壁龛内的胁侍菩萨（图1）。这两尊菩萨面相丰满圆润，肌肤光洁细腻，头部云髻高耸，曲眉丰颊，双目微垂，嘴角上翘，神情恬静慈祥，体态呈"S"形站姿，小腹微凸，宛如贵妇，立于莲花台上。这两尊彩塑菩萨像在整体艺术处理上已经突破了宗教艺术的审美范畴，其形象和形体的塑造，将宗教范式与唐代世俗女性形象融为一体，特别是菩萨胸、腰、臀曲线的节奏感与律动美感的塑造，无疑达到了盛唐时期彩塑艺术的最高审美水准。相较魏晋时期致力于超凡脱俗的神貌，敦煌盛唐时期壁画

图1 莫高窟盛唐第45窟主室西壁龛内的胁侍菩萨

及彩塑中的菩萨像具有了更多的亲切感与人情味，这种造型艺术风格的出现，主要得益于盛唐开放包容与兼收并蓄的社会风尚，以及对传统大胆革新的开拓精神。

2．款式丰富与多元交融

整体来看，敦煌盛唐时期的菩萨像服饰造型主要包含两个方面：一方面为菩萨像服装形制，包括络腋、僧祇支、披帛、长裙、阔腿裤、腰裙、腰襻、裙带及彩绦；另一方面为菩萨像所佩戴装饰品，包括首服（宝冠、宝缯）及配饰（璎珞、颈饰、臂钏、手镯、耳珰、指环）。

（1）菩萨像服装形制：从服装形制来看，敦煌盛唐菩萨像基本衣着搭配形式主要有三种：第一种，络腋+长裙+腰裙；第二种，披帛+长裙+腰裙；第三种，络腋/僧祇支+披帛+长裙+腰裙。

络腋+长裙+腰裙为敦煌盛唐菩萨像服饰中最常见的衣着搭配方式。据《一切经音义》第四十一卷记载："络掖衣（唐云掩腋衣，本制此衣恐污汗三衣，先以此衣掩右腋，交络于左肩上，然后披着三衣。四分律中错用为覆髆者，误行之久矣不可改也）。"[1]可知络腋最初作为僧人内衣穿着。敦煌盛唐菩萨像服饰中的络腋通常为正反双色的条带形织物，穿着样式不仅为经文中所记载的"掩右腋，交络于左肩上"，同时也出现了掩左腋并交络于右肩的式样。络腋自肩部下垂，从腋下绕至身后，再从肩部绕回身前，之后，分为在肩前系结或在肩前直接下垂以及在肩前缠绕三种表现形式（图2）。

（a）莫高窟第166窟主室东壁　　　（b）莫高窟第320窟主室西壁　　　（c）莫高窟第217窟主室西壁
　　南侧观世音菩萨　　　　　　　　龛外南侧观世音菩萨　　　　　　龛外北侧观世音菩萨

图2　敦煌盛唐菩萨像络腋的三种表现形式

---

❶ 一切经音义，CBETA电子佛典集成（CBETA，Chinese Electronic Tripitaka Collection Feb）[M/CD].T54，No.2128，P.581，c21.

敦煌盛唐菩萨像所穿着的长裙在造型上基本可以分为三种：第一种为透明纱罗长裙，裙身轻纱透体，腰间围系华丽的织锦腰裙，另有腰裙外围裹长帛腰襻，在腰前或腰侧系结后两端下垂，如莫高窟盛唐第66窟主室西壁龛外北侧观世音菩萨的服饰（图3）；第二种为单层织锦长裙，裙身华美，腰间同样围系华丽的织锦腰裙，如莫高窟盛唐第45窟主室西壁龛内两身胁侍菩萨的服饰（图1）；第三种为双层织锦长裙，内部衬裙较长，衬裙在腰间翻出下垂，内外裙在腰间系带，并在腰侧翻卷，使外裙两侧裙角提起，底部露出内部衬裙，或有垂至裙侧的璎珞将裙身兜起，如莫高窟盛唐第194窟主室西壁龛内北侧胁侍菩萨的服饰（图4）。敦煌盛唐菩萨像除穿着长裙来搭配腰裙与腰襻外，更有在腰前垂裙带，腰襻外加系彩绦，于腰两侧打结并垂于身前及身侧，更显菩萨服饰的华贵不凡。

在敦煌盛唐壁画及彩塑中，披帛见于菩萨、天王、力士等尊像服饰中，也出现在飞天、乐舞伎等天人服饰中。段文杰先生在研究中认为佛教服饰中的"仙帔"形式是受来自波斯、大秦、中亚的男女"并有巾帔"的影响而形成的特殊装饰❶。日本学者吉村怜将其称为"天衣"❷。并且，在《陀罗尼集经》中的确有将菩萨像所披的长巾状装饰物称为"天衣"的记载："画大般若菩萨像……菩萨身上着罗绮。绣作

襆裆。其腰以下着朝霞裙。于上画作黄色花袭。天衣笼络络于两臂。腋间交过出其两头。俱向于上。微微屈曲如飞飏势。其两手腕皆着环钏。"❸敦煌盛唐菩萨像服饰中的披帛通常披于双肩，在身前交互搭于左右手臂垂下。从披帛的材质来看，可分为透明纱质披帛与正反面双色披帛两种。透明纱质披帛通常较纤细，正反面双色披帛一般中间较宽，两端细窄（图5）。

"披帛+长裙+腰裙"这种上身赤裸，仅披天衣的搭配方式在敦煌早期的壁画中较为多见，显示出早期外来风格的影响在敦煌唐代菩萨像服饰中一直存在延续。

"络腋+披帛+长裙+腰裙"为前两种衣着搭配

图3 莫高窟盛唐第66窟主室西壁龛外北侧观世音菩萨

图4 莫高窟盛唐第194窟主室西壁龛内北侧胁侍菩萨

图5 莫高窟盛唐第205窟主室南壁胁侍菩萨

❶ 敦煌研究院. 敦煌艺术大辞典［M］. 上海：上海辞书出版社，2019：458.
❷ 吉村怜. 古代佛、菩萨像的衣服及其名称［C］. 2005年云冈国际学术研讨会论文集（研究卷）：164–179.
❸ 陀罗尼集经，CBETA[M/CD].T18，No.0901，P.0805，a30.

方式的结合，此种形式在敦煌盛唐的菩萨像服饰中也比较流行，而"僧祇支+天衣+长裙+腰裙"的搭配方式相较前者则为数不多。《大唐西域记》曰："僧却崎（唐言掩腋。旧曰僧祇支，讹也。）覆左肩，掩两腋，左开右合，长裁过腰。" [1] 僧祇支在敦煌隋及初唐菩萨服饰中较为多见，而盛唐菩萨服饰中并不常见。其中较为特殊的当属莫高窟第217窟主室西壁龛外南侧的大势至菩萨，但此菩萨所着僧祇支并不同于经文中所讲的"覆左肩"，而是覆右肩，覆右肩而坦左肩的僧祇支在敦煌壁画中不止此例，并多见于主尊右侧胁侍菩萨所穿着，与左侧胁侍菩萨服饰呈对称呼应。

除以上三种衣着搭配形式外，敦煌盛唐菩萨像服饰中还出现了菩萨着袈裟的形式，如莫高窟盛唐第328窟主室西壁龛顶的说法图中，两身胁侍菩萨身着与主尊佛陀相同形制、相同颜色的袈裟，以象征其身份尊贵（图6）。

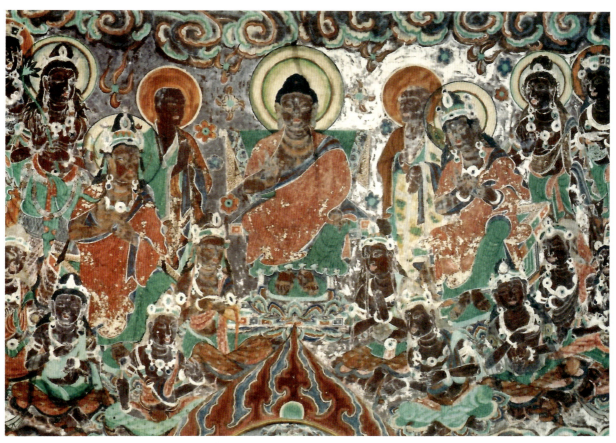

图6　莫高窟盛唐第328窟主室西壁龛顶天衣座弥勒说法图

（2）菩萨像所佩戴装饰品：敦煌盛唐时期，菩萨像服饰的装饰意味更加强烈，菩萨像所佩戴的装饰品也更加繁复。这一时期的菩萨多为头束高髻戴宝冠，高耸的发髻纹理清晰，与当时宫廷妇女雍容华贵的装扮如出一辙。

宝冠有大小之分，其中珠宝冠最为常见，其上搭配七宝、日月装饰、火焰纹宝珠、植物纹装饰等，造型变化极为丰富。日月装饰最早流行于萨珊波斯钱币中的王者头冠之上，由北魏时期传入中国，并在菩萨冠上作为流行的装饰，在云冈石窟及敦煌早期洞窟中多以仰月的造型出现，在敦煌盛唐时期则流行日月造型，由波斯王者的冠饰转而为菩萨的冠饰，似乎体现了中国的佛教信仰者对菩萨的理解

[1] 大唐西域记，CBETA[M/CD]. T51，No.2087，P.0876，a21.

（图7、图8）❶。植物纹装饰的宝冠中最为特殊的当属莫高窟盛唐第45窟主室西壁龛内的菩萨宝冠（图9），此窟西龛内多身菩萨头戴卷叶纹的宝冠，也可称其为"卷云纹冠"❷。此种冠饰也出现在莫高窟盛唐第217窟主室北壁及莫高窟盛唐第188窟主室东壁，为供养贵妇和供养天女所戴之冠（图10、图11）。因此类冠饰在印度佛教人物装饰中未曾出现过，由此可推断此类冠饰应是来源于世俗，为佛教本土化的产物。除此之外，还有两种宝冠较为重要，即化佛冠与宝瓶冠，因其具有辨别菩萨身份的特殊作用。《佛说观无量寿佛经》曰："次亦应观观世音菩萨。……顶上毘楞伽摩尼妙宝。以为天冠。其天冠中有一立化佛。高二十五由旬。"❸ "次观大势至菩萨。……此菩萨天冠有五百宝莲华。……顶上肉髻如钵头摩花。于肉髻上有一宝瓶。盛诸光明普现佛事。余诸身相如观世音等无有异。"❹由此可知，化佛冠与宝瓶冠为判断观世音菩萨与大势至菩萨身份的重要依据（图12、图13）。

图7　莫高窟北魏第285窟主室西壁龛内南侧戴仰月冠的菩萨

图8　莫高窟盛唐第23窟主室西壁龛内南侧戴日月冠的菩萨

图9　莫高窟盛唐第45窟主室西壁龛内戴卷叶纹宝冠的菩萨

图10　莫高窟盛唐第217窟主室北壁戴卷叶纹宝冠的贵妇

图11　莫高窟盛唐第188窟主室东壁北侧戴卷叶纹宝冠的天女

图12　莫高窟盛唐第217窟主室西壁龛外北侧观世音菩萨戴化佛冠

图13　莫高窟盛唐第217窟主室西壁龛外南侧大势至菩萨戴宝瓶冠

同时，敦煌盛唐时期的菩萨像服饰多出现璎珞，相较早期"金玉环带"❺的样式，盛唐时期的璎珞材质更加丰富，珠玉鲜花缀满全身，用色也考虑到了与其服装色彩的搭配统一；在造型方面基本分为项饰璎珞与全身璎珞两种，项饰璎珞仅装饰于颈部与胸部，而全身璎珞则与颈饰璎珞连接下垂，在腹部相汇

❶ 赵声良. 敦煌石窟北朝菩萨的头冠［J］. 敦煌研究，2005〔3〕：8-17.
❷ 阮立. 唐敦煌壁画女性服饰美学研究［M］. 兰州：兰州大学出版社，2015: 64.
❸ 佛说观无量寿佛经，CBETA[M/CD]. T12, No.0365, P.0343, c11.
❹ 佛说观无量寿佛经，CBETA[M/CD]. T12, No.0365, P.0344, a18.
❺ 敦煌研究院. 敦煌艺术大辞典［M］. 上海：上海辞书出版社，2019: 458.

呈"X"形，底部下垂并在侧面将长裙兜住，与服装产生互动关系。无论在造型还是色彩方面，敦煌盛唐菩萨璎珞均注重与菩萨服装、头冠、臂钏、手镯及耳饰的搭配相统一。

3. 材料多样与精湛技艺

社会富足与文化交流促进了唐代纺织业的迅速发展，纺织品种类繁多，织、绣、印、染、绘等技艺精湛，繁盛的纺织品与染织工艺在敦煌盛唐菩萨服饰中得到了充分体现。

敦煌盛唐壁画中，多见菩萨身着透明纱质长裙，裙身轻盈透体，其上点缀小散花纹，应为唐代时期贵重的纱縠织物❶。对比出土于新疆吐鲁番阿斯塔那墓的唐代朵花纹印花纱（图14），其为用防染剂印花的平纹纱，黄色地上显白花❷，与敦煌盛唐菩萨所着纱裙极为相似。另外，敦煌盛唐菩萨服饰中常见唐代时期流行的扎经染色工艺图像，此种工艺因其特殊的织造方式而呈现出与众不同的模糊效果，使其在图像中具备了可识别性，如莫高窟盛唐第217窟主室东壁的菩萨络腋图案，对比日本正仓院藏扎经染色织物，两者的表现形式基本一致（图15、图16）❸。此外，莫高窟第194窟菩萨裙带中又见唐代极为盛行的绞缬工艺。

除了传统的蜡缬、绞缬、凸纹木版印花、碱剂防染印花等工艺外，夹缬、镂空纸版印花等工艺也在唐代流

图14　唐代朵花纹印花纱（新疆吐鲁番阿斯塔那墓出土）

图15　莫高窟盛唐第217窟主室东壁菩萨服饰

图16　扎经染色织物（日本正仓院藏）

行❹。将莫高窟盛唐第45窟主室西壁龛内胁侍菩萨的腰裙图案与日本正仓院藏唐代浅红地花叶纹夹缬薄绢相对比（图17、图18），可知此腰裙表现的正是唐代高超的夹缬工艺。通过上述对比，足以证明敦煌盛唐菩萨服饰中所反映出的工艺与当时纺织品的高度一致性。

---

❶ 谭蝉雪. 敦煌石窟全集·服饰画卷［M］. 香港：商务印书馆（香港）有限公司，2015: 142.

❷ 王乐. 中国古代丝绸设计素材图系·汉唐卷［M］. 杭州：浙江大学出版社，2018: 113.

❸ 王可，刘元风. 6—12世纪扎经染色织物纹样及其东西方交流［J］. 装饰，2021（8）：78-81.

❹ 杨建军. 隋唐染织工艺在敦煌服饰图案中的体现［J］. 服饰导刊，2012（2）：4-10.

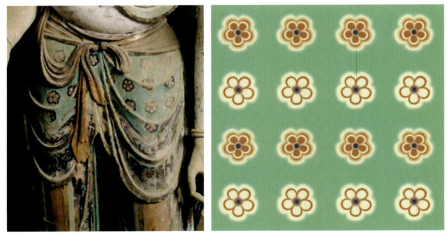 

图17　莫高窟盛唐第45窟主室西壁龛内胁侍菩萨腰裙图案　　　　　　　图18　唐代浅红地花叶纹
夹缬薄绢（日本正仓院藏）

4．绚丽多彩与和谐统一

富丽堂皇、绚丽夺目是敦煌盛唐壁画及彩塑给人最直观的感受，繁荣开放与兼容并包的态度使唐代服饰色彩日趋华丽。

在中国，传统"五方正色"体系一直作为主要的色彩文化观念与色彩象征形式，而这一观念随着文化交融的繁盛在唐代有了突破。敦煌藏经洞及吐鲁番阿斯塔那等地已经出土了大量唐代时期色彩富丽、花色繁复的唐代纺织品。《吐鲁番出土丝织物中的唐代印染》一文中提到："吐鲁番出土的唐代丝织物中，所见到的色谱据不完全统计，不同色阶的红有银红、水红、猩红、绛红、绛紫五色；黄有鹅黄、菊黄、杏黄、金黄、土黄、茶褐六色；青、蓝有蛋青、天青、翠蓝、宝蓝、赤青（紫色有蓝光，古称'绀'色）、藏青六色；绿有葫绿、豆绿、叶绿、果绿、墨绿五色；连同黑、白共达二十四色之多。"❶可见唐代时期的色彩观已经打破传统，实现了多元融合。

在敦煌盛唐壁画及彩塑中最常见的色彩为五色：红色、蓝色、绿色、棕黑色和白色。红色颜料主要为朱砂与铅丹，这两种颜料在当时均从中亚传入；蓝色颜料主要为石青与青金石，石青产自我国祁连山或中原地区，而青金石则从阿富汗、印度等国传入；绿色颜料为石绿与氯铜矿；棕黑色颜料主要为二氧化铅；白色颜料主要为方解石❷。由此说明，丝绸之路的繁盛为文明的交融创造了条件，使既内敛又华贵的东方色彩与风情浓郁的异域色彩在敦煌实现了完美融汇。

红与绿的对比色互相搭配寻求和谐是盛唐时期菩萨服饰色彩应用中最显著的特点。无论是正反红绿双色络腋，还是红色长裙搭配绿色腰裙，又或是红地绿色显花长裙，这种对比强烈的组合在敦煌盛唐菩萨服饰上均展现出完美的契合度，体现出唐代独特的色彩调和形式与色彩调和观念，展现出了敦煌盛唐菩萨服饰色彩在对比中寻求和谐统一的时代风格。

5．花团锦簇与中西合璧

在唐代政治开明、兼收并蓄的社会背景下，敦煌盛唐时期的石窟艺术达到了前所未有的富丽与繁华。壁画及彩塑中的菩萨服饰图案题材丰富、绚丽多彩，既有传统的几何填花纹、团花纹、十字散花纹，又有来自西域与中原相融合而成的卷草纹，还有佛教色彩浓郁的宝相花纹，完全不同于前期的清雅风格，呈现出花团锦簇与中西合璧的时代特色。

整体来看，敦煌盛唐菩萨服饰的图案在洞窟内展现出两种不同的表现特征。

❶ 武敏. 吐鲁番出土丝织物中的唐代印染［J］. 文物，1973（10）：37-47.
❷ 李最雄. 敦煌莫高窟唐代绘画颜料分析研究［J］. 敦煌研究，2002（4）：11-18，110.

第一，同一洞窟内或同一铺经变画或说法图内的菩萨服饰图案，造型与色彩表现基本类似。例如，莫高窟盛唐第217窟主室南壁说法图中的菩萨服饰图案，统一为四瓣或六瓣蓝绿散花，花地分明。这种四等分十字型与六等分的散花在盛唐菩萨服饰中较为常见，多表现于菩萨的络腋、长裙或腰裙中（图19）。

第二，菩萨服饰的图案与同一洞窟壁画的装饰图案表现出一定的关联性。例如，莫高窟盛唐第66窟主室西壁龛外北侧观世音菩萨的腰裙图案，为百花草纹，此图案在敦煌盛唐洞窟中其他菩萨服饰上均未出现，而另见于莫高窟盛唐第66窟主室北壁的边饰图案上（图20、图21）。又如，莫高窟盛唐第194窟主室西壁龛内南侧胁侍菩萨长裙上的卷草图案，与第194窟主室西壁龛沿上的卷草边饰图案基本一致（图22、图23）。可见，在壁画绘制过程中，画匠们已考虑到了人物服饰图案与整体洞窟壁画风格的整体统一。

图19　莫高窟盛唐第217窟主室南壁说法图中的菩萨服饰图案

图20　莫高窟盛唐第66窟主室西壁龛外北侧观世音菩萨的腰裙图案

图21　莫高窟盛唐第66窟主室北壁的百花草纹边饰图案　　图22　莫高窟盛唐第194窟主室西壁龛内南侧胁侍菩萨长裙上的卷草图案　　图23　莫高窟盛唐第194窟主室西壁龛沿上的卷草边饰图案

三、小结

佛教自印度传入中国本土，至敦煌，已跨越了地域与种族、时空与文化的限制，融汇了来自古西亚、中亚、南亚与东南亚文明，吸收了西域少数民族、中原本土文化，形成了风格独特、形式丰富的敦煌石窟艺术，同时结合盛唐特殊的时代风貌与地域文化，也造就了敦煌盛唐菩萨像服饰独一无二的地位及影响。

首先，敦煌盛唐菩萨像服饰文化具有承前启后的意义。一方面，盛唐时期的菩萨像服饰在造型上对前期进行了继承与相应发展。例如：盛唐时期的菩萨像上依旧可以看出对传统佛教艺术造像特征的保留，如上半身裸露、披发等特点，宗教性特征依然显著，但在面容上已与早期有了很大变化，盛唐菩萨像大部分面容丰腴，慈眉善目，雍容华贵；在服装上，继承了隋及初唐时期的大部分形制，但也较前期有了新的变化，如络腋、天衣等形制在盛唐时期依旧盛行，而隋及初唐时期所流行的僧祇支在盛唐菩萨服饰中却比较少见；在配饰上，承袭了隋及初唐时期环佩璎珞的式样，并有了进一步的发展，呈现出珠围翠绕的装饰效果。另一方面，敦煌盛唐菩萨像服饰对后期起到了重要范式作用。敦煌石窟中的菩萨像服饰从北朝发展至隋、初唐、盛唐，在造型、纹样、色彩等方面都发生了更加丰富的变化，至盛唐后期风格已逐步趋于稳定，为中晚唐及后期菩萨像服饰提供了重要的粉本范式。

其次，敦煌盛唐菩萨像服饰在中国传统服饰文化中具有重要地位。敦煌盛唐壁画及彩塑中遗存的大量菩萨像服饰，其形制丰富、图案精美、造型华丽，不仅对研究唐代佛教服饰文化具有重要价值，而且盛唐菩萨像服饰风格变化所表现出的宗教性、民族性与世俗化之间的有序互动和融合，完美展现出中国传统服饰文化在发展过程中的继承性、包容性与创造性，是丝绸之路文化背景下的优秀典范，对当代服饰文化的交流发展具有重要的现实价值。

Stylistic Features of Bodhisattva Costumes at Dunhuang Mogao Grottoes During the High Tang Dynasty

Liu Yuanfeng   Chang Qing

Dunhuang was under the direct jurisdiction of the Tang imperial court during the high Tang Dynasty (705—781). With social stability and unprecedented political and economic openness and prosperity, it created great opportunities for the development of Dunhuang art. The art of the Dunhuang caves during the high Tang Dynasty reached unprecedented heights in terms of both murals and polychrome sculptures due to the prosperity of the Silk Road, creating a unique national style and epoch characteristics of Dunhuang.

A large number of Bodhisattva images survived in Dunhuang's high Tang Dynasty murals and polychrome sculptures, which have a long history, complete chronological order, and a rich variety of forms. Most of them have well-preserved costume forms, patterns, and colours. They show the unique aesthetic concepts and characteristics of the times in the context of Tang culture, which are of great value in exploring the integration and interaction of multicultural and multi-ethnic cultures.

1. An overview of the high Tang Dynasty Bodhisattva images in Dunhuang

The old interpretation of Bodhisattva is "Dao-mind sentient beings" or "Dao sentient beings", etc. And the new interpretation is greatly enlightened sentient beings or enlightened sentient beings, etc. It is said to be the person who seeks the great mind of the Way, just as it is said to be the person who seeks the Way and seeks the great consciousness. Any practioner who practices the six paramita, seeks supreme bodhichitta, benefit all sentient beings, and achieve Buddhahood in the future can become a Bodhisattva.

1.1 Basic classification of Bodhisattva images in Dunhuang during the high Tang Dynasty

The Bodhisattva images seen in the Tang caves in Dunhuang are basically divided into two categories: the first category is the Bodhisattva portraits with names recorded in Buddhist sutras, such as Avalokitesvara Bodhisattva, Mahasthamaprapta Bodhisattva, Manjusri Bodhisattva, Samantabhadra Bodhisattva, Ksitigarbha Bodhisattva, etc.; the second category is like attendant Bodhisattva and Dharma-listening Bodhisattva such kind of offering Bodhisattva who are adjacent to Buddha, listening to the Dharma, without a specific name or inscription.

1.2 Representation of the Bodhisattva images in Dunhuang during the high Tang Dynasty

There are two types of Bodhisattva images in the caves of the high Tang Dynasty in Dunhuang: one is the polychrome statue of Bodhisattva, and the other is the Bodhisattva images from murals. The polychrome sculptures of Bodhisattvas are usually located inside or outside of the main chamber niche, standing, sitting, half cross-legged, or kneeling, who are the attendant Bodhisattvas of the Buddha. There are various ways to present the Bodhisattva image in murals.

The first kind is the Bodhisattva images painted in the main position of relatively independent wall paintings inside the caves. The most notable one is the single Bodhisattva sculpture set outside the west niche of the main chamber in the cave among them. The probability of a single standing Bodhisattva sculpture's appearance in the high Tang period was relatively higher compared with the previous period. Moreover, the location of the Bodhisattva sculpture was conspicuous and the image was prominent, so the costumes were painted much more exquisitely. In addition, the portraits of Manjusri and Samantabhadra often appeared as main figures in the murals of the high Tang Dynasty in Dunhuang. Not only did they appear as single holy portrait of Manjusri and Samantabhadra, but also they were painted in the Manjusri and Samantabhadra sutra transformation tableaux. They all appeared in a symmetrical form, with Manjusri riding on a lion and Samantabhadra riding on a white elephant. Besides, Manjusri images are individually painted in the "Ask the Diseases" chapter of "Vimalakīrti-Nirdeśa-Sūtra".

The second kind is the Bodhisattva images that belong to attendant Bodhisattva or offering Bodhisattva surrounding the Buddha in the cave paintings, which are mainly included in the sutra transformation tableaux or Dharma-preaching scenes. At present, the sutra transformations conventionally acknowledged by academia are those that were established in academic circles referring to a certain Buddhist scripture or several related Buddhist scriptures into a large-scale mural with a complete sequence. Due to the development of Pure Land Buddhism, sutra transformation tableaux reached their peak during the high Tang Dynasty in Dunhuang. They were usually composed of the main Buddha image in the centre, who were surrounded by the attendant Bodhisattva or the offering Bodhisattva, without inscriptions, sitting or standing in multiple combinations and forms. The number of Dharma-preaching scenes in the high Tang Dynasty in Dunhuang was relatively reduced because of the development of sutra transformation tableaux. The themes are mainly included in the Dharma-preaching scenes of Shakyamuni Buddha, Amitabha Buddha, Medicine Buddha, Maitreya Buddha, etc. The common combination form is: one Buddha, two disciples and two Bodhisattvas; one Buddha, two disciples, and four Bodhisattvas; or one Buddha, two disciples, and six Bodhisattvas; or even one Buddha, two disciples, and ten Bodhisattvas.

There are also Bodhisattva images due to specific storylines. For example, the transformative Bodhisattva from the "Vimalakīrti-Nirdeśa-Sūtra: The Feast Brought by the Emanated Incarnation" usually appears in the kneeling posture or standing sideways, holding a bowl and offering rice.

2. Costume features of the Bodhisattva images in the high Tang Dynasty in Dunhuang

The Dunhuang high Tang Bodhisattva statue costume shows a more exquisite style compared to the Sui and early Tang periods, along with the prosperity of the Silk Road and the development of textile skills in the Tang Dynasty. The proportions of Bodhisattva sculptures are vivid and realistic, with rich and varied styles, and the patterns and colours are increasingly complex and flamboyant, showing the same richness as the secular costumes of the high Tang Dynasty.

2.1 Proportional coordination and the beauty of curves

Bodhisattva images of the Dunhuang high Tang period are different from those of the early period, and the most obvious difference is the change of body shape.

First of all, in terms of body proportions, the Bodhisattva in the early Dunhuang caves is large, and the head to body are not in perfect proportion, a feature that became more prominent in the Sui Dynasty statues. In order to create a tall and majestic feeling for the faithful believers when looking up, the Bodhisattva's head is becoming larger, the shoulders are wider, and the upper body proportion is enlarged. The Bodhisattva gradually acquired a similar body proportion compared with a real person until the early Tang period. The Bodhisattva's head-to-body ratio is more realistic in the high Tang Dynasty, and artists also paid more attention to the interpretation of human physiological structure, which is basically the same as that of a real person, even more proportionate and slender.

Secondly, in terms of the expression of body dynamics, the high Tang Dynasty Bodhisattvas statues strengthened their realism with a more naturalistic sense of muscle and joint, as opposed to earlier Solemn ones in Dunhuang, which had a single posture and less variation. In the pursuit of realism as well as health and fitness, the postures of Bodhisattvas statues are increasingly varied. Their bodies lean forward, or twist at the waist, revealing the beauty of graceful curves.

Once again, in the depiction of the Bodhisattva's demeanor, there is a big difference between the Bodhisattva images of the high Tang Dynasty and earlier ones that are exaggerated and imaginative performances. The Bodhisattva's posture becomes more and more delicate, with vivid and lifelike expressions, a plump face, and an increasing degree of femininity. This kind of change reflects the reverence of Chinese society for national cultural characteristics such as women's kindness and softness under the influence of Confucian culture.

The representative among them is the attendant Bodhisattva of the Mogao Grottoes in the high Tang Dynasty, Cave 45 in the main chamber of the west wall niche (Fig. 1). The two Bodhisattvas sculptures have full and rounded faces, smooth and delicate skin, high ushnisha, curved eyebrows and cheeks, slightly dropped eyes, upturned corner of mouth with a serene and benign look. Their bodies are in an "S"-shaped standing posture on the lotus

Fig. 1 Mogao Grottoes, high Tang Dyansty, Cave 45, west niche of the main chamber, attendant Bodhisattva

platform, with a slightly bulging belly, like a noblewoman. The overall artistic treatment of the two polychrome Bodhisattva statues has broken through the aesthetic scope of religious art, and the images and forms are shaped in such a way as to blend the religious paradigm with the secular female image of the Tang Dynasty. In particular, the shaping of the rhythmic and rhythmic aesthetics of the Bodhisattva's chest, waist, and buttocks has undoubtedly reached the highest aesthetic level of painted sculpture art in the prosperous Tang Dynasty. Compared with the extraordinary deities of the Wei and Jin Dynasties, the Bodhisattva images in the murals and polychrome sculptures of the Tang Dynasty in Dunhuang had more intimacy and humanistic sense. The emergence of this type of artistic style is mainly due to the openness and tolerance of the high Tang Dynasty, which displayed a pioneering spirit of bold innovation over tradition.

2.2 Richness of style and diversity

As a whole, the costume features of Bodhisattva images during the high Tang period at Dunhuang consist of two main aspects: first is the costume form of the Bodhisattva, including the Luoye, Sankaksika, silk scarf, long skirt, loose pants, Nivi, waist loop, skirt belt, and colourful sash; second is the ornaments worn by the Bodhisattva, including the head ornament (crown and riband) and accessories (keyūra, necklace, armlets, bracelets, earrings, rings).

2.2.1 Clothing form of Bodhisattva statue

There are three kinds of clothing forms of Bodhisattva in the Dunhuang high Tang Dynasty: the first is Luoye + long skirt + Nivi; the second is the silk scarf + long skirt + Nivi; and the third is the Luoye/Sankaksika + silk scarf + long skirt + Nivi.

The combination of Luoye + long skirt + Nivi was the most common way for Bodhisattva to be dressed in the high Tang Dynasty at Dunhuang. It is recorded in *The Sound and Meaning of the Tripitaka Volume 41* that Luoye was used to cover the axilla for fear of polluting the Three Clothes. Use this dress to cover the right axilla, cross it on the left shoulder, and drape it with the Three Clothes. It is wrongly used to cover the shoulder blade in Dharmagupta-Vinaya, and it has been impossible to change the misconduct for a long time. It can be seen that the Luoye was first worn as a monk's undergarment. The Luoye of the Bodhisattva sculpture in Dunhuang is usually a two-coloured striped fabric on the front and back. The dressing style is not only the style of covering the right axilla and interlacing it on the left shoulder as recorded in the sutras, but also in the style of covering the left axilla and interlacing it on the right shoulder. The Luoye is wrapped from the shoulders down to the back of the body, then wrapped from the shoulders back to the front of the body. It can be divided into three forms: tying a knot in front of the shoulder or hanging directly in front of the shoulder, wrapping in front of the shoulder (Fig. 2).

The long skirts worn by the Bodhisattva images of the high Tang Dynasty in Dunhuang can be basically divided into three types in terms of shape: the first is a long skirt made of transparent gauze, with a gorgeous brocade Nivi around the waist. The skirt is wrapped with long silk waist loops, and the two ends hang down in front of the waist, such as the clothes of Avalokitesvara on the north side outside the west niche of the main chamber of Cave 66 Mogao Grottoes in the high Tang Dynasty (Fig. 3). The second is a single-layer brocade long skirt with a gorgeous body and a gorgeous brocade Nivi around the waist, like the costumes of the two Bodhisattvas in the west niche of the main chamber of Cave 45 in the Mogao Grottoes (Fig. 1). The third is a double-layered brocade long skirt with a longer inner petticoat, and the petticoat turned over and drooped from the waist. The inner and outer skirts are tied around the waist, and they are rolled at the waist side so that the skirt

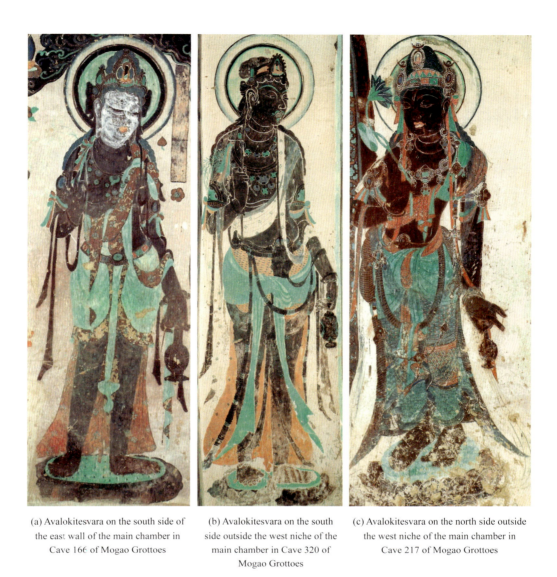

(a) Avalokitesvara on the south side of the east wall of the main chamber in Cave 166 of Mogao Grottoes

(b) Avalokitesvara on the south side outside the west niche of the main chamber in Cave 320 of Mogao Grottoes

(c) Avalokitesvara on the north side outside the west niche of the main chamber in Cave 217 of Mogao Grottoes

Fig. 2 Three representations of the Bodhisattva statues Luoye in the high Tang Dynasty in Dunhuang

corners of the outer skirt are lifted and the inner petticoat is exposed at the bottom. There is a keyūra that hangs down to the side of the skirt and turns the skirt up, such as the costume of the attendant Bodhisattva on the north side of the west niche of the main chamber of Cave 194 of the Mogao Grottoes (Fig. 4). In addition to wearing a long skirt with a Nivi and a waist loop, the Bodhisattva sculpture in Dunhuang also hangs a skirt belt in front of the waist, and the waist loop is tied with a colourful sash. Knotted on both sides of the waist and hanged in front of or beside the body, it is more obvious to show the extravagant dress of Bodhisattva during the high Tang Dynasty.

In the murals and painted sculptures of the Tang Dynasty in Dunhuang, silk scarf can be seen in the costumes of statues such as Bodhisattvas, heavenly kings, and guardians, as well as in the costumes of celestial beings such as flying Apsaras and music dancers. In his research, Mr. Duan Wenjie believes that the form of celestial scarf in Buddhist clothing is a special decoration formed by the influence of men and women from Persia, Rome and Central Asia who "have scarves together". Japanese scholar Rei Yoshimura called it "Celestial garment". Moreover, there is indeed a record in the "Dharani Collection Sutra" that the long scarf-like decorations worn by the Bodhisattva statues are called "Celestial garment": "One should paint the Great Prajna Bodhisattva. The Bodhisattva is dressed in brocade. Bodhisattva is wearing a skirt of the morning glory. Yellow flowers are painted on it. The celestial garment is wrapped around both arms. The interaxillary crosses out of its two ends, which face upward. And it slightly flexed like a soaring momentum. Its two wrists are adorned with bracelets". The silk scarf of the Bodhisattva in the high Tang Dynasty of Dunhuang is usually draped over the shoulders, and hangs down in front of body. Judging from the material of the silk scarf, it can be divided into two types: transparent gauze silk scarf and reversible two-coloured silk scarf. The transparent gauze silk scarf is usually slender, and the two-coloured silk scarf is generally wider in the middle and narrow at both ends (Fig. 5).

Fig. 3 Mogao Grottoes, Cave 66 in the high Tang Dynasty, Avalokitesvara on the north side outside the west niche of the main chamber	Fig. 4 Mogao Grottoes, high Tang Dynasty, Cave 194, attendant Bodhisattva inside the north side in the west niche of the main chamber	Fig. 5 Mogao Grottoes, high Tang Dynasty, Cave 205, south wall of the main chamber, attendant Bodhisattva

It is very common to find the combination of silk scarf + long skirt + Nivi with a naked upper body and only wearing celestial garment in early Dunhuang murals, indicating that the influence of early foreign styles continued on Bodhisattva costumes in the high Tang Dynasty.

The Luoye + silk scarf + long skirt + Nivi is a combination of the first two clothing styles, which were also popular in the Bodhisattva costumes in the high Tang Dynasty in Dunhuang. It is less common to find the matching form of Sankaksika + celestial garment + long skirt + Nivi compared with the former one. According to *Great Tang Records from the Western Regions*, Sankaksika covers the left shoulder and two axilla, while its left side open and close right side, with long cut over the waist. Sankaksika is frequently painted on the Bodhisattva costumes in the Sui and early Tang Dynasty, while it is not common on the Bodhisattva costumes in the high Tang Dynasty. One of the special examples is the Mahasthamaprapta Bodhisattva on the south side outside the west niche of the main chamber of Mogao Cave 217. The Sankaksika is not the same as covering the left shoulder in the sutra, but covers the right shoulder. This is not the only case that covers the right shoulder and bares the left shoulder in Dunhuang murals, which is more commonly seen on the right attendant Bodhisattva costume beside the Buddha, and it corresponds to the left attendant Bodhisattva.

In addition to the above three styles, there is also a costume of a Bodhisattva wearing Kashaya in the high Tang Dynasty in Dunhuang. For example, two Bodhisattvas wear the same form and same colour of Kashaya as Buddha in the Dharma-preaching scene on the top of the west niche in the main chamber of Cave 328, symbolizing their dignity (Fig. 6).

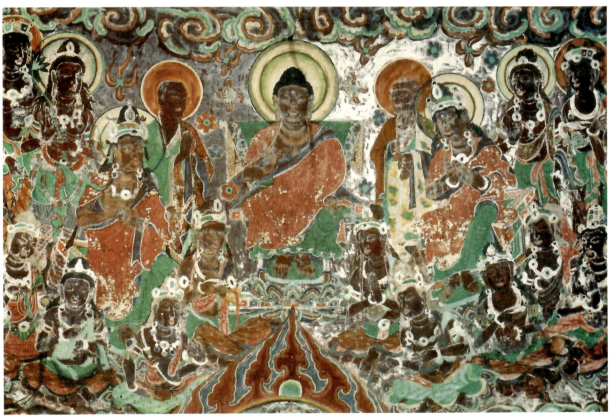

Fig. 6 Maitreya's preaching scene on the top of the west niche in the main chamber, Cave 328 in the high Tang Dynasty, Mogao Grottoes

2.2.2　Accessories worn by Bodhisattva images

The decorative sense of the Bodhisattva costumes was more intense during the high Tang Dynasty in Dunhuang, and the accessories worn by the Bodhisattva were also more complicated. Most of the Bodhisattvas wore crowns with high buns on their heads during this period. The high buns had the same clear textures as court women's elegant and luxurious dresses at that time.

There are different sizes of crowns, among which jewel crowns are the most common ones, with seven treasures, the sun and moon decorations, flame-patterned jewels decorations, plant-pattern decorations, etc. The decoration with the sun and moon was first popular on the crowns of kings on Sassanid Persian coins. It was introduced to China during the Northern Wei Dynasty, and it was used as a popular decoration on the crowns of Bodhisattvas. The shape of the moon was often used in Yungang Grottoes and early Dunhuang caves. The decoration of the sun and the moon was popular, and the crown ornament of the Persian king was changed to the crown ornament of the Bodhisattva, which seemed to indicate the understanding of the Chinese Buddhist believers on the Bodhisattva (Fig. 7, Fig. 8). Among the crowns decorated with plant patterns, the most special one is the crown of the Bodhisattva in the west niche of the main chamber of Cave 45 in the Mogao Grottoes (Fig. 9). There are several Bodhisattvas who wear scrolling leaves crowns in the west niche of this cave, so it is called the "cirrus pattern crown", which also appears on the north wall of the main chamber of Cave 217 in the high Tang Dynasty and the east wall of the main chamber of Cave 188 of Mogao Grottoes. It is the crown worn by the lady donors and celestial woman (Fig. 10, Fig. 11). Consequently, such a crown has never appeared in Indian Buddhist figure decoration, so it can be inferred that such crown ornaments should be derived from the secular world and are the product of the indigenization of Buddhism. In addition, there are two more important crowns, the nirmana-buddha crown and the vase crown, which have a special role in identifying the identity of the Bodhisattva. In the Amitayurdhyana Sutra, the second one should be Avalokitesvara. On top is the wonderful Mani pearl. There is a standing Nirmanakaya Buddha in the heaven's crown, who is in twenty five yojana in height. The Mahasthamaprapta comes next. There are five hundred lotuses in his heavenly crown, and his ushnisha is like a padma. There is a treasure vase atop ushnisha, which holds all the light and shows the Buddha's deeds. The rest of the body is the same as that of Avalokitesvara. It can be inferred that the nirmana-buddha crown and the vase crown are an important basis for judging the identities of Avalokitesvara and Mahasthamaprapta. (Fig. 12, Fig. 13).

Meanwhile, the costumes of the Bodhisattva in the high Tang Dynasty in Dunhuang mostly appeared with keyūra. Compared with the style of the early "golden and jade ring belt", the materials of the keyūra in the high Tang Dynasty were richer. Considering the unification of costume colour, the whole body was covered with pearls, jade, and flowers. In terms of shape, it is basically divided into two types: the necklace keyūra and the whole body keyūra. The necklace keyūra is only decorated on the neck and chest, while the whole body keyūra

Fig. 7 Mogao Grottoes, Cave 285 of the Northern Wei Dynasty, the Bodhisattva wearing the Moon Crown on the south side of the west niche of the main chamber

Fig. 8 Mogao Grottoes, Cave 23 of the high Tang Dynasty, the Bodhisattva wearing the sun and moon crown on the south side of the west niche of the main chamber

Fig. 9 Mogao Grottoes, Cave 45 of the high Tang Dynasty, the Bodhisattva wearing the crown with scrolling leaves in the west niche of the main chamber

Fig. 10 Mogao Grottoes. Cave 217 of the high Tang Dynasty, a noble woman wearing the crown with scrolling leaves on the north wall of the main chamber

Fig. 11 Mogao Grottoes, Cave 188 of the high Tang Dynasty, a celestial woman wearing crown with scrolling leaves on the north side of the east wall of the main chamber

Fig. 12 Mogao Grottoes, the north side of the west niche of the main chamber of Cave 217 in the high Tang Dynasty, the Avalokitesvara wearing the nirmana-buddha crown

Fig. 13 Mogao Grottoes, the south side of the west niche of the main chamber of Cave 217 in the high Tang Dynasty, Mahasthamaprapta wearing a vase crown

is connected with the necklace keyūra, meeting in the abdomen in an "X" shape. It drapes and wraps beside the skirt, creating an interactive relationship with the garment. In terms of shape and colour, the keyūra worn by Bodhisattva coordinates with the Bodhisattva's clothing, crown, armlet, bracelet, and earrings.

2.3 Diverse materials and exquisite craftsmanship

Social affluence and cultural exchanges promoted the rapid development of the textile industry in the Tang Dynasty. There are many kinds of textiles, and the skills of weaving, embroidering, printing, dyeing, and painting are exquisite. The prosperous textiles and dyeing and weaving techniques are fully reflected in the costumes of Bodhisattva in the high Tang Dynasty in Dunhuang.

The Bodhisattva is often seen wearing a long transparent gauze skirt in the murals of the high Tang Dynasty in Dunhuang. The skirt is light and transparent, embellished with small scattered floral patterns. It should have been a precious gauze fabric in the Tang Dynasty, compared with the flower pattern printed voile unearthed in Astana, Turfan, Xinjiang in the Tang Dynasty (Fig. 14). It was plain gauze printed with dye inhibitors, with white flowers on the yellow ground, which is especially similar to the gauze skirt worn by the Bodhisattva in the high Tang Dynasty in Dunhuang. In addition, images of the popular dyeing by enlacing wrap process in the Tang Dynasty are common in the costumes of the high Tang Bodhisattva in Dunhuang. This process produces a distinctive blurring effect due to its special weaving method, making it recognizable in the image. For example, the pattern of the Bodhisattva on the east wall of the main chamber in Cave

Fig. 14 Flower pattern printed voile unearthed in Astana, Turfan, Xinjiang, Tang Dynasty

217 of the Mogao Grottoes, it is basically the same as that of the dyed fabrics of the Japanese Shoso-in (Fig. 15, Fig. 16). In addition, the skirt strap of the Bodhisattva in Cave 194 of Mogao Grottoes also used a popular resist dyeing technique in the Tang Dynasty.

Indigo printing, hollow paper printing and other techniques were also popular in the Tang Dynasty in addition to traditonal techniques of batik, resist dyeing, relief woodblock printing, alkali-resistant dyeing printing. Comparing the pattern of the Nivi of the Bodhisattva in the main chamber of the west shrine in Cave 45 of the Mogao Grottoes with the indigo printed thin silk with the pattern of flowers and leaves on the light red ground

Fig. 15 Mogao Grottoes, Cave 217 in the high Tang Dynasty, Bodhisattva costumes on the east wall of the main chamber

Fig. 16 Warp dyeing fabric, Shoso-in collection, Japanese

in the Shoso-in, Japan (Fig. 17, Fig. 18), it can be seen that the expression of this Nivi should be the superb indigo printing of the Tang Dynasty. Through above comparison, it is efficiently proven that the craftsmanship reflected in the costumes of the Bodhisattva in Dunhuang is highly consistent with the textiles of that time.

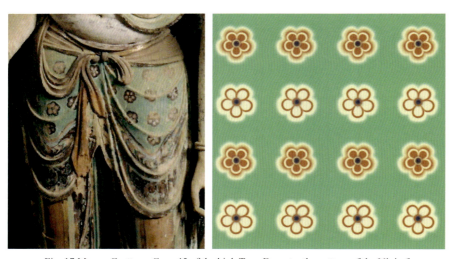

Fig. 17 Mogao Grottoes, Cave 45 of the high Tang Dynasty, the pattern of the Nivi of the attendant Bodhisattva in the west niche of the main chamber

Fig. 18 The indigo printed thin silk with the pattern of flowers and leaves on the light red ground of the Tang Dynasty, Shoso-in collection

2.4   Colour brilliance and harmonious unity

The murals and polychrome sculptures that impressed us in Dunhuang during the high Tang Dynasty were sumptuous and magnificent. The atmosphere of prosperity, openness, and inclusiveness makes the costume of the Tang Dynasty more and more gorgeous.

In China, the traditional "Five colour" system has always been the main cultural concept and colour symbol, and this concept made a breakthrough in the Tang Dynasty with the prosperity of cultural integration. A large number of textiles dated to the Tang Dynasty with rich colours and complex patterns have been unearthed from the Library Cave in Dunhuang and Astana Turfan. Weaving and Printing of Textiles unearthed from Turfan in the Tang Dynasty mentions that according to incomplete statistics, the color spectrum seen in the silk fabrics of the Tang Dynasty unearthed from Turfan, there are five red colour levels, such as silver red, water red, scarlet, purple red, and purple. The yellow colour has light yellow, chrysanthemum yellow, apricot yellow, golden yellow, earth yellow, and tea brown. The blue colour has pale blue, azure, turquoise blue, sapphire blue, red green, and navy blue. Greens include gourd green, bean green, leaf green, apple green and dark green. Together with black and white, there are as many as twenty-four colours being used. It can be known that the colour concept in the Tang Dynasty broke through tradition and achieved multiple integrations.

The most common colours in the Dunhuang high Tang of murals and polychrome sculptures are five colours: red, blue, green, brown-black, and white. The red pigments are mainly cinnabar and red lead, and both of them were introduced from Central Asia at that time. The blue pigments are mainly azurite and lapis lazuli, and azurite was introduced from the Qilian Mountain or Central Plain, while lapis lazuli was introduced from Afghanistan and India. The green pigments are malachite and atacamite. The brown-black pigments are mainly lead dioxide, and the white pigments are mainly calcite. This shows that the prosperity of the Silk Road created conditions for the integration of civilizations, so that the introverted and luxurious oriental colours and the exotic colours have been perfectly integrated in Dunhuang.

The contrasting colours of red and green are matched with each other to seek harmony, which is the most significant feature of the colour application of Bodhisattva costumes in the Tang Dynasty. Whether it's the front and back of the red and green double-colored Luoye, the red long skirt with the green Nivi, or the red and green floral pattern long skirt, this combination of strong contrasts fits perfectly in the Dunhuang Bodhisattva costumes. It reflects the unique form and concept of colour harmony in the Tang Dynasty, and it also shows the era style in which the colours of the high Tang Dynasty Bodhisattva costume seek harmony and unity in contrast.

2.5　Rich multi-colored decorations, as well as a blend of Chinese and Western styles

The cave art of Dunhuang during the Tang Dynasty reached an unprecedented level of opulence and prosperity under the politically enlightened and eclectic social background of the Tang Dynasty. The costumes of the Bodhisattvas from the murals and polychrome sculptures contain a rich and colourful array of motifs, including traditional geometric filler patterns, floral cluster patterns, and cross floral patterns, as well as the scroll pattern, which is a combination of those from the Western Regions and Central Plain. The rosette pattern is present with a strong Buddhist influence. It is completely different from the elegant style of the earlier period, showing the characteristics of the times with a mixture of Chinese and Western styles.

Overall, the patterns of Bodhisattva costumes exhibit two different characteristics within the caves during the high Tang in Dunhuang.

First of all, the patterns of Bodhisattva costumes in the same cave or in the same sutra transformation tableaux or Dharma-preaching scenes are basically similar in shape and colour. For example, the Bodhisattva costume pattern on the south wall of the main chamber of Cave 217 is uniformly four-petal or six-petal blue with green scattered flowers which are clearly defined. Quartering cross type and six-part scattered flowers are extremely common in the Bodhisattva costume of the high Tang Dynasty, which appears on the Bodhisattva's Luoye, long skirt or Nivi (Fig. 19).

Fig. 19 Mogao Grottoes, Cave 217 of the high Tang Dynasty, Bodhisattva costume of a Dharma-preaching scene from the south wall of the main chamber

Secondly, the patterns of Bodhisattva costumes show some correlation with the decorative patterns of the murals in the same cave. For example, the Nivi of the Avalokitesvara on the north side of the west niche in the main chamber in Mogao Cave 66 is a floral tendril pattern in the high Tang Dynasty, which does not appear on other Bodhisattva costumes in the caves of Dunhuang in the high Tang Dynasty, while it was painted on the side decoration of the north wall of the main chamber of Cave 66 in the high Tang Dynasty (Fig. 20, Fig. 21). Another example is the scroll pattern on the long skirt of the Bodhisattva on the south side of the west niche in the main chamber of Cave 194, which is basically the same as the scroll pattern along the west niche of Cave 194 (Fig. 22, Fig. 23). It can be seen that the painters have taken into account the overall unity of the character's dress pattern and mural style in the painting process.

Fig. 20 Mogao Grottoes, Cave 66 of the high Tang Dynasty, the pattern of the Nivi of Avalokitesvara on the north side outside the west niche of the main chamber

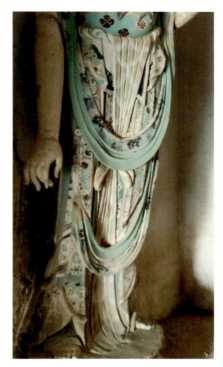

| Fig. 2 The border decoration of a Floral Tendril pattern on the north wall of the main chamber of Cave 66 in the high Tang Dynasty of Mogao Grottoes | Fig. 22 The Rolling Tendril pattern of the long skirt of the attendant Bodhisattva on the south side of the west niche in the main chamber of Cave 194 in the high Tang Dynasty of Mogao Grottoes | Fig. 23 The Rolling Tendril pattern on the edge of the west niche in the main chamber of Cave 194 in the high Tang Dynasty of Mogao Grottoes |

3. Summary

Buddhism was introduced to the mainland of China from India and reached Dunhuang, which has crossed geographical, ethnic, temporal, and cultural boundaries, incorporating civilizations from ancient Western Asia, Central Asia, South Asia, and Southeast Asia, as well as the minority cultures of the Western Regions and the native cultures of the Central Plains which have shaped the unique style and rich forms of Dunhuang's cave art. Combined with the special characteristics of the time and regional culture of the high Tang Dynasty, it also created the special status and influence of the costumes of the Bodhisattva images in the Tang Dynasty.

First of all. the costume culture of the Bodhisattva images in the high Tang Dynasty in Dunhuang has the significance of inheriting the past and connecting the future. On the one hand, the Bodhisattva costumes in the high Tang Dynasty inherited and developed correspondingly from the earlier period in terms of shape. For example: Bodhisattvas in the high Tang period still retain the characteristics of traditional Buddhist art statues, such as the bared upper body, unrolling hair. The religious characteristics are still obvious, but their facial features have changed a lot compared to early period ones. Most of the Bodhisattva statues have plump faces, a benevolent and kind countenance, who are graceful and elegant. In terms of clothing forms, they inherited most of the shapes from the Sui and early Tang Dynasties, but they also had new changes compared to the earlier period. Luoye and celestial garments were still popular during the high Tang Dynasty, while the popular costume of Sankaksika in the Sui and early Tang dynasties are relatively rare in the high Tang Bodhisattva costumes. In terms of clothing accessories, it has inherited the style of ring-shaped Keyūra in the Sui and early Tang

Dynasties, which has further development. It presents a decorative effect surrounded by emeralds and beads in an annular pattern. On the other hand, the costumes of Bodhisattva statues in the high Tang Dynasty in Dunhuang played an important role as a paradigm in the later period. The costumes of Bodhisattva statues in the Dunhuang Grottoes developed from the Northern Dynasties to the Sui, early Tang, and high Tang Dynasties. More abundant changes have taken place in terms of shapes, patterns, colors, etc. By the late high Tang Dynasty, the style had gradually stabilized, and it had provided an important pattern paradigm of Bodhisattva costume for the middle Tang Dynasty and later period.

Secondly, the costumes of Bodhisattva statues in the high Tang Dynasty in Dunhuang remained an important position in Chinese traditional costume culture. There are a large number of Bodhisattva costumes left in the murals and polychrome sculptures of the high Tang Dynasty in Dunhuang, with rich shapes, exquisite patterns, and gorgeous forms. They are not only of great value to the study of the Buddhist costume culture in the Tang Dynasty, but also indicate the orderly interaction and integration of religion, nationality, and secularization shown by the changes in the styles of Tang Dynasty Bodhisattva costumes, perfectly demonstrating the inheritance, inclusiveness, and creativity of traditional Chinese costume culture in the process of development. It is an excellent example in the context of Silk Road culture, which has important practical value for the exchange and development of contemporary costume culture.

敦煌莫高窟盛唐第194窟彩塑菩萨绞缬裙带的复原研究

杨建军　崔　岩

一、引言

敦煌莫高窟盛唐第194窟西壁龛内南侧的立姿菩萨，是敦煌盛唐时期彩塑的代表作品（图1）[1]。该尊彩塑菩萨不仅姿态优美生动，而且锦衫华丽，彩裙、天衣层层套叠。其中，由腰际垂至足底的一条裙带，在红褐色地上显现出规整连续的扇形白色花纹，表现的即是盛唐时期非常流行的绞缬，间接反映出唐代精湛的绞缬工艺及独特美感。

绞缬是古代一种重要的染织工艺，通过针缝、线捆等方法扎结织物达到防染目的，染色后形成晕染渗化效果的花纹，具有偶然性的自然韵律美。在我国东晋时期已经广泛应用于绞缬技术，隋、唐时期技术发达，达到鼎盛时期。本文以敦煌莫高窟盛唐第194窟彩塑菩萨裙带为研究对象，分析其代表的绞缬工艺的发展历史和风格特点，并对此裙带的制作方法和染色步骤进行实验性复原。

二、裙带所示绞缬工艺历史及风格分析

我国绞缬工艺的历史十分久远。文献记载和出土文物表明，我国古代民间至迟在4世纪就已经普遍从事绞缬生产，并且发展出不同的扎结方法。南北朝时期的北齐魏收撰《魏书》卷二十一上《列传第九上》中《献文六王》记载："王公以下贱妾，悉不听用织成锦绣、金玉珠玑，违者以违旨论；奴婢悉不得衣绫绮缬，止于缦缯而已；奴则布服，并不得以金银为钗、带，犯者鞭一百。"根据唐代释玄应等撰《一切经音义》卷十"谓以丝缚缯染之，解丝成文曰缬也"的记载可知，《魏书》中"缬"应该就是"以丝缚缯染之，解丝成文"的绞缬。东晋陶潜在《搜神后记》卷九中也记载："淮南陈氏于田中种豆，忽见二女子姿色甚美，

图1　敦煌莫高窟盛唐第194窟
彩塑菩萨立像

---

❶ 敦煌文物研究所. 中国石窟·敦煌莫高窟（第四卷）[M]. 北京：文物出版社，1987: 42.

着紫缬襦、青裙，天雨而衣不湿。其壁先挂一铜镜，镜中见二鹿。"其女子身着"紫缬襦、青裙"，远远看去如梅花鹿一般。显然，女子穿着的"紫缬襦"应该就是"鹿胎缬"花纹的绞缬上衣。此外，成书于北朝时期的《洛阳伽蓝记》一书，著者杨衒之根据《惠生行记》《宋云家纪》《道荣传》记述了北魏神龟年间（518—520年）宋云、惠生向西域求经的史实。据该书卷五记载，他们从鄯善赴于阗途中遇捍么城，在城南寺中看到"悬彩幡盖亦有万计"。同卷还载"惠生初发京师之日，皇太后勅付五色百尺幡千口、锦香袋五百枚、王公卿士幡二千口"。杨衒之记录的佛教彩幡，对应敦煌莫高窟发现的唐代彩幡实物（图2）[1]，可以得知绞缬工艺在彩幡上的运用非常普遍[2]。另外，从文献记载和出土于新疆吐鲁番、和田等地区的六朝绞缬实物看，除了捆扎法形成的散点式花纹，还有腊梅、海棠、蝴蝶等图案，而玛瑙缬、鱼子缬、龙子缬等制作精美的多种图案，进一步证实早在4世纪我国的绞缬技术已经相当成熟。

绞缬工艺在隋、唐时期非常流行，规模空前。当时绞缬流行的盛况，从诗人李贺"杨花扑帐春云热，龟甲屏风醉眼缬"和"醉缬抛红网，单罗挂绿蒙"的诗句，以及段成式"醉袂几侵鱼子缬，飘缨长胃凤凰钗"和"厌裁鱼子深红缬，泥觅蜻蜓浅碧绫"，杜牧"竹冈森羽林，花坞团宫缬"等诸多描述中可见一斑。除了在新疆吐鲁番地区和甘肃敦煌出土的唐代绞缬实物之外，在唐代三彩陶器、绢画、壁画等艺术作品中，还间接反映着技艺高超的唐代绞缬。其中，敦煌莫高窟盛唐第194窟西壁龛内彩塑菩萨的裙带，就是最具代表性的范例。

绞缬工艺以捆绞、缝绞等防染技法变化出多样的图案效果。敦煌莫高窟盛唐第194窟彩塑菩萨的裙带图案规整有序，边缘朦胧，无疑表现的是缝绞，即以针线穿缝、绞扎折叠数层的面料，通过防染产生规整的网格状、朵花形等连续式图案。我国新疆吐鲁番阿斯塔那古墓曾出土一批绞缬作品，如1959年出土的茄紫绛紫两色叠胜纹绞缬绢裙、1969年出土的棕色叠胜纹绞缬绢，以及1972年出土的朵花绞缬罗等。其中，1969年在新疆吐鲁番阿斯塔那北区117号墓出土的棕色叠胜纹绞缬绢（图3）[3]，还保留有染前折成6

图2　多色花鸟纹缬染幡（唐代，敦煌莫高窟第130窟出土，敦煌研究院藏）

图3　棕色叠胜纹绞缬绢（唐代，新疆维吾尔自治区博物馆藏）

❶ 常沙娜. 中国织绣服饰全集·第1卷·织染卷［M］. 天津：天津人民美术出版社，2004：188.
❷ 杨建军，崔岩. 唐代佛幡图案与工艺研究［J］. 敦煌研究，2014，144（2）：16-20.
❸ 新疆维吾尔自治区博物馆出土文物展览工作组. 丝绸之路·汉唐织物［M］. 北京：文物出版社，1973：50.

层的痕迹和未拆除的缝线，花纹菱格线上的针脚清晰可见。王㐨先生曾对棕色叠胜纹绞缬绢等缝绞方法进行过专门研究，通过模拟复制研究，分析唐代绞缬与缝绞之间的关系，证实了缝绞在唐代绞缬艺术中的运用具有普遍性[1]。那么，将敦煌莫高窟盛唐第194窟彩塑菩萨裙带所描绘的规整连续式扇形花纹，确定为以缝绞制作而成的唐代绞缬图案具有一定的事实依据。

三、裙带所示绞缬工艺的制作方法

上文分析敦煌莫高窟盛唐第194窟彩塑菩萨裙带表现的是缝绞技法，但由于缝绞本身也具有多样性特征，所以折叠面料的方式、缝绞方法的变化，可以呈现千变万化的不同效果。

例如，图3中的绞缬绢是以最为普遍的缝绞工艺之一——平缝方法制成的，制作时先等距折叠布料，然后依照花纹形成的规律用合股线穿缝、抽紧，通过针线抽紧叠压产生的紧密褶皱形成防染区域，染色之后出现白色花纹。从它产生的效果了解到，由于抽紧缝线时拉力的缘故，在图案的白色花纹线中显现出较为明显的针孔痕迹，且针孔周围因抽紧密实防染效果清晰，稍远处则渗色较多，造成白色花纹线条随之出现或宽或窄，或断或连的变化。又如，日本正仓院收藏的奈良时代黄地七宝纹绞缬薄绢（图4）[2]，做工精巧、花纹细腻，虽然制作之初的褶皱早已消失，但在花纹线条处仍可以见到缝绞留下的隐约针孔及抽紧痕迹，花纹线条同样具有时隐时现的断续效果。由此可见，这正是平缝针法缝绞特有的视觉效果，也是无法避开的现状。敦煌莫高窟盛唐第194窟彩塑菩萨裙带的白色花纹线条连贯流畅，没有表现出任何平缝针法因抽紧而形成的断裂式痕迹，从其图案排列整齐、描绘精致，且在纹样轮廓处精心表现出晕染效果看，无疑真实再现了当时流行的华美绞缬，并非随意为之。由此确定，敦煌莫高窟盛唐第194窟彩塑菩萨裙带表现的虽然是缝绞效果，但不是当时最为常见的平缝方法。

通过对比可见，此裙带所示效果与日本传统的"青海波"蓝染绞缬纹样，无论是图案的组合方式，还是工艺所形成的防染效果均十分相似（图5）[3]。所不同的是，"青海波"纹在每个扇形中多了一道线条，

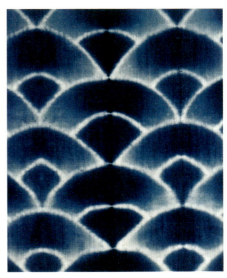

图4　黄地七宝纹绞缬薄绢，8世纪中叶（日本正仓院藏）　　　图5　"青海波"蓝染绞缬纹样
　　　　　　　　　　　　　　　　　　　　　　　　　　　　　　　　　　（日本），榊原朝子

[1] 王㐨. 中国古代绞缬工艺 [J]. 考古与文物，1986（1）：74—88.
[2] 松本包夫. 正仓院藏品与日本飞鸟、天平时代的染织艺术 [M]. 京都：紫红社，1984：87.
[3] 榊原朝子. 日本传统扎染技法 [M]. 京都：紫红社，1999：162.

用以表现波纹的涟漪，而敦煌莫高窟盛唐第194窟彩塑菩萨裙带图案更为简略，基本纹样元素为单纯的扇形。"青海波"纹样的名字源自日本宫廷古乐的一首曲子，后来将以此乐曲为舞曲的舞者服装上装饰的波浪形纹样命名为"青海波"。日本学者片野元彦、榊原朝子等人曾先后对"青海波"纹进行过复原研究。据此分析，"青海波"纹样的源头应该在中国的唐代，而敦煌莫高窟盛唐第194窟彩塑菩萨裙带所表现的连续式扇形花纹，正是盛行于唐代的绞缬图案，很可能在传入日本后便以此为基础逐渐演变为更丰富的"青海波"纹。

经过以上分析，我们得知要制作出与彩塑菩萨绞缬裙带花纹类似的效果，应该至少在叠坯和缝绞这两个程序上与传统做法有所区别和创新。工艺试验中采用宽度为0.4米、长度为1.14米的真丝双绉作为坯绸，制作工艺如下。

1．叠坯

叠坯的方法决定了花纹最后形成的连续效果，而丝绸折叠的平均和精确保证了花纹一致的规律。首先，我们利用坯绸0.4米的宽度，将其等分为8份，每份宽5厘米，并做标记。然后，按照折扇的凹凸方式

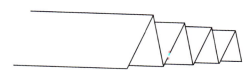

图6　叠坯示意图

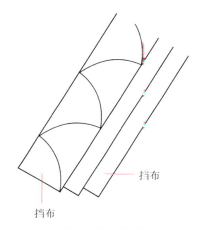

图7　挡布示意图

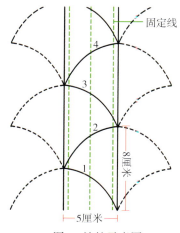

图8　缝绞示意图

将丝绸进行7次折叠，并熨烫定型。如果丝绸较大而不易固定，可以将折叠后绸带的两侧和中间以大针脚缝以固定线，这样会使后面的缝绞工序更易完成，只是需要在染色之前将固定线拆去。折叠定型之后的面料为长条形，横截面呈"M"形（图6）。这种叠坯的方式是以花纹格眼的对角线为轴加以折对，使网格在折对后相重合，并简化成二方连续的带饰图形，这样可以使缝绞和染色加工得到最便捷的工艺效能。

虽然这种叠坯方式可以取得花纹连续网状的效果，但是存在一个问题，即折叠之后的丝绸在染色时外侧受色面积大，而折在里面的部分染色面积相对小，待全部染色完成拆线后会造成丝绸两侧边花纹较明显、中间部分花纹较模糊的弊端。因此，日本的绞缬艺术家片野元彦采取了一种很好的方法来解决这个问题，即在折叠后的丝绸前后各用一块挡布（图7）。挡布可以用棉布制作，其宽窄和叠坯方法均与夹在中间的丝绸一样，厚度应略薄于中部丝绸。它的作用就是将折叠后丝绸外侧的染色不匀问题进行矫正，使染液透过挡布均匀地染到中间的丝绸上，获得完美的染色效果。

2．缝绞

下面对折叠好的丝绸进行缝绞。依据花纹，我们用消色笔在长条带状丝绸上做出标记，形成半个扇面形外缘正反连续的线条。图8显示了缝绞的线迹和顺序，可以看出染色后形成的连续扇面形花纹效果，而一个单位花纹的大小由折叠后的丝绸宽度和一个扇面中轴线的长度决定。鉴于前面已将丝绸折叠为5厘米宽，因此试验中将花纹中轴线长度定为8厘米，可知最终染色形成的一个扇面形花纹单位的长度为8厘米，而宽度为10厘米，是一个稍偏的扇面形状，与彩塑绞缬花纹近似。

将花纹定位后，开始用针引线沿着标记穿缝。走针方法

如图9所示，从*A*点入针，从丝绸底面*B*点出针，然后回针到起点*A*再入针，两个针孔重叠，形成一段针迹。继续从丝绸底面*C*点出针，距离为第一段针迹的两倍，回针至*B*点入针，与*B*点针孔重叠，后面的走针以此类推。这种缝绞方法的特别之处在于每次穿针引线之后都需用力拉紧，使其紧密地缝合折叠后的丝绸，而不是采用惯用的抽紧方法，这样是为了保证花纹线条连贯，而不形成抽紧时的皱褶。

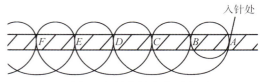

图9　穿缝走针方向示意图

从以上缝绞特点可以看出，这种方法非常适合制作窄长条形的面料。因为这种形状的面料可以将折叠厚度控制在一定范围之内，保证入染的效果；另外，将染得的长条拼接起来连缀成长裙，正是唐代妇女流行的装束，敦煌藏经洞出土唐代绢画《佛传图》中的侍女（图10）❶和莫高窟中唐第231窟东壁门上女供养人的裙装也证明了这一点。

四、裙带所示绞缬工艺染色材料的分析

上文探讨了裙带的显花技术，即了解怎么进行防染和获得特定的花纹效果。彩塑菩萨裙带的色彩涉及彩绘颜料的成分、质地、变色等诸多问题，超出了本文的讨论范围，我们仅从彩塑保存现状来看，其染色部分呈赭黄色，经过上千年的变化，色彩的明度和纯度都受到一定影响，但色彩的倾向比较明确。然后对比现存同时代丝绸文物的色彩，可以得到与其相近色彩的染色方法。例如，出土于我国新疆地区的众多汉唐织物，这批丝织

图10　《佛传图》（局部，唐代，敦煌藏经洞出土，大英博物馆藏）

物品种丰富、时代明确、保存状况较好，具有一定的染色参照性。依据武敏对出土于新疆吐鲁番阿斯塔那墓的土黄地黄白两套色印花绢（图11）❷、茶褐色地绿白两套色印花绢、黄地白花绢、棕色地白花绢等多个标本进行的分析和试验，得出采用黄连根套染莲子壳、黄连根套染核桃皮、栀子套染莲子壳和栀子套染核桃皮这四种套染方法均可以获得类似于赭黄色的丝绸地色，且证实土黄地黄白两套色印花绢的地色与黄连根套染莲子壳染成的标本更为一致❸，说明以这种染材进行染色可以获得类似于敦煌莫高窟盛唐第194窟彩塑菩萨绞缬裙带的染色效果。

除此之外，图4所示日本正仓院8世纪中叶的黄地七宝纹绞缬薄绢，无论是它的缝绞工艺还是色彩显现都更加接近于敦煌莫高窟盛唐第194窟彩塑菩萨绞缬裙带的颜色，即在黄地色中带有一些红色倾向。据日本中江克己研究，当初染制黄地七宝纹绞缬薄绢所使用的染料即为红花，由于其色牢度较低，现在已经褪色变成茶黄色❹。沈从文先生也指出"古代红色染料主要是紫草和红花……红花出西北，所以北朝

❶ 大英博物馆. 西域美术（全3卷）：大英博物馆斯坦因收藏第1卷·敦煌绘画·Ⅰ［E］. 东京：株式会社讲谈社，1982：32.
❷ 新疆维吾尔自治区博物馆出土文物展览工作组. 丝绸之路·汉唐织物［M］. 北京：文物出版社，1973：54.
❸ 武敏. 吐鲁番出土丝织物中的唐代印染［J］. 文物，1973（10）：44.
❹ 中江克己. 日本的染织18 红花染［M］. 东京：泰流社，1978：33.

图11　土黄地黄白两套色印花绢（唐代，新疆维吾尔自治区博物馆藏）

以来有'凉州绯色为天下最'的记载。"❶从敦煌莫高窟盛唐第194窟彩塑菩萨裙带所表现的绞缬看，虽经过上千年变化，但色彩倾向仍然比较明确。再有，盛唐时期的贵族阶层非常流行红花染绞缬，而菩萨作为人们心目中至高无上的大智慧者，为其塑像自然是集世间之美于一身。故而由此推断，敦煌莫高窟盛唐第194窟彩塑菩萨裙带的绞缬原型，理应是用当时非常珍贵的红花染料染制而成。

红花中同时包含黄色素和红色素。黄色素学名为"Safflorgelb"，含量较多，占20%～30%；红色素又名"红花素"，学名为"Carthamine"，含量较少，仅占0.3%～0.6%❷。由于唐代以后流行用红花的红色素染红色，一般情况下传统红花染工艺主要指这种染红色的技术。红花的红色素具有弱酸性，不溶于水或酸性液，而溶于碱性液，因此其萃取、染色方法较为独特。从我国对红花染工艺掌握和使用的历史来看，经历了一个较长的发展时期。在红花传入我国中原之前，中亚地区和我国西北地区常把红花中的黄色素提取出来进行染色。不成熟的染色技术使得无法全部提炼红花中的红色素，故而染得的颜色介于红色和黄色之间，而且时间长久导致的褪色问题也比较明显。这段历史有许多资料可以证明，六朝时期的红即为汉代的"缘"，《说文解字》对这个字的解释是："帛赤黄色也。"❸另外举出三染之别。郭璞注《尔雅》云："缘，今之红也。"说明当时的红并不是现代三原色中的红，而是介于赤黄之间的橙色。现在新疆、青海等地考古发现的北朝至初唐的一些红色织锦多数褪成黄色，或许也说明了当时制备红花素染液尚且不纯的问题❹。直到唐宋时期，人们已经可以将红花中的红色素进行提纯并染制鲜艳的红色，古人形容为"真红""猩红"，这是相较之前带有黄色倾向的红色而言的。因为从唐代之后，红花的栽培遍及全国，红花染已经大多用比较上乘的红花素来完成了。而依据红花包含黄色素和红色素两种色素，通过酸性液和碱性液两种不同性质的媒介提取色素，从而染出从黄色、橙色、粉红色至大红色等一系列色彩的特点，因此我们用传统红花染工艺来进行敦煌莫高窟盛唐第194窟彩塑菩萨绞缬裙带的染色复原实验。

五、红花染工艺复原实验

实验材料：散红花500克，丝绸（真丝双绉）200克，稻草灰1.6千克，乌梅40克。

1. 制备助剂

染色之前需要准备助剂：用于萃取红花红色素的碱性溶液和用于中和红色素溶液的酸性溶液。传统工艺中，前者多用草木灰制得，后者为乌梅水。实验时，先把40克乌梅用2升热水（约80℃）浸泡3天以上，过滤上层透明乌梅水待用（pH 3～4）。把1.6千克稻草灰用16升沸水浸泡2小时以上，过滤表层透明

❶ 沈从文. 谈染缬：蓝底白印花布的历史发展［C］//沈从文. 龙凤艺术. 北京：北京十月文艺出版社，2010：180.
❷ 中国医学科学院药物研究所，等. 中药志（第三册）［M］. 北京：人民卫生出版社，1961：317.
❸ 许慎. 说文解字［M］. 北京：中华书局，1963：274.
❹ 赵丰. 红花在古代中国的传播、栽培和应用［J］. 中国农史，1987（3）：70.

灰水（头遍灰水）备用（pH 11～12）。

2．萃取红色素

前文提到红花同时包含黄色素与红色素，因此需要先将红花中的黄色素去除。将500克散红花用15升水浸泡，2小时后用棉布或麻布过滤并挤净黄色素液。把红花再用15升水浸泡，静置12小时后用棉布或麻布过滤并挤净黄色素液，接着水洗花瓣6～10遍，尽量去除花瓣中的黄色素。

去除红花中的黄色素之后，再萃取其中的红色素。红色素能够溶于碱性溶液，因此在花瓣内注入10升灰水（pH 11～12），3小时后用棉布或麻布过滤并挤净汁液，取得头遍染液。再在花瓣内注入5升灰水（pH 11～12），3小时后用棉布或麻布过滤并挤净汁液，取得二遍染液。将头遍、二遍染液混合，取得约13升红色素染液，再过滤去除杂质。这时的红色素溶液需要再用酸性物质进行中和才能完成，因此在染液中加入1.8升乌梅水，搅拌均匀备用（pH 7左右）。

3．绞缬丝绸浸水

将已经缝绞好的丝绸条带放入清洁的水中，大约浸渍15分钟就可以浸透。如果制作时的挡布采用的是棉布，或质地较厚，可以加长浸泡时间，使其完全浸透。这个简单的步骤是为了防止干燥的丝绸投入染液造成染色不匀，同时预湿后能使丝绸纤维膨化而利于上色。王㐨先生的研究指出，在绞缬工艺中的浸水步骤非常关键，因为关系到防染的成败和染花的艺术效果[1]。因为当缝绞或者结扎好的坯绸进入水中时，水分就会沿着纤维间的微隙向内渗透，直到饱和状态。织物纤维吸湿后急剧膨胀，使缝绞的地方产生一定的内应力，因此在靠近针眼及绑扎的地方会挤压得更加严实，利于预期花纹的显现。

4．染色

把丝绸条带在40℃温水中浸泡30分钟，绞净水分浸入染液，染色15分钟。由于所染丝绸条带经多层折叠并针缝，染色时需要在染液中不断揉压，促使染液渗入。取出，在染液中又注入约90毫升乌梅汁，使pH值变为6左右，之后将丝绸条带浸入染液，再揉压染色15分钟。把300毫升乌梅水加入15升温水（约20℃）中，制成固色液（pH 5左右）。把染色后的丝绸条带在固色液中固色15分钟，其间在固色液中不断揉压，促使固色液渗入。

红花染采用常温染色法，染液量需要浸没丝绸条带，并有相当的宽裕。染色时需要用筷子拨动丝绸，令染液均匀上色。

5．整理

染色结束后，将丝绸条带从染液中取出，先用清水进行彻底冲洗，将浮色漂尽，再用干毛巾将丝绸条带上的多余水分吸去，最后将缝绞的线拆去。展开绸带，慢慢显现出染得的花纹，随后晾干、烫平，获得最后的绞缬作品（图12）。对比敦煌莫高窟盛唐第194窟彩塑菩萨的绞缬裙带，我们通过工艺试验得到的绞缬丝绸花纹与其基本一致，而染色所呈现的色彩更加鲜艳，更接近于红花染丝绸面料的初貌。

图12　敦煌莫高窟盛唐第194窟彩塑菩萨
绞缬裙带复制纺织品

[1] 王㐨. 中国古代绞缬工艺［J］. 考古与文物，1986（1）：75.

六、结语

通过对敦煌莫高窟盛唐第194窟彩塑菩萨的绞缬裙带的分析，可以看到敦煌唐代彩塑匠师除了对于人物动作和神态的真实塑造，还着力表现了菩萨所穿的华丽服饰，以及各种服饰面料的质地、图案和工艺，清晰刻画出唐代绞缬工艺中缝绞和染色方法的面貌。对于研究唐代绞缬工艺历史和风格特征，还原绞缬工艺的具体制作方法，探究敦煌唐代彩塑风格特征与唐代绞缬工艺及其在敦煌服饰中的体现，都提供了宝贵的资料和新的研究视角。

Restoration Research of the Polychrome Bodhisattva Resist−dyeing Skirt Strap in Cave 194 in the Dunhuang Mogao Grottoes of the High Tang Dynasty

Yang Jianjun   Cui Yan

1. Introduction

The standing Bodhisattva on the south side of the west niche in Cave 194 of the Mogao Grottoes in Dunhuang is a representative work of polychrome sculpture in the Tang Dynasty in Dunhuang (Fig. 1). This polychrome sculpture of Bodhisattva not only has a graceful and vivid posture, but also has a gorgeous brocade robe, with colourful skirts and celestial garments stacked in layers. Among them, a skirt strap that hangs from the waist to the soles shows a regular and continuous fan-shaped white pattern on the reddish-brown ground, which was very popular in the Tang Dynasty. In a roundabout way, it reflects the Tang Dynasty's exquisite resist-dyeing technique and unique beauty.

Resist-dyeing was an important dyeing and weaving technique in ancient times, through needle sewing, thread bundling, and other methods to achieve the purpose of preventing dyeing. After dyeing, it forms a pattern with a blurring and permeating effect, which has an accidental beauty of natural rhythm. The resist-dyeing technique was widely used in the East Jin Dynasty of our country, and the technology was developed in the Sui and Tang Dynasties and reached its peak. This paper takes the polychrome Bodhisattva skirt strap in Cave 194 of the high Tang Dynasty in the Mogao Grottoes in Dunhuang as the research object, analyzing the development history and style characteristics of the resist-dyeing technique, and we restore the production methods and dyeing steps of the skirt strap experimentally.

Fig. 1 Cave 194 of the Mogao Grottoes in Dunhuang, high Tang Dynasty, a standing polychrome sculpture of Bodhisattva

034

2. Analysis of the history and style of the resist-dyeing technique shown in the skirt strap

The history of Chinese resist-dyeing technique is very long. Documentary records and unearthed cultural relics show that ancient Chinese folks were generally engaged in the production of resist-dyeing at the latest in the 4th century AD, and they developed different binding methods. During the Northern and Southern Dynasties, Wei Shou, from the Northern Qi Dynasty, wrote *Wei Shu,* Volume 21, Biography of the Ninth, Xianwen Six Kings which records that the lower concubines are not allowed to wear splendid gold jade and pearls. Offenders should be punished according to imperial edict. Female slaves and servants are not allowed to wear twill and figured fabrics who can only wear unadorned silk. Slaves wear rough silk, and they cannot use gold or silver as hairpins or belts, and offenders should be whipped 100 times. According to *The Sound and Meaning of Tripitaka* Volume 10, written by Shi Xuanying, it is dyed with silk. It can be seen from the record that Xie in *Wei Shu* should be the resist-dyeing clothes, which are dyed with silk ties, unravelling them. Tao Qian of the Eastern Jin Dynasty also recorded in Volume 9 of *Soushen Houji* that a person named Chen from south of Huai River was planting beans in the field, and suddenly he saw two women who were very beautiful, wearing purple Ru and cyan skirts. But their clothes were not wet in the rain. There is a bronze mirror, and two deer were mirrored. The woman was dressed in purple Ru and cyan skirt, and she looked like a deer from a far distance. Obviously, the purple Ru worn by the woman should be a resist-dyeing coat with a deer pattern. In addition, the book *Luoyang Qielan Ji*, written in the Northern Dynasty by Yang Xuanzhi, describes the historical facts about Song Yun and Hui Sheng's pilgrimage to the Western Regions in the Northern Wei Dynasty (518-520) based on *Hui Sheng Xing Ji, Song Yun Jia Ji,* and *Dao Rong Biography*. According to the volume 5 of the book, they arrived in Hanmo City on their way from Shanshan to Khotan, and they saw thousands of hanging colourful flags and banners in the temple south of the city. The same volume also records that Huisheng was about to leave the capital on the first day, and the Empress gave a thousand five-coloured banners with a hundred-foot length, five hundred brocade bags, and two thousand banners for princes and nobles. The Buddhist coloured banners recorded by Yang Xuanzhi correspond to unearthed banners in Dunhuang from the Tang Dynasty (Fig. 2), it can be seen that the application of the resist-dyeing technique on colourful flags is very common. In addition to the recorded documents and resist-dyeing materials unearthed in Turpan, Khotan, and other regions in Xinjiang, there are also patterns such as wintersweet, begonia, and butterfly, apart from the scattered pattern formed by the bundling method. A variety of exquisite patterns, such as agate Xie, fish Xie, and dragon Xie, are produced, which further proves that the resist-dyeing technique in our country has been quite mature as early as the 4th century AD.

The resist-dyeing technique was very popular in the Sui and Tang Dynasties, and it reached an unprecedented scale. At that time, the popularity of resist-dyeing technique could be learned from Li He's poems "Yanghua flutters the tent in spring clouds, tortoise shell screen drunk eyes" and "Drunk valerian throws the red net, single Luo hangs from green fog", as well as Duan Chengshi's poem "Drunk robe and a few invading fish roes, Valerian, phoenix hairpin with flying tassels", and "I hate cutting fish, deep red Valerian, looking for dragonfly and light blue silk in mud", and in Dumu's poem "Ridge are abundant in bamboo with weapons and armour, flowery orchard and silk fabric dyed with pattern". In addition to the resist-dyeing materials unearthed in Turpan, Xinjiang and Dunhuang, Gansu, the Tang Dynasty tri-coloured pottery, silk paintings, murals, and other artistic works also indirectly reflect the highly skilled resist-dyeing technique. Among them, the skirt strap of the polychrome Bodhisattva in the western niche of Cave 194 from the high Tang Dynasty in the Mogao Grottoes is the most representative example.

The resist-dyeing technique presents various patterns with bundling and stitching techniques. The pattern of the polychrome sculpture of Bodhisattva in Cave 194 of the high Tang Dynasty in the Mogao Grottoes is neat and orderly, and the edges are hazy, which undoubtedly shows the stitching process. That is, the fabrics are stitched, twisted, and folded with needles and threads. Continuous gridding and flower patterns were obtained through anti-dyeing methods. A number of resist-dyeing silks have been unearthed from the Astana ancient tomb in Turpan, Xinjiang, such as the Eggplant Purple and Dark Reddish Purple Stacked Resist-dyeing Rough Silk Skirt unearthed in 1959, and the Brown Resist-dyeing Rough Silk with Folded Pattern unearthed in 1969, as well as the Flower Resist-dyeing Cloth unearthed in 1972. Among them, the Brown Resist-dyeing Rough Silk with Folded Pattern (Fig. 3) unearthed in Tomb No. 117 of Astana North District, Turpan, Xinjiang, still retains the traces of 6 folded layers and the stitches that have not been removed. The stitches on the patterned rhombus are clearly visible. Mr. Wang Xu has conducted special research on stitching and bundling methods concerning the Brown folded resist-dyeing rough silk. Through simulation and replication research, he analysed the relationship between resist-dyeing and stitching in the Tang Dynasty, and he confirmed that the stitching method was universally applied in the Tang Dynasty. Then, it has a certain factual basis to determine that the regular and continuous fan-shaped pattern depicted on the polychrome sculpture of the Bodhisattva skirt strap in the Cave 194 of Mogao Grottoes was a resist-dyeing pattern made of stitching in the Tang Dynasty.

Fig. 2 Multicoloured flag with floral and bird pattern from Tang Dynasty, excavated in Cave 130 of Mogao Grottoes in Dunhuang, Dunhuang Academy Collection

Fig. 3 Brown Resist-dyeing Rough Silk with Folded Pattern, Tang Dynasty, Xinjiang Uygur Autonomous Region Museum collection

3. The production method of the resist-dyeing process shown in the skirt strap

The above analysis of the polychrome sculpture of the Bodhisattva skirt strap in Cave 194 of the Mogao Grottoes in the high Tang Dynasty shows the technique of stitching and twisting method. Since the stitching and twisting methods also have diverse characteristics, the forms of folding fabric and the stitching and twisting methods would show an ever-changing effect.

For example, the resist-dyeing rough silk in Fig. 3 is made by one of the most common stitching and twisting processes, the flat seam method. When made, the fabric is folded at equal distances, then stitched and tightened with plural threads according to the principle formation pattern. The tight folds created by the needle and thread form a stain-resistant area, and white patterns appear after dyeing. From the effect it produces, we know that due to the tension when tightening the cloth, obvious pinhole marks appear in the white pattern. The anti-dyeing effect around the pinholes is clear due to the tightening force, and it permeated a little more in the far distance, causing the white pattern lines to appear wide or narrow, broken or connected. Another example is the Nara period Yellow Ground Seven Treasure Pattern Resist-dyeing Silk (Fig. 4) collected by Shoso-in, Japan. It shows exquisite craftsmanship and has delicate patterns. Although the wrinkles at the beginning of production have disappeared, the stitches and tightening traces can still be seen in the pattern lines. The intermittent lines also have a disappearing and reappearing effect. It can be seen that this is the unique visual effect of the flat seam created by the stitching and twisting method, and it is also an unavoidable situation. The white patterns on the skirt strap of the polychrome sculpture of the Bodhisattva in Cave 194 at the Mogao Grottoes in Dunhuang are coherent and smooth, and they do not show any fractured traces formed by the tightening and twisting of flat seams. The patterns are neatly arranged and delicately depicted, and the outlines of the patterns are meticulously placed. Showing the effect of permeating, it is undoubtedly a true reproduction of the popular resplendent resist-dyeing silk at that time, and it is not randomly applied. From this, it can be known that although the polychrome sculpture of the Bodhisattva in Cave 194 of the high Tang Dynasty in the Mogao Grottoes showed the effect of stitching and twisting, it was not the most common flat seam method at that time.

By comparison, it can be seen that the effect of this skirt strap is very similar to that of the traditional Japanese blue resist-dyeing "Qinghai Wave" pattern, in terms of the combination of patterns and the anti-dyeing effect formed by the process (Fig. 5). The difference is that the "Qinghai Wave" pattern has a line in each fan shape to express the ripples of water, while the pattern of the polychrome Bodhisattva skirt strap in Cave 194 in the Mogao Grottoes is much simpler, and the basic pattern elements are simple fan shapes. The name of the "Qinghai Wave" pattern originated from a piece of ancient Japanese court music. Later, the wavy pattern decorated on the dancers' costume with this music was named "Qinghai Wave." Japanese scholars Katano Motohiko and Sakakihara have successively carried out restoration research on the "Qinghai Wave" pattern. According to this analysis, the source of the "Qinghai Wave" pattern should be in the Tang Dynasty in China, and the continuous fan-shaped pattern represented by the polychrome Bodhisattva skirt strap in the Cave 194 of Mogao Grottoes in Dunhuang is exactly the resist-dyeing pattern that prevailed in the Tang Dynasty. It may have gradually evolved into a richer "Qinghai Wave" pattern after it was introduced to Japan.

Fig. 4 Yellow Ground Seven Treasure Pattern Resist-dyeing Silk (mid-8th century, in the collection of the Shoso-in, Japan)

Fig. 5 The blue resist-dyeing "Qinghai Wave" pattern, (Japan) Sakakihara Sakurako

Through the above analysis, we know that in order to create a similar effect to the pattern of the polychrome sculpture Bodhisattva's resist-dyeing skirt strap, there should be at least two procedures of stacking and stitching that are different from the traditional practice and innovative. In the process test, a silk crepe de chine with a width of 0.4 meters and a length of 1.14 meters was used as the greige, and the production process was as follows.

3.1　Stack greige

The method of stacking greige determines the final effect of the continuous pattern, and the average and precise folding of the silk ensures the principle of the consistent pattern. First of all, we used the greige of 0.4m width, which was divided into 8 equal parts, and each part was 5cm wide and marked. Then we folded the greige seven times according to the concave and convex pattern of the folding fan, and ironed it into shape. If the silk is too large and difficult to fix, we sewed the two sides and the middle of the folded ribbon with large stitches to fix the thread, which would make the subsequent sewing and twisting process easier to complete, but the fixing thread needs to be removed before dyed. The stacked fabric after shaping is a long strip with an "M" shape in cross section, as shown in Fig. 6. This method of stacking greige is to fold the diagonal line of the pattern grid as the axis, so that the grids overlap after the folding and they are simplified into two continuous striped patterns, which can make the stitching and dyeing process have the most convenient process performance.

Although this method of stacking blanks can achieve the effect of a continuous mesh pattern, there is a problem. That is, the folded silk has a large colour receiving area outside the greige during dyeing, while the dyeing area of the folded part inside is relatively small. After dyeing and removing the thread, the pattern on both sides of the greige is more obvious, while the pattern in the middle part is blurred. Therefore, the Japanese resist-dyeing artist Genhiko Katano has adopted a good method to solve this problem; that is, to use a blocking cloth in front of and behind the folded silk (Fig. 7). The blocking cloth can be made of cotton, of which width and stacking method are the same as the silk sandwiched in the middle. The thickness of the blocking cloth

038

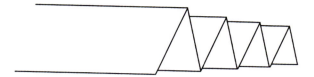

Fig. 6 Stack greige diagram

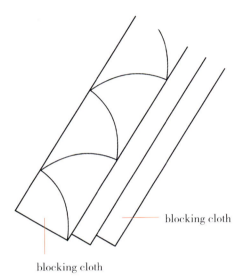

blocking cloth

blocking cloth

Fig. 7 Blocking cloth diagram

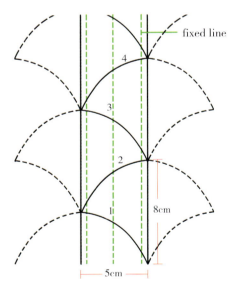

fixed line

8cm

5cm

Fig. 8 Stitching and twisting diagram

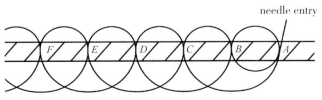

needle entry

Fig. 9 Diagram of stitching direction

should be slightly thinner than the central silk. Its function is to correct the uneven dyeing problem on the outer side of the silk after folding, so that the dyeing liquid can be evenly dyed on the middle silk through the blocking cloth to obtain a perfect dyeing effect.

3.2 The process of stitching and twisting

Next, sew the folded silk. According to the pattern, we mark the long ribbon-shaped silk with an achromatic pen to form a continuous line on the front and back of the outer edge of the half-sector shape. Fig. 8 shows the traces and sequence of stitching, and it can be seen that the continuous fan-shaped pattern effect was formed after dyeing. The size of a unit pattern is determined by the width of the folded silk and the length of the central axis of a fan. Since the silk has been folded to 5cm in width previously, the length of the central axis of the pattern is set at 8cm in the test. It can be seen that the length of a fan-shaped pattern unit formed by the final dyeing is 8cm, and the width is 10cm, which is a slightly oblate pattern. The shape of the fan is similar to the resist-dyeing pattern.

Once the pattern is set in place, the needle leads are started to thread the stitches along the markings. The stitching method is shown in Fig. 9. The needle is inserted from point A, and it is withdrawn from point B on the bottom surface of the silk. Then the needle is returned to the starting point A and inserted again. The two needle holes overlap to form a stitch. Continue to pull out the needle from point C on the bottom surface of the silk until the distance is 2 times of the first stitch. Return to point B and insert the needle, overlapping point B's needle hole. The following stitches were the same as the previous ones. The special feature of this sewing method is that after each stitch is threaded, the needle is pulled tightly so that it is tightly sewn to the folded silk, rather than using the usual method of pulling it tightly, which is to ensure that the pattern lines are consistent without forming wrinkles when pulled tightly.

As can be seen from the above stitching and twisting characteristics, this method is very suitable for making narrow and long fabrics. Because these kinds of fabrics could limit stacking thickness within a certain range to ensure the effect of dyeing. Furthermore, the long dyed strips were stitched together to form a long skirt, which was a popular attire for women in the Tang Dynasty, as evidenced by the dresses of the maids in the Tang Dynasty silk painting *Buddha's biography*, unearthed from the Library Cave (Fig. 10) and the female donor on the east wall of Cave 231 in the middle Tang Dynasty in the Mogao Grottoes of Dunhuang.

Fig. 10 *Buddha's biography* (part), Tang Dynasty, unearthed from the Library Cave of Dunhuang, now in the British Museum

4. Analysis of dyeing materials for the resist-dyeing process shown in skirt strap

The above paragraphs explored the technique of showing a flower pattern on the skirt strap, that is, understanding how to carry out anti-dyeing and obtain specific pattern effects. The colour of the polychrome Bodhisattva's skirt strap involves many issues, such as the composition, texture, and discolouration of the pigment, which are beyond the scope of this paper. We only look at the current state of preservation of the polychrome sculpture, whose dyeing part is in ochre-yellow. After thousands of years of change, the brightness and purity of the colour are affected to a certain extent, but the tendency of the colour is relatively clear. Compare the colour of the surviving contemporaneous silk relics, and we can get its similar dyeing methods. Many fabrics excavated in Xinjiang area dating back to the Han and Tang Dynasties are rich in variety, which are preserved in good condition, and they can provide a certain reference for dyeing methods. Based on Wu Min's analysis and tests on a number of specimens such as yellow and white printed silk in an earthy yellow ground (Fig. 11), green and white printed silk on a tea-brown ground, white flowered silk on a yellow ground, and white flowered silk on a brown ground, which were excavated in the Astana tomb in Turpan, Xinjiang, it was concluded that the four dyeing methods of dyeing with goldthread root over lotus seed shell, goldthread root over walnut skin, gardenia over lotus seed shell and gardenia over walnut skin could obtain similar color to the ochre-yellow. The ground

Fig. 11 Two sets of yellow and white printed silk in an earthy yellow ground, Tang Dynasty, in the collection of the Xinjiang Uygur Autonomous Museum

colour of the two sets of yellow and white printed silk with yellow roots over-dyed lotus shells was proved to be more consistent with the specimens dyed with this dyeing material, indicating that the dyeing effect can be obtained with this dyeing material similar to the dyeing effect of the polychrome sculpture of the Bodhisattva resist-dyeing skirt strap in Cave 194 of the high Tang Dynasty at Dunhuang Mogao Grottes.

In addition, the resist-dyeing of rough silk with seven-precious patterned on the yellow-ground from the mid-eighth century of the Shoso-in Temple in Japan in Fig. 4 is closer to the colour of the resist-dyeing skirt strap of the Bodhisattva in Cave 194 of the Tang Dynasty at Dunhuang, both in its sewing and twisting process and in its colour appearance, i.e., with some red tendencies in the yellow ground colour. According to Japanese scholar Nakae Katsumi's research, resist-dyeing rough silk with seven precious patterns on yellow ground used saffron as a dyeing material, but it has faded into tea yellow because of its low colour fastness. Mr. Shen Congwen has pointed out that the ancient red dyeing material was mainly from comfrey and safflower, and safflower was from the northwest China. It was recorded that the scarlet colour from Liangzhou was the world's best one. With regard to the resist-dyeing skirt strap depicted on the polychrome sculpture of Bodhisattva in Cave 194 of the Mogao Grottoes, the colour tendency is still relatively clear after thousands of years of change. In addition, safflower resist-dyeing was very popular among the aristocracy of the Tang Dynasty, and the Bodhisattva achieved supreme wisdom in people's minds. They are naturally a collection of the world's beauty all in one. Therefore, it can be inferred that the prototype of the polychrome Bodhisattva's resist-dyeing skirt strap in Cave 194 of the high Tang period at Dunhuang Mogao Caves must have been dyed with the very precious saffron dyeing material at that time.

Safflower contains both yellow and red pigments. The scientific name of the yellow pigment is Safflorgelb, which has a high content, accounting for 20%-30%; the red pigment, also known as safflower, is scientifically called Carthamine, which has a low content, accounting for only 0.3%-0.6%. Since the red pigment of safflower became popular after the Tang Dynasty for dyeing red, the traditional safflower dyeing process mainly refers to this technique of dyeing red in general. Safflower red pigment is weakly acidic, which is insoluble in water or acidic liquid, but it is soluble in alkaline liquid. That means its extraction and dyeing methods are relatively unique. Judging from the history of our country's mastery and usage of safflower dyeing technology, it has gone through a long period of development. Before safflower was introduced into the Central Plains of our country, the yellow pigment in safflower was commonly extracted and dyed in Central Asia and Northwest China. The immature dyeing technology makes it impossible to fully extract the red pigment from safflower, so the dyed colour is somewhere between red and yellow, and the problem fading of caused by time is also obvious. There are many materials in this history that can prove that the red colour in the Six Dynasties period is the "Yuan" of the Han Dynasty. The book *Origin of Chinese Characters* explains Yuan as a reddish yellow. In addition, the distinction of three dyeing methods is cited. *Erya*, interpreted by Guo Pu, explains that Yuan is red. This shows that the red at that time was not the red of the modern three primary colours, but the orange between red and yellow. Most of the red brocades unearthed in Xinjiang, Qinghai, and other places dating back to the Northern Dynasties and the early Tang Dynasty have faded to yellow, which may also explain why the safflower dye liquid was not pure at that time. People could extract and purify the red pigment in safflower and dye it bright red until the Tang and Song Dynasties, when ancient people described it as "true red" or "scarlet", which is compared with the previous red with a tendency to yellow. The cultivation of safflower has spread all over the country since the Tang Dynasty, and most of the safflower dyeing has been done with relatively high-quality Carthamine. Based on the fact that saffron contains both yellow and red pigments, and that the pigments are extracted through two different mediums, acidic and alkaline liquid, to produce a range of colours from yellow, orange, pink, and crimson, we used the traditional saffron dyeing process to perform a dyeing restoration experiment on the polychrome Bodhisattva skirt strap of Cave 194 of the high Tang Dynasty in the Mogao Grottes at Dunhuang.

5. Restoration experiment of safflower dyeing process

Experimental materials: 500g of scattered safflower, 200g of silk (silk crepe de chine), 1.6kg of straw ash, and 40g of dark plum.

5.1 Preparation additives

Additives need to be prepared before dyeing: an alkaline solution for extracting safflower red pigment and an acidic solution for neutralizing the red pigment solution. The former is mostly made from straw ash, and the latter is made of dark plum water in traditional methods. During the experiment, soak 40g of dark plums in 2L of hot water (about 80°C) for more than 3 days, and filter the upper layer of clear dark plum water for use (pH 3-4). Soak 1.6kg of straw ash in 16L of boiling water for more than 2 hours, then filter the clear grey water on the surface (the first gray water) for use (pH 11-12).

5.2 Extraction of red pigment

As mentioned above, safflower contains both yellow pigment and red pigment, so the yellow pigment in safflower needs to be removed first. Soak 500g of safflower in 15L of water, then filter with cotton or linen after 2 hours and squeeze out the yellow pigment solution. Soak the safflower in 15L of water, let it stand for 12 hours, filter it with cotton or linen, and squeeze out the yellow pigment solution. Then wash the petals 6 to 10 times to remove the yellow pigment in the petals as much as possible.

After removing the yellow pigment from the safflower, the next step is to extract the red pigment. The red pigment can be dissolved in an alkaline solution, so inject 10L of grey water (pH 11-12) into the petals. Filter and squeeze the juice with cotton cloth or linen cloth after 3 hours to obtain the first dyeing solution. Then inject 5L of grey water (pH 11-12) into the petals, filter and squeeze the juice with cotton or linen after 3 hours to obtain the second dyeing solution. Mix the two dyeing solution together to obtain about 13L of red dyeing solution, then filter to remove impurities. At this point, the red pigment solution needs to be neutralized with an acidic substance, so add 1.8L of dark plum water to the dyeing solution, and stir it evenly for later use (about pH 7).

5.3　Soaking the resist—dyeing silk in water

Put the sewed silk strips into clean water and soak them for about 15 minutes. If the blocking cloth is made of cotton, or the texture is thick, we can prolong the soaking time to make it completely soaked. This simple step is to prevent the dry silk from causing uneven dyeing, and it can make the silk fiber expand after pre-wetting, which is conducive to dyeing synchronously. Mr. Wang Xu's research pointed out that the immersion step in the resist-dyeing process is especially critical because it is related to the dyeing outcome and the artistic effect of the dyeing pattern. When the sewed or bundled crepe silk enters the water, the water will penetrate inward along the micro-gap between the fibers until it is saturated. The fibers of the fabric swell greatly after absorbing moisture, which causes some internal tension in the sewn and twisted areas, so that they are pressed together more tightly near the seams and knotted areas, which is conducive to the appearance of the expected pattern.

5.4　Dyeing

The silk strips were soaked in warm water at 40℃ for 30min, then drowned in the dyeing solution for 15min. Since the dyed silk strips were folded and stitched into multiple layers, the dyeing solution needed to be pressed continuously to promote the penetration of the dyeing solution. Take them out and fill the dyeing solution with 90mL of plum water, making the pH value around 6, after which the silk strips were then dipped into the dyeing solution and pressed for 15min. 300 mL of plum water was added to 15L of warm water (about 20℃) to make a solid solution (pH 5 or so). The dyed silk strips are dyed in the solid solution for 15min, during which they are continuously kneaded and pressed in the solid solution to promote the penetration of the solid solution.

Saffron dyeing is done by the dyeing method at room temperature, and the silk strips need to be submerged in excessive dyeing solution. The silk needs to be plucked with chopsticks so that it is evenly coloured when dyed.

Fig. 12 Resist-dyeing skirt strap of replica textile polychrome sculpture of Bodhisattva in Cave 194 of the high Tang Dynasty in Mogao Grottoes, Dunhuang

5.5　Organizing

After finishing dyeing, the silk strips are pulled out of the dyeing solution and rinsed thoroughly with water to remove the floating colour. Then a dry towel is used to absorb excessive water from the silk strips; finally, the sewn and twisted threads are removed. Unfold the silk strips and the dyed pattern is slowly revealed, then dried and ironed it to obtain the final work (Fig. 12). Compared with the resist-dyeing skirt strap of the

Bodhisattva in Cave 194 of the high Tang Dynasty in Mogao Caves at Dunhuang, the pattern of the resist-dyeing silk obtained through our tests is basically the same. The dyeing presents more vivid colours, which is closer to the initial appearance of the saffron-dyed silk fabric.

6. Conclusion

Through the analysis of the resist-dyeing skirt strap of the Bodhisattva in Cave 194 of the high Tang Dynasty in the Mogao Grottoes at Dunhuang, it can be seen that artists in Dunhuang not only portray the realistic movements and demeanor of the figure, but also focus on the gorgeous costumes worn by the Bodhisattva, as well as the texture, patterns, and techniques of the various costume fabrics. The sewing and dyeing methods of the Tang Dynasty resist-dyeing process are also clearly portrayed. It provides valuable information and new perspectives for studying the history and stylistic features of the Tang Dynasty resist-dyeing process, recovering the specific production methods of the resist-dyeing process, and researching the stylistic features of Tang Dynasty polychrome sculptures in Dunhuang and their embodiment in Dunhuang costumes.

敦煌莫高窟盛唐第194窟南亚及东南亚王子服饰研究

王　可

　　敦煌莫高窟第194窟壁画"各国王子问疾图"中描绘了维摩诘讲经说法，"各国国王或王子"前来问疾的场景。这组"奇装异服"的形象正是长安诸蕃客使的写实，体现了大唐盛世万邦来朝的繁盛景象。这组形象中走在最前方的几位王子的服饰便是本文研究的对象，通过针对其服装形制、纹样、色彩，以及面料工艺等进行实验性的复原研究，为研究丝绸之路沿线的相关民族服饰提供参考。

一、第194窟南亚及东南亚王子身份分析

　　"各国王子问疾图"自贞观十六年（642年）开凿的莫高窟第220窟以来，南亚和东南亚王子的形象就无一例外地出现在朝贡者的群像中，而且几乎都是位于队列之首（除了敦煌中唐时期吐蕃占领瓜州时将吐蕃赞普及侍从的形象置于首要位置）。敦煌莫高窟第194窟主室南壁绘有维摩诘经变一铺，八位穿着单薄的南亚和东南亚王子形象就走在队列最前方，在服饰及配饰穿搭上这几位形象都比较相似，本文拟对图1中①号和②号两位人物形象进行复原。

　　针对这一王子或使臣形象，首先对其身份族属问题做一探究。玄奘在《大唐西域记·卷一·三十四国》中描绘他所见到的古印度人："服则横巾右袒，首则中髻四垂……短制左衽，断发长髭"，在《大唐西域记·卷二·印度总述》中有更为细致的描写："衣裳服玩，无所裁制……男则绕腰络腋，横巾右袒。女乃襜衣下垂，通肩总覆。顶为小髻，余发垂下。或有剪髭，别为诡俗。首冠花鬘，身佩璎珞……国王大臣服玩良异，花鬘宝冠以为首饰，环钏璎珞而作身佩……人多徒跣，少有所履。染其牙齿，或赤或黑，齐发穿耳，修鼻大眼，斯其貌也。"[1]从这段描述中，对比敦煌莫高窟第194窟壁画中的①号人物，多数描写都比较吻合。不论是"首则中髻四垂"，还是"顶为小髻"，①号人物都描绘出玄奘所见到的古印度人在头顶上梳有发髻，还

图1　南海诸国王子

---

❶ 玄奘，辩机. 大唐西域记汇校 [M]. 范祥雍，汇校. 上海：上海古籍出版社，2018：83.

有嘴边上被修剪过的胡须，同时头戴花鬘宝冠，手脚都带有环钏，金环贯耳，赤足步行，眼眶深陷，鼻梁高窄的样貌。其中提到了其肤色或赤或黑，而①号人物虽呈现较白的肤色，但是通身绘制了赤色毛发，笔者认为这是画师在描绘古印度人时有意为之。另外在服装的描写上也有些许不符。玄奘在描绘其所看到的古印度人穿着的服装时强调了衣服并没有裁制过，也就是使用整块布来进行围裹。男性将织物缠绕于腰间的同时祖右肩而绕于腋下，对比这样一种对服装的描绘，与莫高窟第194窟②号人物的穿着更为相像，而①号人物则像是对女性穿着的遮至膝前而通肩总覆的短衣这样一种描绘。虽然男性特征明显的①号人物穿着的是玄奘所见的女装样式，笔者仍然认为这个人物形象是来自南亚的古印度王子或王侯。原因有两点：一是因为印度是佛教的发源地，随着佛教的传播，至隋唐时期两国的交往更为密切，古印度先后派遣使团到唐朝多达25次，因此将古印度王子和使节的形象置于队列最前方便是情理之中了；二是有学者认为，唐大历年间第194窟的"各国王子礼佛图"开创了一个新的粉本，并推测画师是"按据史传，想象风采"❶，所以能够看到描绘的古印度王子或王侯的形象与史料记载的相似却在和图像描绘的细节上略有偏差。另外，在现在印度的某些地区，仍有人采用这种穿着方式。因此推测①号人物形象应是从南亚古印度而来的王子或王侯。

而②号人物形象在古代绘画作品中和一些出土陶俑中能看到近似的形象。梁元帝所绘制的《职贡图》中有一个狼牙修国使的形象［图2（a）］，与阎立本所绘制的《职贡图》［图2（b）］中婆利国和罗刹国前来朝贡的人物形象很相似，他们从外貌形象上和服饰搭配上都与第194窟中②号人物形象［图2（c）］相似。

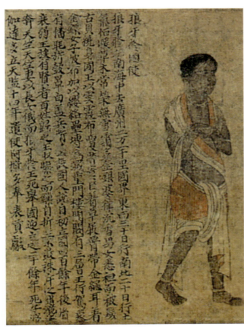  

（a）狼牙修国使　　　　　　　　（b）东南亚国家人物形象　　　　　（c）②号人物

图2　②号人物形象与《职贡图》中的人物比较

在描画狼牙修国使的作品上有一题记："狼牙修国在南海中……男女悉祖而被发，古贝绕身。国王以云霞布覆体，贵臣着草屐，腰带金绳，耳着金银。女子披布，加以璎珞。"❷类似这样一种描绘，在记

❶ 李昀. 万国衣冠拜冕旒：敦煌壁画中的朝贡者形象［C］//中山大学艺术史研究中心. 艺术史研究：19. 广州：中山大学出版社，2017：169–205.

❷ 姚义斌. 中华图像文化史·魏晋南北朝卷［M］. 北京：中国摄影出版社，2016：206.

载东南亚国家民俗风情的文献中也可得见，如表1中罗列的相关史料。

表1 东南亚各国服饰相关史料

古代国家	现国家	人物描绘	出处
林邑	越南	王戴金花冠……衣朝霞布、珠玑璎珞，足蹑革履，时复锦袍……其人深目高鼻，发拳色黑。俗皆徒跣，以幅布缠身，冬月衣袍。妇人椎髻……人皆奉佛，文字同于天竺	列传·卷八十三
		王著白氎古贝，斜络膊，绕腰，上加真珠金锁，以为璎珞，卷发而戴花。夫人服朝霞古贝以为短裙，首戴金花，身饰以金锁真珠璎珞……其人拳发色黑，俗皆徒跣，得麝香以涂身，一日之中，再涂再洗。拜谒皆合掌顿额……自林邑以南，皆卷发黑身，通号为"昆仑"	列传·卷一百四十七
		男女皆以横幅古贝绕腰以下，谓之干漫，亦曰都漫。穿耳贯小环。贵者着革屣，贱者跣行。自林邑、扶南以南诸国皆然也。其王者着法服，加璎珞，如佛像之饰	列传·卷七十八
真腊	柬埔寨	王著朝霞古贝，瞒络腰腹，下垂至胫，头载金宝花冠，被真珠璎珞，足履革屣，耳悬金珰。常服白叠，以象牙为屩。若露发，则不加璎珞。臣下服制，大抵相类……人形小而色黑，妇人亦有白者。悉拳发垂耳，性气捷劲	列传·卷八十三
狼牙修	马来西亚	其俗，男女皆祖而被发，以古贝为干漫，其王及贵臣乃加云霞布覆胛，以金绳为络带，金环贯耳。女子则被布，以璎珞绕身	列传·卷七十八
婆利	文莱	其国人披古贝如帊，及为都缦。王乃用斑丝者，以璎珞绕身	列传·卷七十八
		其人皆黑色，穿耳附榼……男子皆拳发，被古贝，布横幅以绕腰	列传·卷一百四十七
骠国	缅甸	其衣服悉以白氎为朝霞，绕腰而已。不衣缯帛，云出于蚕，为其伤生故也	列传·卷一百四十七

从以上有关东南亚国家人物形象描绘的文献中可见其人有着黑色的皮肤，卷曲的头发，多跣足而金环贯耳，所穿着的服饰也通过图像精准地反映出来，整幅布横向绕腰，斜络膊而下垂至胫，谓之干漫，亦曰都漫。《一切经音义》卷八十一中有一词语"敢曼"，是这样释义的："敢曼，梵语也。遮形丑之下裳，如此方之裤袴。一幅物，亦不裁缝，横缠于腰下，名曰合曼也。"❶这里的"干漫""都漫""敢曼"应该都是这种由整幅布不加剪裁，通过围裹而成的下装，下文将这类下装均称为"敢曼"。这种装束在出土的昆仑俑身上也能看到，唐代郑仁泰墓❷和唐代薛从简墓❸中出土的昆仑俑（图3）所刻画的人物形象也与第194窟中的②号人物形象很相似。上文在提及林邑国的文献中写道："自林邑以南，皆卷发黑身，通号为'昆仑'。"《南海寄归内法传》中也有记载："南海诸洲有十余国……诸国周围或可百里，或数百里，或可百驿。大海虽难计里，商舶串者准知。良为掘伦，初至交广，遂使总唤昆仑国焉。唯此昆仑，头卷体黑。自余诸国，与神洲不殊。"❹可见"昆仑"这一称谓并不指某一国，而是指南海各岛屿上的众

---

❶《续修四库全书》编纂委员会. 续修四库全书［M］. 上海：上海古籍出版社，2002：491.
❷ 陕西省博物馆，礼泉县文教局唐墓发掘组. 唐郑仁泰墓发掘简报［J］. 文物，1972：7.
❸ 陕西省文物管理委员会. 陕西省出土唐俑选集［M］. 北京：文物出版社，1958：51.
❹ 义净. 南海寄归内法传校注［M］. 王邦维，校注. 北京：中华书局，1995：34.

多国家。通过以上对东南亚贡使图像、昆仑俑和东南亚古代相关文献的对比互证，本文认为第194窟中的②号人物形象应是东南亚王子或王侯。

二、第194窟南亚和东南亚王子服饰图案与工艺研究

　　虽然第194窟南亚和东南亚王子的图像已有掉色或者斑驳的情况，但是仍能整理出纹样细节。两个人物形象服饰中共出现了四种纹样（图4），可以看出基本是以"S"形为纹样母题，通过提取或是归纳得到的几何纹样。这些纹样在绘制上与一种染织工艺所呈现出来的视觉效果非常相似，那就是扎经染色工艺。

郑仁泰墓出土的昆仑俑　　薛从简墓出土的昆仑俑

图3　唐代昆仑俑

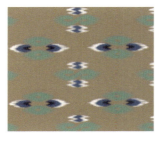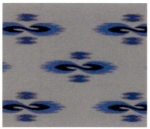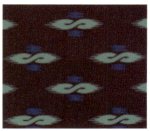

图4　南亚和东南亚王子服饰图案（笔者整理）

　　扎经染色织物是众多纺织品中极具独特魅力的一种，它与传统防染工艺和传统织造技艺不同，是将传统的防染技艺和织造技艺结合在一起进行织造的，有着防染技艺结合织造技艺的独特性和与众不同的视觉效果，因此，可以构建出图像研究与实物研究的证据链。扎经染色工艺核心是在经线上按照图案要求先进行扎染，然后织造，由于织造过程中经线上的图案难以完全对齐，会呈现出经向梳齿状参差不齐的效果，反映在图像上就是由似素描线条般的排线来区分色块或是替代图案龙骨线。

　　除了敦煌莫高窟第194窟的南亚和东南亚王子穿着的以"S"形为纹样母题的扎经染色织物以外，类似的纹样还出现在其他洞窟中的菩萨、南亚或东南亚王子以及昆仑奴的服饰上。表2为整理敦煌莫高窟中出现的"S"形纹样所得，有以单独纹样出现的，也有以对称纹样出现的，还有以复合纹样出现的。

表2　敦煌莫高窟中具有扎经染色织物"S"形纹样特征的图像

纹样类型	代表洞窟	纹样
单独纹样	159	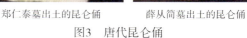

续表

纹样类型	代表洞窟	纹样
对称纹样	9	
复合纹样	44	

这样一种以"S"形为纹样母题的扎经染色织物在中国青海省出土的唐代织物和日本传世的唐代织物中也可以看到。如图5所示，日本正仓院收藏的这两件扎经染色的唐代织物都是以"S"形加以变形为纹样母题通过对称或是翻折得到的相对复杂的几何纹样，且通过多次捆扎和染色在"S"的曲线部分获得两种颜色，壁画中描绘的此类扎经染色图案不论是从结构上、设色上还是视觉效果上都与出土或传世的唐代扎经染色织物高度相似。因此，敦煌莫高窟第194窟中的南亚和东南亚王子所穿着的织物应为扎经染色织物。

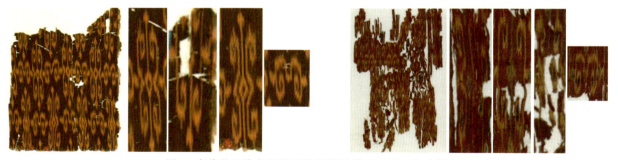

图5　唐代扎经染色织物及其纹样局部（日本正仓院藏）

三、第194窟南亚和东南亚王子形象的艺术再现

上文提及了南亚和东南亚王子穿着的服装是"无所裁制"的整幅织物，穿着方式是直接将"布横幅以绕腰"，并且通过图像、实物与文献的多元对比互证认为其所穿着的织物是通过扎经染色的工艺实现的。那么，南亚和东南亚王子形象艺术再现的难点主要是解决织物工艺和穿着方式两个方面。

1．扎经染色织物制作方法

扎经染色工艺自唐代起一直活态传承至今，我国新疆维吾尔族所织的艾德莱斯绸和海南黎族织的绗锦都是扎经染色织物，但是在织造方法及纹样色彩上却大相径庭。在对两地的实地调研后发现新疆艾德莱斯绸纹样粗犷奔放，色彩绚丽鲜艳，充满着韵律感与流动感，在经线方向能够明显地呈现出参差不齐的模糊纹样。而海南的绯锦都是只染一种颜色，以深蓝色或蓝黑色为主，纹样细腻，古朴雅致。通过对比两地扎经染色织物的风格，笔者认为新疆艾德莱斯绸的纹样风格与第194窟南亚和东南亚王子所穿着的扎经染色织物更为接近。故本文选取南亚王子上衣扎经染色纹样（图6）基于新疆艾德莱斯绸工艺进行实验性复原，具体工艺步骤如下：

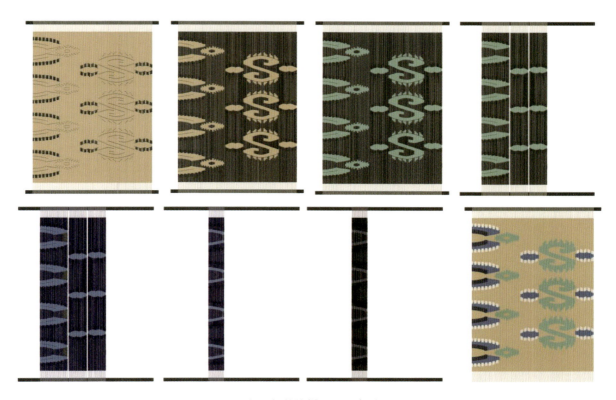

图6　捆扎纹样过程示意图

（1）导线：将16筒纱通过溜眼，手动分经后固定在整经机上，绕70圈后两头拴住导纱线取下放置一边备用，一共绕100捆线。绕好后将这100捆线有序地置于扎花架上，此时要将两边的导纱线对齐以免图案出现错乱。

（2）画图：用一根湿润的粗棉线按照纹样轮廓摆放在扎花架上，再用笔点画做好图案标记。

（3）捆扎：根据标记好的图案位置先将纹样白色部分用塑料薄膜（以前使用玉米皮，现代使用塑料薄膜）牢牢捆扎住，全部捆扎完毕后取下所有经线放入热水中浸泡一晚，使经线完全湿透有助于后续的染色。

（4）染色：准备好染液，将经线两头的导纱线一一对应捆绑住，做好标记以便再次捆扎时经线顺序不错乱，再放置到染色架上，摇动染色架的摇臂使之带动经线不断地浸入染液中充分染色，完成后取下洗掉浮色后阴干，此时除去被捆扎位置均完全染色。

（5）捆扎—染色—清洗—阴干：将第一次染色完毕的经线按顺序放回扎花架上（此时扎花架的杆应穿过导纱线），再次重复"捆扎—染色—清洗—阴干"这一过程，依次染青绿色、蓝色和深蓝色。

（6）拆线：将染完色的经线置于扎花架上，去除掉所有塑料薄膜，挂起阴干。

（7）整经：将染好的经线再次放入扎花架上，依次挑出每捆线的16根线头握在手中，按导线顺序拆开成捆的经线合成一捆，每到扎结导纱线的位置用线捆扎固定一次，以防织造过程中纹样错位。

（8）绕线：取一根长棍，将整理好成为一捆的经线头部绑在长棍上，开始进行"8"字形缠绕，直到绕完所有经线成为一个大蚕茧的状态。

（9）排经：此时虽然每捆经线都已分经，但是图案在此时还停留在核心纹样阶段，需要手工挑纱按最终纹样顺序排列经线。

（10）上机：两人配合将排好顺序的经线一一穿综，再将剩余经线挂在另一端，就可以开始织造了。

虽然壁画属于图像资料，但是能够发现扎经染色织物因其特殊的染织方式而有极具辨识度的纹样特征，通过新疆艾德莱斯绸的工艺实验制作的扎经染色织物，对比南亚王子上身所着的织物可见纹样基本一致，并且能够完全呈现出排线式参差不齐的视觉效果（图7）。

图7　南亚王子服饰图案与扎经染色复原织物（笔者整理）

2. 穿着方式

第194窟南亚和东南亚王子所穿着的"敢曼"在如今的南亚和东南亚还有很多人穿着。其中，古印度时期就已经出现并流传至今的印度传统男装"托蒂"（Dhoti）❶和东南亚的泰国所穿着的"帕·裙噶本"（Pha Chungkaben）❷与"敢曼"就很相似。通过壁画和史料中的记载可以看出这种不经过裁缝，横缠于腰下的"敢曼"呈现出裤装的形态，这与同样是由一块长方形的布料，通过在腰间打结缠绕，余料穿裆绕于后腰而自然形成两条裤腿的"托蒂"和"帕·裙噶本"，不论是从穿着方式上还是视觉形态上都如出一辙。因此，南亚及东南亚王子的"敢曼"艺术再现参考了印度"托蒂"和泰国"帕·裙噶本"的穿着方法。

南亚和东南亚王子"敢曼"的具体穿着方法步骤如下：

南亚王子穿着"敢曼"时将1米宽、3米长的布料取中置于身后，从两侧把布向身前围，对齐A与B两

❶ 万达纳·布哈达瑞. 印度的服装、纺织品和珠宝［M］. 新德里：帕卡什出版，2004.
❷ 田中千代. 世界民俗衣装：探寻人类着装方法的智慧［M］. 李当岐，译. 北京：中国纺织出版社，2001：118.

端，在前中心将C与C′系结，系紧后将腰部的布料向外、向下翻卷，起到固定作用的同时还可以卷进一些日常所需的小物件，充当口袋。再将B与B′等量折叠成褶后，把布端穿过两腿之间折进后腰。最后把A与C折成若干个直缀，将直缀中间位置折进前腰，使之自然形成裤腿的同时还能固定在腰间自然下垂遮挡裆部（图8）。

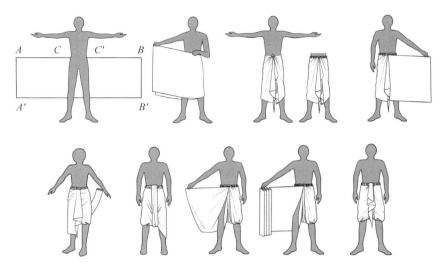

图8　南亚王子"敢曼"穿着步骤图（笔者手绘）

东南亚王子穿着"敢曼"时和南亚王子的初始步骤相同，只是在腰间扎结固定后，A与B两端需合并在一起，将A与B沿AB—A′B′中间点向下翻折，再不断向一个方向向下卷，以起到固定贴合作用，最后将布端穿两腿之间绕到后侧，折进腰部固定（图9）。这样按照史料记载的"一幅物，亦不裁缝，横缠于腰下"的服装形态就呈现出来了。

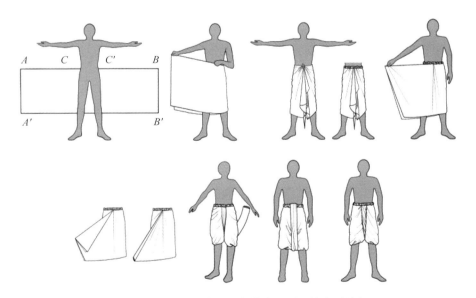

图9　东南亚王子"敢曼"穿着步骤图（笔者手绘）

通过对"一幅布"的穿着方式进行实践性复原，可见服装本身虽然无形可言，但是通过系结、打褶、缠绕在身体之上根据身体结构自然形成包裹的穿着方式，体现出南亚和东南亚人物形象的服装独特性，也展现了这种形成"无形之形"的服饰所充满的智慧。

3．整体造型

在对织物进行工艺实践复原和对穿着方式分析解读后，还需要整理出南亚及东南亚王子所佩戴的冠饰和首饰，最后选择合适的模特来穿着和演绎，艺术再现敦煌莫高窟第194窟南亚和东南亚王子形象艺术再现图片详见本书第295页和第297页。

四、结语

在对敦煌莫高窟第194窟"各国王子问疾图"中南亚及东南亚王子的形象进行分析，结合历史文献和相关出土实物，辅以织物的复原及穿着方式的再现，完成了南亚及东南亚王子形象的艺术再现。通过这一研究加实践的过程，更加凸显出敦煌服饰艺术资料不仅是中华民族服饰的资料宝库，也是世界各国服饰艺术资料的重要补充，对于研究世界服饰史、纺织史等方面提供一个新的路径。

Costume Research on the South Asia and Southeast Asia Princes in Cave 194 in the Dunhuang Mogao Grottoes of the High Tang Dynasty

Wang Ke

The mural "Pictures of Princes Enquiring Diseases" in Cave 194 of the Mogao Grottoes in Dunhuang depicts the scene of Vimalakirti's sermons and "kings or princes of various countries" coming to enquire about diseases. The images of the ambassadors in their exotic costumes represent a realistic portrayal of the ambassadors in Chang'an, reflecting the prosperous scene of the high Tang Dynasty. The costumes of the princes who are at the forefront of this group are the objects of this study. They provide a reference for the study of the costumes of related ethnic groups along the Silk Road through experimental restoration research on their costume styles, patterns, colours, and fabric techniques.

1. Analysis of the prince's identity in South Asia and Southeast Asia in Cave 194

"Pictures of Princes Enquiring Diseases" was depicted in Cave 220 of Mogao Grottoes, excavated in the 16th year of Zhenguan (642), and the images of South and Southeast Asian princes appeared in the group portraits of the tributaries without exception. Almost all of them were at the head of the queue (except for the DunHuang mid-Tang Dynasty, when the Tubo occupied Guazhou, where the images of Tsenpo and servants were given top priority). The south wall of the main chamber in Cave 194 of the Mogao Grottoes in Dunhuang was painted with the Vimalakīrti-Nirdeśa Sutra. Eight figures of South Asian and Southeast Asian princes in thin clothes were walking at the front of the queue. These figures were all dressed up in clothing and accessories in similar ways. This paper intends to restore the two figures of ① and ② in Fig. 1.

For this image of a prince or an envoy, we should first explore their identities and races. Xuanzang described the ancient Indians whom he saw in *The Great Records of the Western Regions in the Tang Dynasty, Volume 1, Thirty-Four Kingdoms:* The clothes are horizontal scarves with the right side bared, the head is in a bun with four drops-short attire with left side overlapping, short hair, and a long moustache. In *The Great Records of the Western Regions in the Tang Dynasty-Volume 2-General Description of India,* it is described in more detail: "The clothes have no tailoring. The men wind a strip of cloth around the waist and up to the armpits leaving the right shoulder bare. The women wear a long robe which covers both shoulders and falls down loose. All the hair on the crown of the head is made into a coil, with all the rest of the hair hanging down. Some clip their moustaches or have other fantastic fashions. Garlands are worn on the head and necklaces on the body. The king and ministers wear differently who use Kusuma-mala and crown as jewellery. Bracelets and

Fig. 1 Princes of ancient southern sea countries

keyūra are worn on their bodies. They mostly go bare-footed, and few wear sandals. Dye their teeth with red or black colour. They bind up their hair and pierce their ears. They have an ornament on their nose, and have large eyes. Such is their appearance." Compared with Figure ① in the murals in Cave 194 of the Mogao Grottoes in Dunhuang, most of the descriptions are quite consistent. Whether it is "the head bun is in the middle" or "the top is a small bun", Figure ① depicts the ancient Indians seen by Xuanzang with a bun on the top of their heads and a trimmed beard around their mouth. At the same time, he wears a flower garland and a crown, with bracelets on his hands and feet. Pierce their ears with gold rings. He walks bare-footed, with deep-set eyes, and a high narrow nose. It is mentioned that the skin color of the person is red or black. Although the Figure ① has a white skin color, the whole body is painted with red hair. The author believes that the artist did this on purpose when he depicted the ancient Indians. There are also some inconsistencies in the description of the clothing. When Xuanzang described the clothes he saw in ancient India, he emphasized that the clothes were not cut, that is, the whole cloth was used for wrapping. The man wraps the fabric around his waist and up to the armpits, leave the right shoulder bare. Compared with such a depiction of clothing, the Figure② in Cave 194 of Mogao Grottoes is dressed more similarly, while the Figure ① looks like the depiction of women wearing shorts that hang over their knees and cover their shoulders. Although the male Figure ① is wearing the women's clothing seen by Xuanzang, the author still believes that this figure is an ancient Indian prince or marquis from South Asia. There are two reasons as follow: one is that India is the birthplace of Buddhism. During the Sui and Tang Dynasties, as Buddhism spread, the two countries' exchanges grew closer. Ancient India dispatched missions to the Tang Dynasty as many as 25 times. It makes sense that the images of Indian princes and envoys should be placed in front of the queue. Secondly, some scholars believe that the "Pictures of Various Countries' Princes Venerating Buddhas" in Cave 194 during the Dali period created a new version of the stencil, and they speculate that the painter was painted according to historical legends and imaginative style, so we can see the depiction of ancient Indian princes or marquises is a slight deviation from the the image. In addition, in some parts of India, some people still use this way of wearing. Therefore, it is assumed that the Figure ① is a prince or a king from ancient India in South Asia.

And the Figure ② can be seen in ancient paintings and some excavated terracotta figurines with a close resemblance. The image of an ambassador from the Langya Xiu [Fig. 2(a)] in the *Tribute Picture* painted by Emperor Yuan of Liang is similar to the figures from the Poli nation and Luocha nation in the *Tribute Picture* painted by Yan Liben [Fig. 2(b)], and they are similar to the figure in Cave 194 [Fig. 2(c)] in terms of appearance and costume.

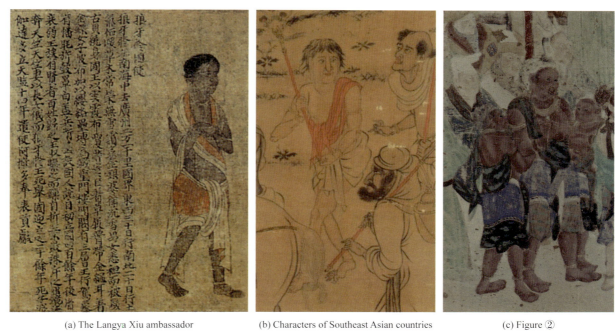

(a) The Langya Xiu ambassador   (b) Characters of Southeast Asian countries   (c) Figure ②

Fig. 2 Comparison between the Figure ② and the figures in the *Tribute Picture*

There is an inscription on the painting depicting the Langya Xiu ambassador: "Langya Xiu lies in the South China Sea. Men and women all bared their shoulders with hanging hair. And ancient shells are wrapped around their bodies. Their king covers his body with cloudy cloth, and noble officials wear straw sandals. Gold ropes are around their waists, and they wear gold and silver earrings. The women wear clothes with bracelets and keyūra." Descriptions like this can also be found in the documents recording the folk customs of Southeast Asian countries. The relevant historical materials are listed in Table 1.

Table 1 Historical Materials Related to Clothing in Southeast Asian Countries

Ancient nation	Modern nation	Description of figures	Reference
Lin Yi	Vietnam	Their king wears a golden crown and Zhaoxia clothes who are decorated with keyūra and jewellery. He puts on leather shoes and brocade robes. They have deep eyes and a high nose with curly black hair. It is customary to bare feet, wrapped in a piece of cloth and dressed in robes in winter. Women have cone bun. Everyone worships Buddha, and the characters are the same as India	Lie Zhuan, Volume 83

Ancient nation	Modern nation	Description of figures	Reference
Lin Yi	Vietnam	The king wears felt and ancient shells, slanting clothes and wrapping them around his waist. Pearls and jewellery were covered on it which were regarded as keyūra. He also wears flowers on his curly hair. The lady wears ancient shell as a short skirt, wearing golden flowers on the head, and she is decorated with golden pearls and keyūra. Their people have black and curly hair, and it is customary to bare feet. They smeared musk on their body, wash and smeared over and over again. All worshippers put their palms together and kotow. From the south side of Linyi, they all have curly hair and black bodies, and they were commonly called "Kunlun"	Lie Zhuan, Volume 147
		Both men and women wear ancient shells around their waists, which is called "Gan man" or "Du man". Pierced ear with little ring. The rich wear leather shoes, and the poor bare feet. It is the same with all the countries south of Linyi and Funan. The king is dressed in dharma robes, which is decorated with keyūra, like the ornaments of Buddha sculpture	Lie Zhuan, Volume 78
Zhen La	Cambodia	The king wears the ancient shells of Zhaoxia, covering his waist and abdomen and hanging down to the shin. A golden crown was on his head, and his body was covered with pearls and keyūra. He also wears leather shoes, and his ears are pierced with golden bells. He wears white folded clothes, using ivory as his sandals. If the hair is exposed, tassels are not added. The clothes of government officials are roughly similar. Their body is small and black in color, and some women are also in white skin. All of them have curly hair and their temperament is quick and vigorous	Lie Zhuan, Volume 83
Langya Xiu	Malaysia	It is customary for both men and women to be bared and dishevelled hair, with ancient shells as "Gan man". Their king and nobles cover shoulder blades with Yunxia cloth, and golden ropes were used to tie. Golden rings pierced through their ears. The woman was clothed and wrapped around her body with keyūra	Lie Zhuan, Volume 78
Po Li	Brunei	Their people wear ancient shells like robes, which are called "Du man". Their king wears spot silk and wrapped his body with keyūra	Lie Zhuan, Volume 78
		All of them are black, with pierced ears and attached thorns. The men have curly hair, covered with ancient shells, and whole piece of cloth was wrapped around their waists	Lie Zhuan, Volume 147
Biao nation	Myanmar	Their clothes are all made of white felt, just around their waists. They don't wear silk since silkworms produce it, which is harmful to them	Lie Zhuan, Volume 147

From the above documents about the depiction of people in Southeast Asian countries, we can see that they have black skin, curly hair, bared feet, and gold rings in their ears. Clothes worn by the images are also accurately reflected, and the whole cloth is around the waist horizontally and roll shoulder down to shinbone, which is called "Gan man" or "Du man." There is a word "Gan man" in Volume 81 of *The Sound and Meaning of the Tripitaka*, which is explained in this way: "Gan man", which is a Sanskrit word, covers the body of a lower garment, like trousers. A piece of cloth, which should not be tailored and sewn, is wrapped around the waist, and it is also called "He man". "Gan man", "Du man", and "Gan man" should be this kind of lower garment made of the whole cloth without tailoring. The following article will call this kind of clothes as "Gan man". This type of attire can also be seen on the unearthed Kunlun figurines, and the tomb figures unearthed from the tombs of Zheng Rentai and Xue Congjian in the Tang Dynasty (Fig. 3) are similar to the Figure② in Cave 194. In the above document referring to the Linyi country, it is written that all of them have curly hair and black skin, and they are commonly called "Kunlun." It is also recorded in the Records of *Buddhist Practice Sent Home from the Southern Sea* that there are more than ten countries in the South China Sea area, and those countries cover a territory of more than hundreds of miles. Although it is difficult to count the area of the sea, the crew on merchant ship know it. In fact, it was called Juelun state, when they first arrived there, all these countries are named Kunlun. And all these people have curly hair and black skin. The rest of countries are different from China. It can be seen that the title "Kunlun" does not refer to a particular country, implying many countries in the islands of the South China Sea.

Kunlun figurine unearthed from Zheng Rentai's tomb   Kunlun figurine unearthed from Xue Congjian's tomb

Fig. 3 Kunlun figurines of the Tang Dynasty

By comparing the above images of Southeast Asian tributes, Kunlun tomb figurines, and ancient Southeast Asian literature, this paper believes that the Figure ② in Cave 194 should be a Southeast Asian prince or marquis.

2. Research on the patterns and craftsmanship of the South Asia and Southeast Asia princes' costumes in Cave 194

Although the images of the princes of South Asia and Southeast Asia in Cave 194 have faded or mottled, the details of the patterns can still be sorted out. There are four patterns in the costumes of the two figures (Fig. 4). It can be seen that the geometric patterns are basically based on the "S" shape as the pattern motif, and they are obtained by extraction or induction. These patterns are similar to the visual effect presented by a dyeing and weaving process, namely the tie-dyeing process.

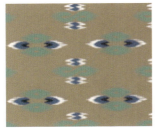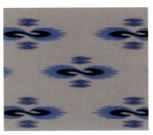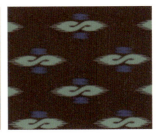

Fig. 4 Costume patterns from South Asia and Southeast Asia prince organised by the author

Tie-dyeing fabric is one of the most unique and attractive types of textiles. It is different from traditional resist-dyeing techniques and weaving techniques, which are woven by combining traditional resist-dyeing techniques and weaving techniques. The uniqueness of weaving techniques and distinctive visual effects could be acquired, so it can build a chain of evidence between image research and physical research. The core part of the tie-dyeing process is to dye the warp yarn first according to the pattern requirements, then weave it. Since the pattern on the warp yarn is difficult to align completely during the weaving process, the jagged effect in the wrap yarn direction will appear. Reflected on the image are the sketch-like lines to distinguish the color blocks or replace the keel line of the pattern.

In addition to the tie-dyeing fabrics with the "S" shape as the pattern motif worn by the South and Southeast Asian princes in Cave 194 of the Mogao Grottoes in Dunhuang, similar patterns also appear in other caves on Bodhisattvas, South or Southeast Asian princes, and Kunlun slaves. The "S" shaped patterns appearing in the Mogao Grottoes in Dunhuang are sorted out as shown in Table 2. Some appear in single patterns, some appear in symmetrical patterns, and some appear in composite patterns.

Table 2 Images featuring the "S" shape pattern of tie-dyeing fabrics
in the Mogao Grottoes in Dunhuang

Pattern type	Representative cave	Pattern
Separate pattern	159	
Symmetrical pattern	9	
Composite pattern	44	

Such a tie-dyeing fabric with the "S" shape as the motif can also be seen in the fabrics unearthed in Qinghai Province, China and the fabrics handed down from Japan in Tang Dynasty. As shown in Fig. 5, the two tie-dyeing Tang Dynasty fabrics in the collection of Shoso-in, Japan are both relatively complex geometric patterns obtained by symmetry or folding in the shape of an "S" and deformed into a pattern motif. Two kinds of colors are obtained on the curved part of the "S" by tying and dyeing many times. Such tie-dyeing patterns depicted in the murals are similar to the unearthed or handed down tie-dyeing textiles in the Tang Dynasty in terms of structure, color, and visual effect. Therefore, the fabrics worn by the South and Southeast Asia princes in Cave 194 of the Mogao Grottoes in Dunhuang should be tie-dyeing textiles.

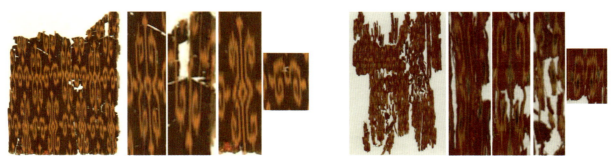

Fig. 5 Tie-dyeing fabrics and their patterns of the Tang dynasty in the Shoso-in collection

3. An artistic reproduction of the images of the prince from South and Southeast Asia in Cave 194

It is mentioned that the clothes worn by princes from South Asia and Southeast Asia are whole fabrics without tailoring, and the way of wearing them is to directly wrap the cloth around the waist. Through multiple comparisons of images, textiles, and documents, it is believed that the fabric worn by them is achieved through the process of tie-dyeing. The difficulty in reproducing the image of South Asian and Southeast Asian princes is primarily in resolving the two aspects of fabric technology and wearing style.

3.1   Reproduction method of tie-dyeing fabrics

The tie-dyeing process has been alive and passed down since the Tang Dynasty. The Atlas silk woven by the Uyghur people in Xinjiang and the brocade woven by the Li people in Hainan are both tie-dyeing fabrics, but they are quite different in weaving methods, patterns and colors. After on-the-spot investigation of the two places, it was found that the Xinjiang Atlas silk pattern is rough and unrestrained with bright colors, full of rhythm and flow. And it clearly shows uneven and fuzzy patterns in the direction of the warp yarn. The Ikat brocades in Hainan are only dyed in one color, mainly dark blue or blue-black, with delicate patterns and simple elegance. By comparing the styles of tie-dyeing fabrics in the two places, the author believes that the pattern style of Xinjiang Atlas is closer to the tie-dyeing fabrics worn by princes of South Asia and Southeast Asia in Cave 194. Therefore, this paper selects the tie-dyeing pattern of the South Asian prince's upper garment (Fig. 6) for experimental restoration based on the Xinjiang Atlas silk process. The specific process steps are as follows:

(1) Preparing yarns: pass 16 bobbins of yarn through the slippery eye, divide the warp manually, and fix it on the warping machine. After winding for 70 laps, tie the guide yarn at both ends, remove it, and set it aside for use. A total of 100 bundles of yarn are wound. After winding, arrange the 100 thread bundles on the tying frame in an orderly fashion. Align the guide yarns on both sides to avoid confusion in the pattern.

(2) Drawing: Use a wet, thick cotton thread to place it on the tie frame according to the outline of the pattern, then use a pen to draw the pattern mark.

(3) Binding: according to the marked position of the pattern, bind the white part of the pattern with plastic film (corn husks were used in the past; plastic film is used in modern times). Remove all the warp threads and put them in hot water after all the tying is completed. Soak all yarns overnight in medium to fully wet them out, which will aid in subsequent dyeing.

(4) Dyeing: Prepare the dye solution, bind the guide yarns at both ends of the warp thread one by one, and

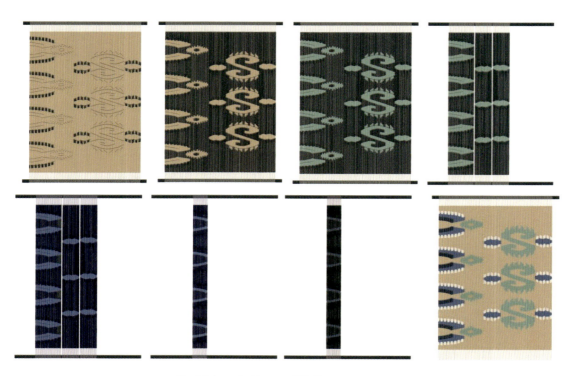

Fig. 6 Schematic diagram of binding pattern process

make a mark so that the warp thread order is not disordered when bundling again. Place it on the dyeing rack and shake the rocker arm of the dyeing rack to drive it. The warp threads are continuously immersed in the dye solution and fully dyed. After completion, they are washed to remove the floating color and dried in the shade. All the warp threads are completely dyed, apart from the bundled parts.

(5) Binding-dyeing-cleaning-drying in the shade: put the warp yarns dyed for the first time back on the flower tie frame in order (the rod of the flower tie frame should pass through the guide yarn at this time), repeat the process of bundling-dyeing-washing-drying in the shade again. Dyed turquoise, blue, and dark blue in turn.

(6) Removal of stitches: Place the dyed warp threads on a flower tie frame, remove all plastic films, and hang them in the shade.

(7) Warping: Put the dyed warp threads on the tying rack again, pick out 16 threads from each bundle in turn and hold them in hands. Unpack the bundles of warp threads in the order of the wires to form a bundle. The position of the thread is fixed once with thread bundling to prevent the pattern from being dislocated during the weaving process.

(8) Winding: Take a long stick and tie the ends of the warp threads that have been arranged into a bundle on the long stick. Wind in the form of an "8" until all the warp threads are wound like a large cocoon.

(9) Arranging the warp: although each bundle of warp threads has been divided, the pattern is still at the core pattern stage at this time. And it is necessary to manually pick the yarn to arrange the warp threads in the order of the final pattern.

(10) Set on the machine: two people work together to thread the warp yarns in order, one by one, then hang the remaining warp threads on the other end to start weaving.

Although the murals belong to the image data, it can be found that the tie-dyed fabrics have highly recognizable patterns because of their special dyeing and weaving methods. When comparing tie-dyeing fabric through the Xinjiang Atlas silk experimental process with textiles worn by prince from South Asia, it can be found that the patterns of the fabrics are basically the same, and the visual effects of uneven lines can be completely presented (Fig. 7).

Fig. 7 Pattern of the South Asian prince's clothing and reproduction fabric by tie-dyeing arranged by author

3.2 Dressing style

The "Gan man" worn by the princes of South and Southeast Asia in Cave 194 is still worn by many people in South and Southeast Asia today. Among them, the Dhoti, a traditional Indian male garment that has been worn since ancient India, and the Pha chungkaben, worn in Thailand in Southeast Asia, are similar to the "Gan man". The mural and historical records show that "Gan man," which is wrapped around the waist without tailoring, is similar to "Dhoti" and "Pha chungkaben" which are also made of a rectangular piece of fabric that is knotted and wrapped around the waist, with the rest of the material wrapped around the back waist to form two legs naturally in terms of dressing styles and visual form. Therefore, the artistic reproduction of the "Gan man" of the princes from South and Southeast Asia refers to the wearing methods of the Indian "Dhoti" and the Thai "Pha chungkaben".

The steps of wearing "Gan man" by South and Southeast Asian princes are as follows.

The South Asian prince wears the "Gan man" by placing a one-meter-wide and three-meter-long fabric behind his body, wrapping the cloth around his body from both sides. Align the two ends of the *AB*, tying the *CC'* knot in the centre of the front. Tie it tightly, and roll the fabric at the waist downward, which can be used as a pocket while rolling in some small items needed for daily life. After folding *BB*'s equal parts into pleats, tuck the cloth end through the legs and into the back waist. Finally, fold the *AC* into several straight stitches, and fold the middle of the stitches into the front waist, so that they naturally form trouser legs and can be fixed at the waist to sag naturally to cover the crotch (Fig. 8).

When a Southeast Asian prince wears a "Gan man", the initial steps are the same as those for a South Asian prince, except that the two ends of the *AB* need to be merged together after the knot is tied and fixed at the waist. The *AB* is folded downward along the middle point of the *AB-A'B'*, and rolled downward in one direction

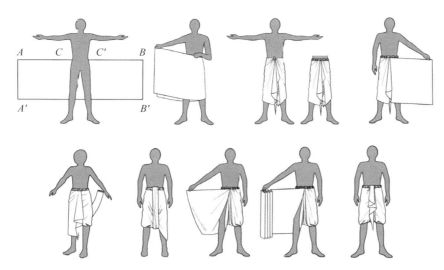

Fig. 8 Wearing steps of "Gan man" of South Asian prince hand-painted by author

to make a fixed knot. Let the end of the cloth go through the two legs to the back side and fix it into the waist (Fig. 9). According to the historical records, the garment form of a piece of cloth wrapped horizontally around the waist without tailoring was presented in this way.

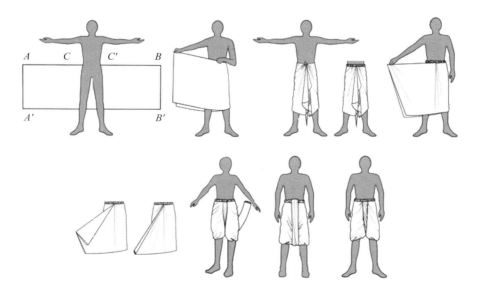

Fig. 9 Wearing steps of "Gan man" of Southeast Asian prince hand-painted by the author

By practically reproducing the way of wearing "a piece of cloth", we can find that the costume itself has no fixed forms, but the way of wearing it by tying, pleating, and wrapping according to the structure of the body reflects the uniqueness of the South and Southeast Asian costume, and it also shows the wisdom of this costume that forms an invisible form.

3.3 Overall shape

After the reproduction of the fabric and the analysis of the way of wearing, it is necessary to sort out the crown ornaments and accessories worn by the princes of South Asia and Southeast Asia. Finally, we will choose an appropriate model to wear and perform it through the artistic representation of princes from South and

Southeast Asia in Cave 194 of the Mogao Grottoes in Dunhuang. Please see pages 295 and 297 for the artistic representation.

4. Conclusion

With regard to the analysis of the images of the princes from South and Southeast Asia in Cave 194 of the Dunhuang Mogao Caves, we have achieved the artistic representation of the images of the princes from South and Southeast Asia, combined with historical documents and related excavated objects, as well as the reproduction of fabrics and wearing styles. Through the process of research and practice, the fact is highlighted that Dunhuang costume artistic materials are not only a treasure trove of Chinese costume materials, but also an important supplement to the costume materials of other countries around the world, providing a new path for the research of world costume and textile history.

Dunhuang Mogao Grottoes Cave 172 of the High Tang Dynasty

敦煌莫高窟盛唐

第172窟

　　第172窟是创建于盛唐时期的覆斗顶形窟，经宋、清重修，是唐代的代表洞窟之一。主室窟顶藻井为团花井心，藻井边缘绘圆形网幔，四角各绘一飞天，四披绘千佛。西壁开平顶敞口龛，龛内彩塑一倚坐佛、二弟子、四菩萨，龛外两侧各一天王，皆为盛唐塑成，清代重修。龛顶上绘三身佛说法图，下绘菩提宝盖。龛内西壁浮塑佛光，两侧各一弟子。南、北壁各绘三弟子。龛沿内侧绘菱纹边饰，外侧绘一整半破团花边饰。龛下绘壸门。南壁西侧绘观世音菩萨一身，下绘男女供养人共两身，中央绘观无量寿经变一铺，西侧绘未生怨，东侧绘十六观。北壁西端绘三身观世音菩萨，中央绘观无量寿经变一铺，西侧绘未生怨，东侧绘十六观。东壁门上绘净土变一铺，门南北两侧的中央分别为普贤变、文殊变，上部为数身菩萨。前室及甬道存宋代壁画。

　　此窟的观无量寿经变为盛唐时期的代表作之一。南壁、北壁壁画题材皆为观无量寿经变。壁画上方为"天乐不鼓自鸣"，琵琶、箜篌、排箫、腰鼓等乐器系着飘带凌空飞行，画面正中有三座大殿，大殿前绘阿弥陀佛及诸菩萨。画家巧妙地采用鸟瞰透视的方法，使得整体构图层次有序、宏伟壮观。壁画中诸人物肌肤虽已变色，但姿态万千。众菩萨服饰华丽，大多为高髻宝冠，项饰璎珞，戴耳珰、臂钏、手镯，肩披青纱，着长裙。但壁画中也出现了无冠、无髻、发束两肩的菩萨形象。整窟壁画各处笔笔细描，气势开阔，体现出画师扎实的绘画功底和华贵大气的审美特征。

（文：杨婧嫱）

Cave 172 is a truncated pyramidal ceiling cave built in the high Tang Dynasty, which was repaired in the Song and Qing Dynasties, and it is one of the representative caves of the Tang Dynasty. The caisson of the main chamber has a round flower center and the edges of the caisson are painted with circular net fringe, and four corners all have a Flying Apsaras, and Thousand Buddhas are painted on the four slopes. There is a niche with flat ceiling in the west wall, which has painted sculptures of one sitting Buddha, two disciples and four Bodhisattvas, and a Maharāja-deva on each side of the niche, they are all made in the high Tang Dynasty and repaired in the Qing Dynasty. The top of the niche is painted with three Buddhas Dharma assembly and below them painted a Bodhi canopy. On the west niche wall is Buddha light relief, with one disciple on each side. On the south and north niche walls are painted with three disciples respectively. The inner side of the niche edge is painted with rhombic pattern decoration, and the outer side is painted with a whole and a half repeated round flower pattern. Below the niche is painted with Kunmen pattern. Avalokitesvara Bodhisattva is painted on the west side of the south wall, and a male and a female donors are painted on the lower part. The central part of the south wall is painted with Amitayurdhyana Sutra illustration, and Ajatasattu's story on the west side and Sixteen Visualizations on the east side. The west end of the north wall is painted with three Avalokitesvara Bodhisattvas, and the central part of the north wall is painted with Amitayurdhyana Sutra illustration, and Ajatasattu's story on the west side and Sixteen Visualizations on the east side. Above the east door is painted with a Pure Land illustration, and the middle parts of the south and north sides of the door are painted with Samantabhadra Bodhisattva tableau and Manjusri Bodhisattva tableau respectively, and the upper parts have several Bodhisattvas. There are murals of Song Dynasty in the front chamber and the corridor.

Amitayurdhyana Sutra illustration in this cave is one of the representative works of the high Tang Dynasty. The themes of the south wall and the north wall are same. At the top of the murals are self-playing musical instruments, such as Pipa, Konghou, Panpipe and Waist Drum flying in the air and tied with streamers. There are three main buildings in the middle of the illustrations, Amitabha Buddha and Bodhisattvas are painted in front of the main halls. The artist skillfully adopted the method of bird's-eye view and perspective to make the overall composition orderly and magnificent. Although the skin color of the figures in the mural has changed, their postures are various. The Bodhisattvas in the murals are magnificent in clothes, and most of them have high hair bun and wear treasure crown, necklace, earrings, armlets, bracelets, green silk scarves on shoulders and long skirts. However, there are also some Bodhisattva images which have no crown, no hair bun, instead their hairs drape on shoulders. The murals in the whole cave are presented in details and with majestic layout, reflecting the painter's mature painting skills and the grand aesthetic taste.

(Written by: Yang Jingqiang)

The attendant
Bodhisattva's clothes
on the north wall of the
main chamber in Cave 172 dated to the high
Tang Dynasty at Mogao Grottoes

胁侍菩萨服饰
莫高窟盛唐第172窟主室
北壁

图为盛唐第172窟主室北壁所画的观无量寿经变中右边的胁侍菩萨。菩萨相貌秀美，双眸微垂，眉心点有白毫，留有胡须。右手托举翡翠花瓶，端坐于莲花台上，左腿下垂，脚踩莲花。菩萨身披薄纱天衣，绿色丝带系于肚脐之上，腰间还有镶嵌珠宝的装饰链条。下身穿着深绿色的织锦阔裙，裙上的几何形纹饰经典且精美，并采用了截金的技法（根据绘制的图形纹样，将金箔切成不同的形状贴附其上），使织锦纹饰更加绚丽多彩。

菩萨头束云髻，佩戴日月宝冠，花冠的正面上部和两侧均有绿松石镶嵌其上。身体其他部位的装饰也非常讲究，其项链、臂钏、耳环、手镯都有绿松石镶嵌其中，特别是由项链左侧延伸下来的编织而成的精致璎珞环钏，在整窟服饰中起到了画龙点睛的重要装饰作用。

（文：刘元风）

The attendant Bodhisattva on the right side of the Amitayurdhyana Sutra illustration on the north wall of the main chamber in Cave 172 dated to the high Tang Dynasty has a beautiful appearance, slightly drooping eyes, a round Urna between the eyebrows and bearded. His right hand holds a jade vase, sitting on the lotus seat, with left leg drooping and foot resting on a lotus. The Bodhisattva wears silk scarf, a green ribbon is tied above navel, and a decorative chain inlaid with jewelry is also around His waist. The lower body is wearing a dark green brocade wide skirt, and the geometric patterns on the skirt are classic and exquisite, and the technique of Jiejin (referring to cut gold leaf into needed shapes and paste them on painting) was adopted to make the brocade patterns more gorgeous and colorful.

The Bodhisattva wears a cloud hair bun and a sun-moon crown with turquoises inlaid on the upper and both sides. The decoration on other parts of the body is also very delicate. His necklace, armlets, earrings and bracelets are also inlaid with turquoise, especially the exquisite keyūra bracelets from the left side of the necklace, which played an important decorative role among all the clothes in the whole cave.

(Written by: Liu Yuanfeng)

The attendant
Bodhisattva's skirt pattern
on the north wall of the main chamber in
Cave 172 dated to the high Tang Dynasty
at Mogao Grottoes

胁侍菩萨裙子图案
莫高窟盛唐第172窟主室
北壁

盛唐第172窟主室北壁观无量寿经变壁画中右边胁侍菩萨的织锦阔裙上布满精美的装饰纹样。膝盖以下的裙饰最为完整清晰，这部分裙面被横向二方连续纹样分为三个大装饰带，依次饰以菱形纹、三角纹、花草纹，其中的三角纹与南壁壁画中舞伎足下的三角纹地毯遥相呼应。色彩以青绿为基调，石青、石绿、土红、深褐四种不同明度的主色形成四个清晰的色彩层次，又以米白、金提亮色调，诸色穿插运用，构筑成均衡、稳定的色彩关系。

这组装饰纹样最大的亮点是上部由菱形连缀而成的几何纹，其特别之处不仅在于截金技法的运用，更在于纹样组织的巧思。这组几何纹既可看作一个个有六个菱形花瓣的正面花型，又可看作层层罗列的正方体。"共用形"既实现了单元纹样连接，又创造出令人迷幻的错视效果。与直线交叉形成的平面格子纹相比，这种以几何作图的错位连线法或四方连续的1/2错位跳接法创造出的纹样无疑更具趣味性和吸引力，当属传统几何纹中的特色品类，这种设计方法也是现代平面设计常用的图形创意方法。

（文：孙晓丽）

The wide brocade skirt on the attendant Bodhisattva who is on the right side of the Amitayurdhyana Sutra illustration is covered with exquisite decorative patterns, and the decorations below the knees are the most complete and clearest. This part of the skirt surface is divided into three large decorative bands by transverse two in a group repeated patterns, which are successively decorated with diamond pattern, triangular pattern and flower and leaf pattern. The triangular pattern echos with the triangular pattern carpet under the dancer's feet in the mural on the south wall. The basic tones are cyan and green, and the four main colors azurite, malachite green, earth red and dark brown have different lightness which formed into four clear color layers, and used rice white and gold to brighten the tone, also with other colors being used alternately to form a balanced and stable color relationship.

The most brilliant design of this group is the diamond geometric pattern in the upper part. Its particularity lies not only in the application of gold-cutting technique, but also in the ingenious idea of pattern composition, which the geometric pattern can be considered as either a flower pattern with six diamond petals or cubes piled up layer by layer. The multi-meaning-pattern not only able to connect pattern units, but also creates an illusionary perspective effect. Compared with the plane lattice pattern formed by the intersection of straight lines, this kind of pattern formed by the dislocation connection method of geometric drawing or the four in a group repeated 1/2 dislocation interval method is undoubtedly more interesting and attractive. It belongs to the special category of traditional geometric patterns, which is also a common used creative graphic design method in modern time.

(Written by: Sun Xiaoli)

图：孙晓丽　Painted by: Sun Xiaoli

The attendant
Bodhisattva's clothes
on the north wall of the main chamber
in Cave 172 dated to the high Tang
Dynasty at Mogao Grottoes

胁侍菩萨服饰
莫高窟盛唐第172窟主室
北壁

盛唐第172窟主室北壁画观无量寿经变壁画一铺，其中有一佛、二菩萨，左、右菩萨的服饰有其盛唐服饰文化的代表性。

左边的胁侍菩萨面容端庄恬静，宽眉秀目，鼻直口圆，留有胡须，左手持琉璃宝匣，右手轻拈睡莲花，端坐于莲花台上，右腿下垂脚踏莲花。菩萨身披绿色络腋，肩披薄纱天衣，下身穿绿色织锦阔裙，裙子上的条形几何纹样极为精美，既有花卉形态的条形纹样，又有几何形态的条形纹样，腰部系织锦腰带，两侧镶嵌绿松石。同时，腰部还系有蓝绿色的飘带且随裙垂落。

菩萨头戴日月宝冠，其冠体正中和两侧各镶嵌祖母绿宝石，耳环、项链、臂钏、手镯均有珠宝装饰其中，长长的璎珞随身飘垂。整套服饰华丽典雅。

（文：刘元风）

There is an Amitayurdhyana Sutra illustration on the north wall of the main chamber in Cave 172 dated to the high Tang Dynasty, which has one Buddha and two Bodhisattvas. The clothes of the left and right Bodhisattvas are representatives of the high Tang Dynasty clothing culture.

The attendant Bodhisattva on the left has a dignified and quiet face, wide eyebrows and beautiful eyes, a straight nose and a round mouth, bearded. He holds a treasure box in His left hand and a lotus in His right hand, siting on the lotus seat with His right leg drooping and foot resting on a lotus. The Bodhisattva wears green Luoye, silk scarf covers on His shoulders, and a wide green brocade skirt on His lower body. The strip geometric patterns on the skirt are very exquisite, both in flower form and geometric form. He has a brocade belt around His waist with turquoise inlaid on both sides. At the same time, blue-green ribbons are tied at the waist and fall with the skirt.

The Bodhisattva wears a sun-moon crown, which is inlaid with emeralds at the center and on both sides. Earrings, necklaces, armlets and bracelets are decorated with jewelry, long keyūra hanging down along the body. The clothes of the whole cave are gorgeous and elegant.

(Written by: Liu Yuanfeng)

图: 刘元风　Painted by: Liu Yuanfeng

The attendant
Bodhisattva's skirt pattern
on the north wall of the main chamber in
Cave 172 dated to the high Tang
Dynasty at Mogao Grottoes

胁侍菩萨裙子图案
莫高窟盛唐第172窟主室
北壁

　　盛唐第172窟主室北壁观无量寿经变壁画中左边胁侍菩萨的织锦阔裙上，饰有严谨精美的几何纹样。这组几何纹样为宽窄相间的横带结构。上、下两个大装饰带内分别填饰单线几何纹和宽边菱形纹，单元大小和线条粗细的差异使这两组成形方法相似的纹样各具特色。上、中部两组用于划分空间的边条纹样均为花草纹和菱形纹二方连续的拼合形式，其中的花草纹虽造型简洁，却为严整的几何纹环境注入了清新活力。色彩统一于壁画基调，以青绿为主色。绘制上最突出的特色是"截金技法"的运用，上部大面积几何纹因金光闪闪的线条和小花而成为整组纹样最灿烂夺目的部分，唐代织金工艺的辉煌效果由此可见一斑。

　　这组几何纹样在题材、构图、色彩配置和绘制手法上，都与右侧胁侍菩萨织锦阔裙纹饰保持着明显的对应关系，但二者又存在一定差异，这充分体现了中国传统图案"多样统一"的创作观念和灵活的组织方法。

（文：孙晓丽）

　　In the mural of Amitayurdhyana Sutra illustration on the north wall of the main chamber in Cave 172 dated to the high Tang Dynasty, the attendant Bodhisattva's wide brocade skirt on the left side is decorated with rigorous and exquisite geometric patterns. This group of geometric patterns have alternating wide and narrow transverse band structure. The upper and lower two large decorative bands are respectively filled with single line geometric pattern and wide edge diamond pattern. The differences in unit size and line thickness made the similar forming method patterns have their own characteristics. The upper and middle pattern stripes which are used to divide the space are the combination of flower and leaf pattern and diamond pattern two in a group repeated, although the shape of flower and leaf pattern is simple, they injected freshness and vitality into the strict atmosphere of the geometric pattern. The color is unified in accordance with the basic tone of the mural, with cyan and green as the main colors. The most prominent feature of the painting is the application of gold-cutting-technique, which made the large-area geometric pattern on the upper part become the most brilliant part of the whole pattern due to the glittering lines and small flowers. From this, we can see the brilliant effect of gold weaving technique in the Tang Dynasty.

　　In terms of theme, composition, color configuration and drawing techniques, this group of geometric patterns maintain an obvious corresponding relationship with the brocade wide skirt pattern on the right attendant Bodhisattva, but there are some differences between the two, which fully reflect the creative concept of diversity and unity of Chinese traditional pattern and flexible arrangement.

(Written by: Sun Xiaoli)

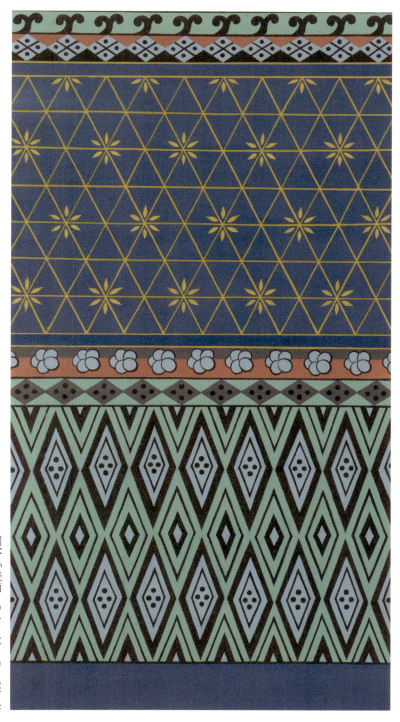

图": 孙晓丽　Painted by: Sun Xiaoli

The attendant
Bodhisattva's clothes
on the east side of the south wall in the
main chamber of Cave 172 dated to the high
Tang Dynasty at Mogao Grottoes

胁侍菩萨服饰
莫高窟盛唐第172窟主室
南壁东侧

盛唐第172窟主室南壁东侧画观无量寿经变壁画一铺，其中主尊右侧有胁侍菩萨一身，只见菩萨的面形圆润而清秀，左手托举琉璃盏，稳坐在莲花台上，双脚踩在莲花上。左肩斜披绿色络腋，身披红白两色薄纱天衣，下穿深褐色长裙，绿色飘带自腰部垂下。菩萨头戴花冠，头冠呈现花枝状向上、向左右翘起，花朵由下向上有节奏地排列，造型极具特色，冠缯从头部两侧垂下。身体各个部位装饰的项链、耳环、臂钏、手镯与璎珞动静相宜，丰富多姿。

在画面的具体表现方面，点、线、面有序结合，服饰结构用线上，有些部位的线是勾勒出来的，有些部位的线则是在涂色时留出来的，线的阴阳结合，生动多变。色彩以沉稳的重色调为主，点缀少许的亮丽色彩。同时，在平涂、勾线的基础上融入西域绘画的色彩明暗变化与立体感，也是一种新的尝试，使整体服饰效果自然而飘逸，清新而美妙。

（文：刘元风）

In the Amitayurdhyana Sutra illustration on the east side of the south wall in the main chamber of Cave 172 dated to the high Tang Dynasty, on the right side of the main Buddha has an attendant Bodhisattva. His face is round and beautiful, holding a flower pot in His left hand, sitting firmly on lotus seat and stepping on a lotus by both feet. The left shoulder is diagonally covered by green Luoye, wearing red and white silk scarf on the upper body, a dark brown long skirt on the lower body, and green ribbons hanging down from the waist. The Bodhisattva wears a flower crown, and the crown is in the shape of flower branches, left and right upturned, the flowers are arranged rhythmically from bottom to top, the shape is very unique and the crown laces hanging down from both sides of the head. Necklaces, earrings, armlets, bracelets and keyūra decorated in various parts of the body are balanced in movement and stillness, which is rich and colorful.

In terms of the picture details, the points, lines and planes are orderly combined. The clothes structure lines in some parts are outlined, and in some parts are left when painting. The combination of Yin and Yang of lines are vivid and changeable. Colors are mainly composed by calm dark colors, dotted with a little bright colors. At the same time, this is also a new attempt to integrate the color light and dark changes and three-dimensional sense of Western painting on the basis of flat coloring and line drawing, which makes the overall clothing effect natural and elegant, fresh and beautiful.

(Written by: Liu Yuanfeng)

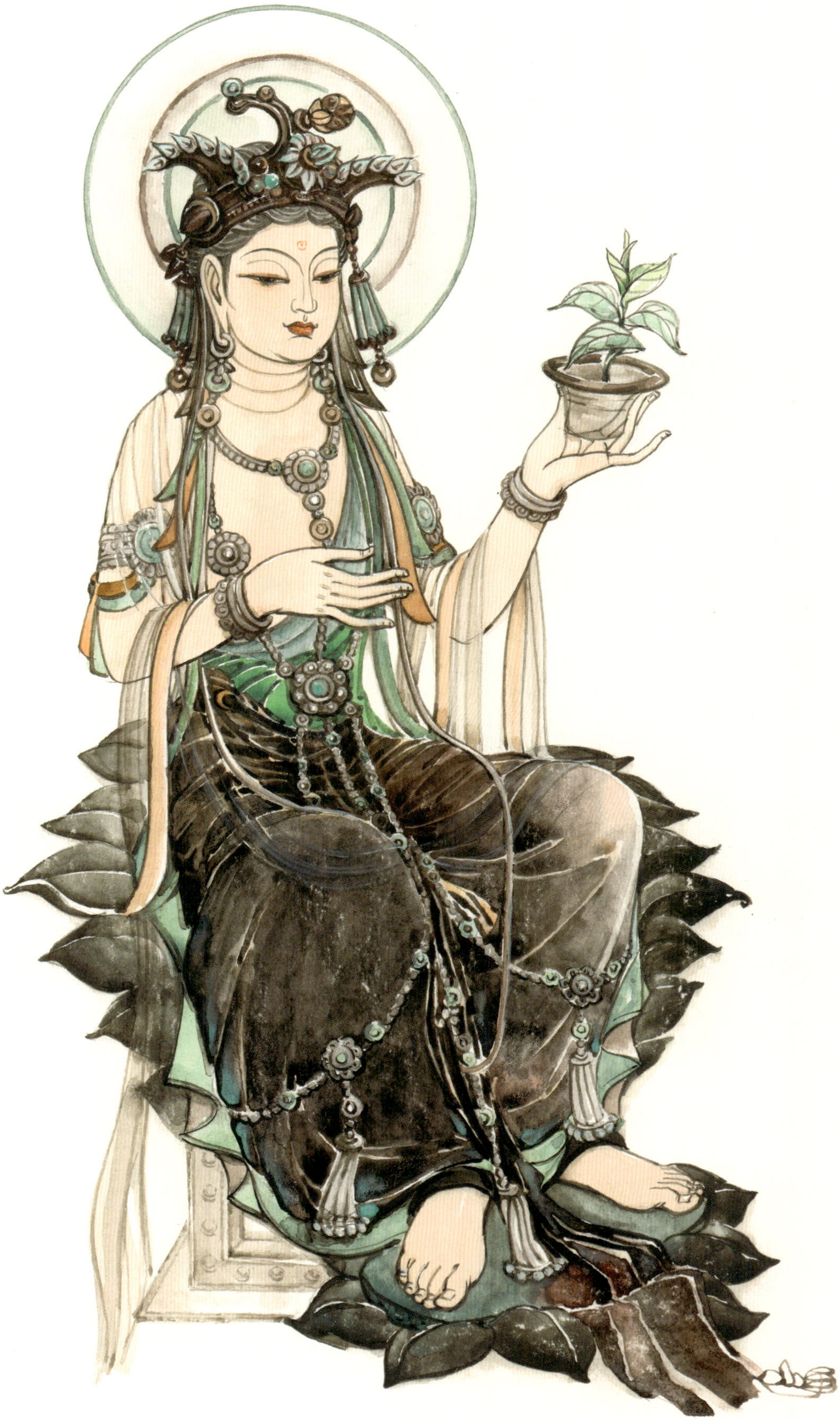

图：刘元风 Painted by: Liu Yuanfeng

Buddha's clothes
on the south wall of the main chamber in
Cave 172 dated to the high Tang Dynasty
at Mogao Grottoes

佛陀服饰
莫高窟盛唐第172窟主室
南壁

盛唐第172窟主室南壁画观无量寿经变壁画一铺，其中听法佛陀面相丰腴，眼帘下垂，留有胡须，聚精会神地静坐于莲花台上，呈现其对佛法的恭敬与谦顺。佛陀内穿绿色丝织右袒衫，腰间有系带，右袒衫的领缘和底摆处镶有精美的卷草花纹的边饰，外披赭褐色通肩袈裟（佛教之法衣，为佛陀、罗汉、僧侣所穿着，其形制为长方形，由布料拼缝而成。按佛教之戒律，袈裟不可用绢帛等贵重面料，以示节俭），袈裟的领子呈一个硕大的圆形并一直垂至腰部以下，且领子翻出蓝灰色的衬里。

在佛陀衣饰造型结构上，右袒衫的领形于胸口呈新月形露出，与袈裟的非规则的几何形构成线与面的对比，整体服饰上既丰富多变又相映成趣。

（文：刘元风）

There is an Amitayurdhyana Sutra illustration on the south wall of the main chamber in Cave 172 dated to the high Tang Dynasty, in which the Dharma listening Buddha has a plump face, drooping eyes and bearded. He sits quietly on the lotus seat with focused mind, showing His respect and humility to Dharma. The Buddha wears a green right-bared shirt inside which fastened at waist, and the collar edge and bottom of the right-bared shirt are inlaid with exquisite scrolling vine pattern. The outside covered with ochre brown shoulder-covering kasaya (Buddhist robe, which is worn by Buddhas, Arhats and monks, is rectangular and sewn by pieces of cloth. According to Buddhist commandments, the material of kasaya can not be expensive materials to show frugality). The collar of the kasaya is a huge circle and hangs down beyond waist, and the collar turns out so that we can see blue gray lining.

In the modeling structure of Buddha's clothes, the collar shape of the right-bared shirt is exposed in a crescent shape on the chest, which is in contrast with the irregular geometric shape of the kasaya. The overall clothes is rich, changeable and interesting.

(Written by: Liu Yuanfeng)

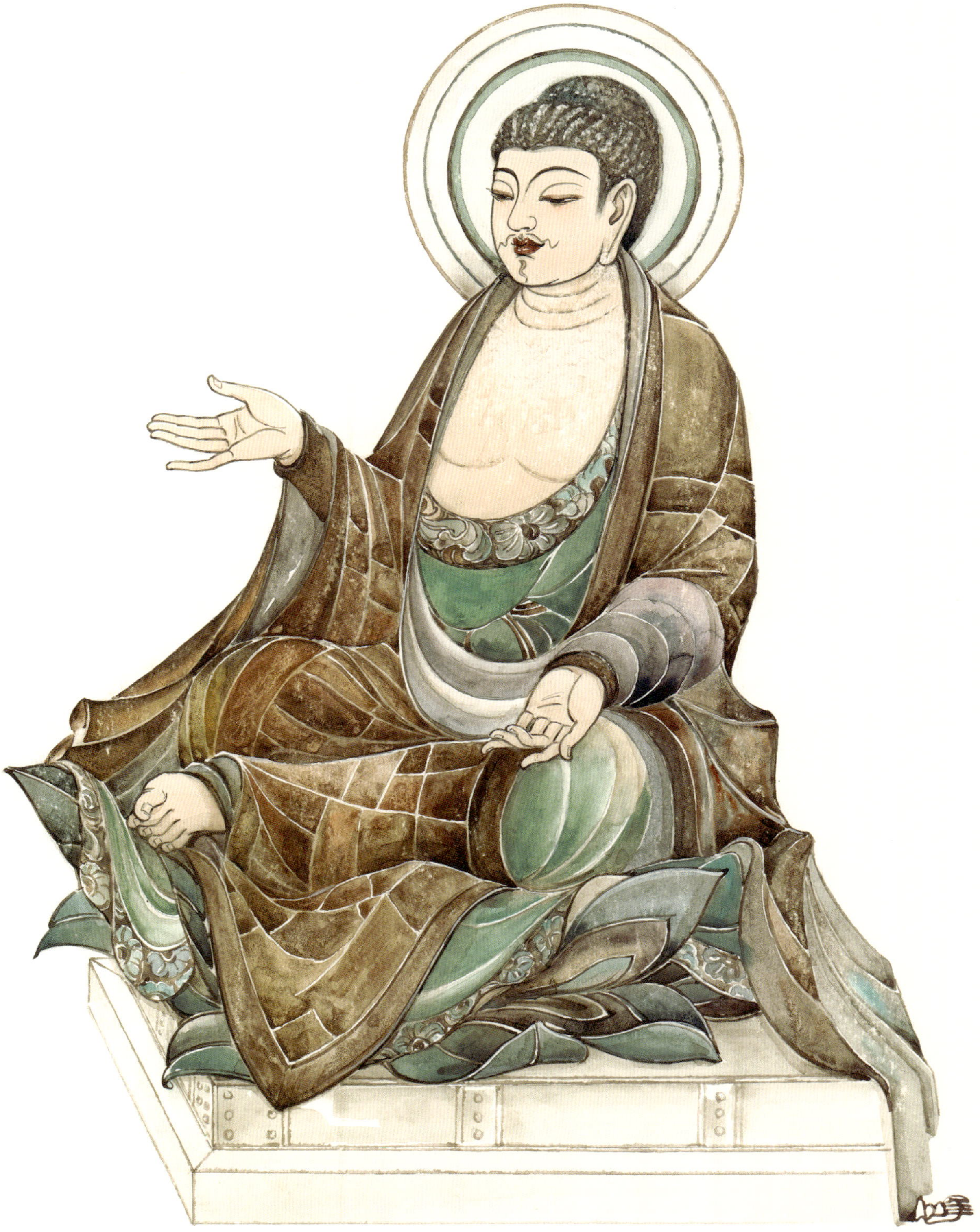

图：刘元风 Painted by: Liu Yuanfeng

Avalokitesvara
Bodhisattva's clothes
on the south side of the east wall in the main
chamber of Cave 172 dated to the high Tang
Dynasty at Mogao Grottoes

观世音菩萨服饰

莫高窟盛唐第172窟主室

东壁南侧

盛唐第172窟主室东壁南侧的观世音菩萨，面形俊俏，朱唇翠眉，眉心画白毫。左手提净瓶，右手轻拈项链坠玉珠，跣足站于莲花毯之上。上身斜披红绿两色络腋（络腋正面为红色，背面为绿色），彩带由左肩垂落绕小臂飘拂，下身穿深红色罗裙，罗裙外套穿红色腰裙，腰裙底边装饰绿色的垂穗。腰部除系红色腰带之外，另有绿色的腰襻围裹并在右侧打花结。菩萨头束高髻，余发披肩，佩戴化佛冠，并有珠宝镶嵌左右，与项链、臂钏、手镯浑然一体。

在绘画的艺术处理上，色彩冷暖对比配置鲜艳夺目，用线独具特色，勾线与留线（涂色时将结构线留出，其效果更显生动）相呼应，充分体现出盛唐菩萨服饰艺术所特有的审美倾向。

（文：刘元风）

The Avalokitesvara Bodhisattva on the south side of the east wall in the main chamber of Cave 172 dated to the high Tang Dynasty has a handsome face, red lips and green eyebrows, and the center of the eyebrows is decorated with a round Urna. His left hand carries a water bottle, and the right hand gently twiddles the necklace jade bead, standing barefoot on lotus cushion. The upper body is diagonally covered with red and green Luoye (the front is red and the back is green), and the ribbon falls from left shoulder and flying around the forearm. The lower body is wearing a dark red Luo skirt, a red waist wrap covers outside, and the bottom of the waist wrap is decorated with green tassels. In addition to wearing a red belt around the waist, there is also green broadband wrap and has a flower knot on the right. This Bodhisattva's head has a high hair bun, the rest hair covers shoulders, wearing a crown with Buddha image, and jewels are inlaid on left and right sides, which complement with necklace, armlets and bracelets as a whole.

In artistic treatment of this painting, the contrast configuration of cold and warm colors are dazzling, lines are unique, and painted lines echo with the blank lines (the structural lines were left when painting because the effect is more vivid). This fully reflects the unique aesthetic tendency of Bodhisattva clothes art during the high Tang Dynasty.

(Written by: Liu Yuanfeng)

图：刘元风　Painted by: Liu Yuanfeng

The Bodhisattva's clothes
on the north side of the east wall in the main
chamber of Cave 172 dated to the high Tang
Dynasty at Mogao Grottoes

菩萨服饰
莫高窟盛唐第172窟主室
东壁北侧

　　盛唐第172窟主室东壁门上北侧的菩萨，清雅娇羞的面孔，眉间饰白毫，左手握净瓶，右手轻拈柳枝，略侧身跣足站在莲花毯上。菩萨身穿僧祇支，肩披天衣，天衣的正面为蓝色，背面为绿色。下身穿土红色曳地长裙，底摆处翻出绿色的贴边。前腰处有白色的丝质裙带扣结后飘落，从冠缯处延伸向下的细长圆环形条带与各色彩带一起绕身飘洒。

　　菩萨头戴花冠，三朵镶嵌祖母绿的莲花纹装饰其正中，华丽的璎珞经由前胸飘拂而下，并兜揽于长裙的两侧，与身上的飘带一起共同营造出整体服饰飘飘欲仙的视觉美感。

（文：刘元风）

The Bodhisattva on the north side of the east wall in the main chamber of Cave 172 dated to the high Tang Dynasty has an clean and shy face, who is decorated with a Urna between the eyebrows, holding a water bottle in the left hand, gently twiddling the willow branch in the right hand, and standing on a lotus carpet slightly sideways and barefoot. He wears Sankaksika, and the shoulders are covered with silk scarf, the front of the silk scarf is blue and the back is green. The lower part of the body is wearing a long earth red skirt, with green welt at the bottom. There is a white skirt belt at the front waist, which falls down after being buckled, and the slender circular strip extending downward from the crown laces flying around the body together with many colorful ribbons.

This Bodhisattva wears a flower crown, and three lotus patterns inlaid with emerald decorate its center. The gorgeous keyūra falls down through the front chest and holds both sides of the long skirt. Together with the ribbons on the body, it creates the visual beauty of the overall dress.

(Written by: Liu Yuanfeng)

图: 刘元风 Painted by: Liu Yuanfeng

Śakro devānām indrah's clothes
on the north side of the east wall in the main
chamber of Cave 172 dated to the high Tang
Dynasty at Mogao Grottoes

帝释天服饰
莫高窟盛唐第172窟主室
东壁北侧

　　赴会图中的这身帝释天头戴通天冠，冠带长垂，身穿朱色大袖袍，内着白色曲领中单，下着裳，穿蔽膝，腰间系大带，脚上着舄，手持歧头麈尾扇，披巾搭于双臂。帝释天手中的麈尾扇是始于东汉、兴于魏晋的独特服饰品，有歧头、尖头、圆头等造型，据释藏《音义指归》引《兼名苑》记载："鹿之大者曰麈，群鹿随之，皆看麈所往，随麈尾所转为准，故古之谈者挥焉。"可见，麈尾扇既是文人清谈的用具，也是指挥权的象征。麈尾扇自中唐开始就很少在现实生活中被使用了，但还经常出现在古代帝王、逸士的画像中，成为他们挥斥方遒的重要道具。

　　目前，洞窟中这铺壁画变色严重，已经很难辨认这身帝释天的五官形象，以及是否有胡须。因此，参照总体造型相近的莫高窟第159窟等洞窟中的帝释天造型，也同样画了面部有胡须的形象。

（文：李迎军）

　　The Śakro devānām indrah in the attending Dharma assembly group is wearing a Tongtian crown, long crown laces hanging down, a vermilion robe with large sleeves, a white curved collar Zhongdan, and the lower body wears Chang, covered with Bixi in front of legs, a large belt around the waist, feet in shoes, holding a two-horns-shaped Zhuwei fan, and a silk scarf over His arms. The Zhuwei fan in Śakro devānām indrah's hand is a unique clothing accessory that appeared in the Eastern Han Dynasty and fashioned in the Wei and Jin Dynasties. It had shapes such as flat head, pointed head and round head. According to the Buddhist text *Yin Yi Zhi Gui* cited from *Jian Ming Yuan*: "The biggest deer in a herd is called Zhu, and the other deer all follow the deer, from behind the herd follows the tail, where the tail goes the herd follows, so the ancient literati loved to have one when they give talks." From this record we can see that Zhuwei was not only a tool used by literati when talking, but also a symbol of leadership. Zhuwei fan has rarely been used in real life since the middle Tang Dynasty, but it often appears in the portraits of ancient emperors and literati, and has become an important prop to show their passion and energy.

　　At present, the mural color has changed seriously, so it is difficult to identify the facial features of the emperor including if he has beard. Therefore, referring to Śakro devānām indrah images in caves such as Cave 159 of Mogao Grottoes with similar overall style, the image with beard is adopted.

(Written by: Li Yingjun)

图：李迎军　Painted by: Li Yíngjūn

The offering
Bodhisattva's clothes
on the south wall of the main chamber
in Cave 172 dated to the high Tang
Dynasty at Mogao Grottoes

供养菩萨服饰
莫高窟盛唐第172窟主室
南壁

此图中的供养菩萨位于盛唐第172窟主室南壁观无量寿经变东侧下部，为一组佛率众听法图中的供养菩萨。由于原壁此处画面有一定的残损，诸多细节不够清晰，本图尝试进行一定程度的还原，并且由于单幅出现，为了保证画面完整，进而对菩萨腿部和下部飘带细节进行推测后的延伸创作。原作此处位于栏杆后部，画面中前面有另一身供养菩萨，呈伏地叩拜姿态，对后面有一部分遮挡。该身供养菩萨双手托举花盘，上身裸露，但由于飘带宽大，造型丰富，并不显得空洞，下部推测应着裙装。耳部上方发饰有璎珞和悬垂装饰，耳饰亦为扇形，后背颈部向下也有璎珞，发辫自脑后长垂。此身菩萨原壁残留的图像主体色调与第172窟主室南壁一致，为青绿色系，十分清雅。飘带经过翻卷缠绕，于菩萨身上形成丰富的衣着层次，十分优美。

（文：张春佳）

This offering Bodhisattva is located in the lower part of the east side of Amitayurdhyana Sutra illustration on the south wall of the main chamber in Cave 172 dated to the high Tang Dynasty. This is a group of people led by Buddha in the Dharma assembly, unfortunately it was damaged partially, and many details are not clear enough. This painting is a attempt to restore in some extent. Because it's a single image, the original work is located at the back of the railing, in front of her is another offering Bodhisattva, who is in the posture of prostrating on the ground and blocked the back partially. In order to make the integrity of the painting, the Bodhisattva's legs and lower streamers are added based on previous study. The original image is located at the back of the railing. In the front of the picture, there is another Bodhisattva in a prostrate posture, partially blocking the back. He holds a flower plate by both hands, and the upper body is bare, and because the silk scarf is long and wide and full of change, she still looks beautiful. The lower body probably wears a skirt, and there are keyūra and pendants on the hair above the ears, and the earrings are also fan-shaped. On the back and neck also have keyūra, and the braids hang down from the back of head. The original main color of this image is consistent with the south wall painting in the main chamber of Cave 172, both are cyan and green, which is very pure and elegant. The silk scarf is rolled and wound to form rich layers, which is very beautiful.

(Written by: Zhang Chunjia)

图：张春佳　Painted by: Zhang Chunjia

此图为盛唐第172窟主室南壁观无量寿经变一铺中西侧下方的供养菩萨。菩萨右侧身跪坐，眉目俊秀，神情专注，双手托着盛放饭食的盘子于面前，虔诚沉静。

菩萨头顶束大髻，曲发披肩，垂于后背，头戴日月冠，由人间帝王冠饰蜕变而来，上饰新月，月中托日，这是波斯萨珊王朝的常见冠饰。菩萨双耳垂珰，戴臂钏、手镯，隐约可见全身上下饰有璎珞。右肩斜挎天衣，下着围腰与长裙。另有披巾从肩部缠绕至双臂并垂落于地面，披巾的正反两面分别为蓝色、绿色，于环绕披拂中显现菩萨的飘逸仙姿，双色随线条变幻，视觉效果丰富。

（文：赵茜、吴波）

This painting shows the offering Bodhisattva in the lower part of the west side in Amitayurdhyana Sutra illustration on the south wall of the main chamber in Cave 172 dated to the high Tang Dynasty. The Bodhisattva kneels down on His right side, with handsome face and focused expression, holding a plate full of food in front by both hands, looks pious and quiet.

This Bodhisattva combs high hair bun, curly hair covers shoulders, hanging on His back, and He wears a sun and moon crown which was transformed from emperor crown, and decorated with crescent and sun which was a common crown decoration in the Sassanian Dynasty of Persia. He wears earrings, armlets and bracelets, the whole body is decorated with keyūra. The right shoulder covered by heavenly clothes, and the lower body wears long skirt and waist wrap. In addition, a silk scarf is wrapped from shoulders to arms and falls on the ground, and the front and back sides of the silk scarf are cyan and green respectively, to set off an elegant and fairy posture of the Bodhisattva by winding and flying. The two colors varies with the lines and have rich visual effects.

(Written by: Zhao Xi, Wu Bo)

The offering Bodhisattva's clothes on the west side of the south wall in the main chamber of Cave 172 dated to the high Tang Dynasty at Mogao Grottoes

供养菩萨服饰

莫高窟盛唐第172窟主室南壁西侧

此图为盛唐第172窟主室南壁观无量寿经变一铺中西侧下方的供养菩萨。菩萨微微含胸，双手捧红莲。

供养菩萨头顶束大髻，余发呈条片状垂于后背，戴花蔓冠，在宝冠的中央有立体花蔓钿饰，在宝冠的两侧各有一圆形钿饰，戴手镯、臂钏，臂钏造型也似花朵。菩萨右肩似斜挎天衣，搭饰披巾，披巾在身后形成"U"字形垂落于地。菩萨束腰带、着长裙，并兼有璎珞装饰。从服饰色彩上看，宝冠、天衣、臂钏、围腰、璎珞和长裙均似为棕色系，披巾为正反蓝绿两色，整体色调简朴素雅。

（文：赵茜、吴波）

This painting shows the Bodhisattva in the west side lower part of Amitayurdhyana Sutra illustration on the south wall of the main chamber in Cave 172 dated to the high Tang Dynasty. The Bodhisattva is slightly slouching and holding a red lotus by both hands.

The offering Bodhisattva combs a big hair bun, and the rest hair hangs on His back in stripe shape, a flower vine crown on head, which has three-dimensional flower vine ornaments in the center, and a circular ornament on both sides of the crown. Bracelets and armlets, and the shape of the armlets is also like flower. The Bodhisattva's right shoulder covered by heavenly clothes, and matched with silk scarf. The silk scarf forms an "U" shape behind and falls to the ground. The Bodhisattva ties a belt and wears a long skirt, which is decorated with keyūra. From the perspective of dress color, the treasure crown, heavenly clothes, armlets, waist wrap, keyūra and long skirt all seem to be brown, and the silk scarf is blue in front and green in back. with simple and elegant overall tone.

(Written by: Zhao Xi, Wu Bo)

The offering Bodhisattva's clothes on the west side lower part of the south wall in the main chamber of Cave 172 dated to the high Tang Dynasty at Mogao Grottoes

供养菩萨服饰

莫高窟盛唐第172窟主室南壁西侧下方

图：吴波 Painted by: Wu Bo

The offering Bodhisattva's clothes
on the east side lower part of the south wall in the main chamber of Cave 172 dated to the high Tang Dynasty at Mogao Grottoes

供养菩萨服饰
莫高窟盛唐第172窟
主室南壁东侧下方

此图为盛唐第172窟主室南壁观无量寿经变东侧下方的供养菩萨。菩萨结跏趺坐，面目清秀腴润，长眉入鬓，神色自若。右手持长茎莲花，左手放于腿上。

菩萨梳高髻，戴宝冠，冠缯自头后长垂于胸前，在宝冠的中央镶宝珠，两侧饰有花钿。项饰宽厚，细圈间缀有圆形钿饰，戴同色双环手镯。菩萨外穿大袖罗衫，宽松畅意，其内左肩斜挎天衣，又在双臂上搭饰披巾，下着长裙。菩萨的罗衫为蓝色，披巾一面蓝一面绿呈双色配置，内搭红棕色天衣，宝冠与项饰也均为红棕色，整体色彩协调雅致。罗衫、天衣、披巾、长裙组合缠绕形成层次丰富的视觉效果。

（文：赵茜、吴波）

This painting shows the offering Bodhisattva in the east side lower part of Amitayurdhyana Sutra illustration on the south wall of the main chamber in Cave 172 dated to the high Tang Dynasty. The Bodhisattva sits in lotus position, with clean and beautiful face, long eyebrows, and looks peaceful and natural. He holds a long stem lotus in the right hand and puts the left hand on leg.

The Bodhisattva combs a high hair bun and wears a crown, the crown laces hang from the back of His head down to His chest. The center of the crown is inlaid with precious jewel, and the two sides are decorated with flowers. The necklace is wide and thick, with round flower ornaments between thin rings, and double rings bracelets with same color. The Bodhisattva wears a large sleeved Luo shirt, which is loose and comfortable, the left shoulder covered by heavenly clothes, and a scarf on His arms and a long skirt on the lower body. The Bodhisattva's Luo shirt is blue, the silk scarf is blue on one side and green on the other side, matched with reddish brown heavenly clothes inside. The crown and necklace are also reddish brown, so the overall color is harmonious and elegant. Luo shirt, heavenly clothes, silk scarf and long skirt are combined and wound to form a rich visual effect.

(Written by: Zhao Xi, Wu Bo)

The Dharma listening Bodhisattva's clothes
on the east side of the main Buddha on the north wall of the main chamber in Cave 172 dated to the high Tang Dynasty at Mogao Grottoes

听法菩萨服饰
莫高窟盛唐第172窟
主室北壁主尊东侧

此图为盛唐第172窟主室北壁观无量寿经变中主尊东侧的听法菩萨。

菩萨半跏趺坐，高鼻秀眼，右手托着盛放花朵的盘子，神态静和；梳高髻，头戴宝冠，余发垂于肩背，宝冠两侧也有钿饰装扮；双耳垂珰，戴项饰，手镯；双肩搭饰披巾，于身体两侧垂落，胯间有围腰结构，并在身前系结，围腰下着大袴，形制束口，也称"大袑""倒顿""嶒袴"。整体服饰以蓝绿色为主，头冠、项饰、围腰、长裙均为冷色，头发为暖色，主次分明，色彩明快。

（文：赵茜、吴波）

This painting shows the Dharma listening Bodhisattva on the east side of the main Buddha in Amitayurdhyana Sutra illustration on the north wall of Cave 172 dated to the high Tang Dynasty.

The Bodhisattva sits with both legs folded, high nose and narrow eyes, holding a plate full of flowers by His right hand, looks peaceful. He combs high hair bun and wears a treasure crown, the rest hair hanging over His shoulders and back. There are also flower ornaments on both sides of the treasure crown. Earrings, necklace, and bracelets, and shoulders are covered by silk scarf and falling to both sides of the body. Waist wrap around waist and tied in front of the body, under the waist wrap is a big trousers with narrow cuffs, also known as "Dashao", "Daodun" and "Baoku". The overall dress is mainly cyan and green, the crown, necklace, waist wrap and long skirt are cold colors, and the hair is warm color, which have clear priorities.

(Written by: Zhao Xi, Wu Bo)

图'' 吴波 Painted by: Wu Bo

The donors' clothes
on the west side of the south wall in the
main chamber of Cave 172 dated to the
high Tang Dynasty at Mogao Grottoes

供养人服饰
莫高窟盛唐第172窟主室
南壁西侧

此图为盛唐第172窟主室南壁观无量寿经变西侧"未生怨"中的一组供养人，该图位于"未生怨"画面的中下方。

图中三位女子，均身穿大袖襦裙，宽大的袖口有"吴带当风"的飘逸之感。盛唐时期的女装有大袖衫，袖宽往往大于1.3米。右首身形高大女子梳圆环椎髻，为敦煌盛唐至五代壁画中常见的贵妇发髻，流行很长一段时期，彰显此女身份尊贵。贵妇头戴的冠饰似属于虔诚的听法妇女习见头饰之一，在女信徒中颇为流行，而双手所持之物状如花环，应是在听法之际表供养之意。身后跟随的两位侍女均梳双丫髻，为盛唐时期未成年女性的常见发型。

（文：赵茜、吴波）

This painting shows a group of donors in the Ajatasattu's story on the west side of Amitayurdhyana Sutra illustration on the south wall of the main chamber in Cave 172 dated to the high Tang Dynasty. This painting is located in the lower part of the Ajatasattu's story illustration.

The three women in the painting are all wearing large sleeves Ru skirts, and the wide cuffs have a sense of celestial elegance. During the high Tang Dynasty, women had large sleeves shirts, and the sleeves width were often wider than 1.3 meters. The tall woman on the right has a circular hair bun, which was a common noble woman's hair bun in Dunhuang murals from the high Tang Dynasty to the Five Dynasties. It had been popular for a long time to show woman's pride. The headdress worn by the noble woman seems to be one of the common headdresses for devout Dharma listening women. It was quite popular among female believers, and the object held by her hands is like a wreath, which should represent to give offering when listening Dharma. The two maidens behind are all combed in Shuangya hair bun, which was a common hairstyle of underage women during the high Tang Dynasty.

(Written by: Zhao Xi, Wu Bo)

图：吴波　Painted by: Wu Bo

Prince Ajatashatru and
Queen Vaidehi's clothes
on the west side of the north wall in the
main chamber of Cave 172 dated to the
high Tang Dynasty at Mogao Grottoes

阿阇世太子、韦提希
夫人服饰
莫高窟盛唐第172窟主室北
壁西侧

这两张图选自第172窟主室北壁西侧，表现"观无量寿经"里的"未生怨"。此铺"未生怨"由下端起首，描绘阿阇世太子"欲害其母"的情节。

阿阇世太子左手向前想要抓住韦提希夫人，右手持剑挥舞。身后有一侍从见状连忙上前制止太子。阿阇世太子头戴通天冠，内搭配曲领中单，外穿右衽交领袍服，领子与大袖装饰绿色缘边。腰部围系蔽膝和腰带，蔽膝上绘有连续的植物纹样。

画面中间的韦提希夫人见太子持剑追赶，惊慌失措，伸开双臂，迈腿逃跑。韦提希夫人头梳多寰高髻，身着大袖长襦，裙长曳地。宽大的袖子和长裙在她仓皇而逃时大幅度飘曳于身后。

（文：董眣云、吴波）

These two paintings are selected from the west side of the north wall in the main chamber of Cave 172, showing the Ajatasattu's story from Amitayurdhyana Sutra. The story starts from the bottom and depicts the plot of prince Ajatashatru "going to kill his mother".

Prince Ajatashatru moved forward and tried to grasp Queen Vaidehi by his left hand, and waved a sword in his right hand. When seeing this, a guard hurried forward to stop the prince. The prince Ajatashatru wears a Tongtian crown, and a curved collar Zhongdan shirt inside, and a right lapel cross collar robe outside. The collar and large sleeve cuffs are decorated with a circle of green trim. The waist is wrapped by Bixi and tied a belt, and the Bixi is painted with continuous plant pattern.

In the middle of the painting, when Queen Vaidehi saw the prince chasing with a sword, she was panicked, then stretched out her arms and ran. Queen Vaidehi combs multi circular high hair bun, wears a big sleeves long Ru, and the long skirt trained behind. The wide sleeves and long skirt fluttered behind when she fled in a hurry.

(Written by: Dong Yiyun, Wu Bo)

图：吴波　Painted by: Wu Bo

与莫高窟同时期壁画上绝大多数弟子采用右袒方式穿着袈裟不同的是，壁画上这身弟子的袈裟没有披在肩上，而是双手各持袈裟的一端正欲披挂的状态。这样别出新意的造型表达不仅使这身弟子的整体形象独树一帜，还让原本遮挡在右袒式袈裟内的服装结构清晰地显现出来——上身内着右衽偏衫，下着多褶四方连续花长裙，腰间以细长腰带系结。

佛教自印度传入中国时，袈裟里面搭配穿着的是僧祇支，造型呈长方形，穿着时从左肩缠至右腋下，袒右肩。由于袒露肩膊的着装并不适用于中原固有的着装观念，因此出现了"中式僧祇支"——偏衫。竺道祖在《魏录》中记载："魏宫人见僧祖一肘不以为善，乃作偏袒，缝于（於）僧祇支上相从，因名偏衫。今开脊接领者盖魏遗制也。"偏衫是佛教服饰本土化的产物，虽源于魏但并未在魏时完全取代僧祇支，从敦煌壁画、雕塑中可以看出，至盛唐时仍然是僧祇支与偏衫并用的情形。

（文：李迎军）

The disciple's clothes
on the south wall of the west niche in the main chamber of Cave 172 dated to the high Tang Dynasty at Mogao Grottoes
弟子服饰 莫高窟盛唐 第172窟主室西壁龛内 南侧

Different from the way most disciples wear kasaya with right shoulder bared at the same period, this disciple's kasaya in the mural is not on His shoulders, but in a state which held by His hands and ready to put on. This unique art expression not only makes the overall image of this disciple different, but also clearly shows kasaya inside design which is mostly covered in other cases — with a right lapel shirt on the upper body, and a multi pleated long skirt on the lower body with four in a group repeated flower pattern, and tied a long narrow belt around the waist.

When Buddhism was introduced into China from India, kasaya was matched with Sankaksika inside in rectangular shape, wrapped from left shoulder to right armpit and bare right shoulder. Since bare shoulder was not suitable for the inherent dress habit in the Central Plains, so the "Chinese Sankaksika" appeared — Pian shirt. Zhu Daozu wrote in *Wei Lu*: "When people in the Wei palace saw monks bare one shoulder, they didn't think it was good, so they made Piantan which modified from Sankaksika, so called Pian shirt. Nowdays people have lapel and put collar followed Wei tradition." Pian shirt is the result of Localization of Buddhist clothes, and it started from the Wei Dynasty, but did not completely replace Sankaksika in the Wei Dynasty, from Dunhuang murals and sculptures we can see that Sankaksika and Pian shirt still coexisted during the high Tang Dynasty.

(Written by: Li Yingjun)

莫高窟第172窟主室西壁龛内三面墙壁共绘有八身弟子像，每身弟子都有部分形象被壁面上浮塑的佛光、项光遮挡，但显露的部分造型生动、画风细腻，仍呈现出极高的艺术表现力。八身弟子神态各异、栩栩如生，绘于西壁浮塑佛光北侧、虔诚肃立在佛祖身侧的这身弟子左手持经卷，右手伸食指似在深思，又似在探讨佛学奥义强调重点。整身弟子造型以精细的线条勾勒，笔意流畅，设色雅致，服装刻画清晰翔实，对服装上图案的描绘尤为细致——身披蓝、绿、红三色右袒式五瓣小团花图案田相袈裟，条相交错处的方格内饰有"卍"字纹，内着的褶裙上也饰有精巧的四瓣花四方连续纹样。

（文：李迎军）

The disciple's clothes
on the west wall of the west niche in the main chamber of Cave 172 dated to the high Tang Dynasty at Mogao Grottoes
弟子服饰 莫高窟盛唐 第172窟主室西壁龛内 西侧

The three walls in the west niche of the main chamber in Cave 172 at Mogao Grottoes are painted with eight disciples. Some of the images are blocked by Buddha light relief, but the exposed parts still look vivid and delicate, showing high artistic expression. The eight disciples have different and lifelike expressions. This one is painted on the north side of the Buddha light relief on the west wall, and He stands piously beside Buddha, holding a scripture in left hand and extends His index finger of right hand, who seems thinking deeply or discussing the profound meaning of Buddhism. His whole body outlined by fine lines, with smooth brushwork, elegant colors, clear and accurate clothing depiction, and the patterns on the clothing are particularly detailed—He wears a blue, green and red right shoulder bared field pattern kasaya with five petaled small round flower pattern, in the square frames have "卍" pattern, and the pleated skirt inside is also decorated with exquisite four petaled flower pattern four in a group repeated.

(Written by: Li Yingjun)

The Buddha's
Sankaksika trim pattern
on the south wall of the main chamber
in Cave 172 dated to the high Tang
Dynasty at Mogao Grottoes

佛陀僧祇支缘
边图案
莫高窟盛唐第172
窟主室南壁

第172窟主室南壁绘制观无量寿经变一铺，中央端坐阿弥陀佛。佛陀身披田相袈裟，内着石绿色僧祇支，现择取缘边图案整理绘制。图案为二方连续式的百花草纹，无明显骨架结构，而是连续的花叶一脉贯穿。图案花型虽然不复杂，但是色彩丰富，以石青、石绿及熟褐相间，再点缀以红色花心，显得花团锦簇，春意盎然。

（文：崔岩）

The south wall of the main chamber in Cave 172 is painted with Amitayurdhyana Sutra illustration, with Amitabha Buddha sitting in the center. The Buddha is dressed in field pattern kasaya, with malachite green Sankaksika inside. Here we choose the edge pattern to study. The pattern is two in a group repeated flower and leaf pattern, without obvious frame structure, but continuous flowers and leaves run through one vein. Although the flower pattern is not complex, it is rich in color, alternated with azurite, malachite green and dark brown, and then dotted with red flower centers, which looks colorful and lively.

(Written by: Cui Yan)

The Bodhisattva's
clothes trim pattern
on the north side of the east wall in the
main chamber of Cave 172 dated to the
high Tang Dynasty at Mogao Grottoes

菩萨服饰缘边
图案
莫高窟盛唐第172
窟主室东壁北侧

第172窟主室东壁北侧为文殊变，文殊菩萨结跏趺坐于青狮背驼莲花宝座之上，虽然肌肤及部分服饰已氧化变色，但菩萨最外层所着透明服饰缘边仍清晰可辨，纹样细致精美。现将菩萨服饰的缘边图案进行绘制整理。此文殊菩萨上身服饰缘边为浅土红底色，图案主体为赭色填充的菱形纹样，四边及对角线相交勾勒白边，墨绿色圆点点缀四边或四角，两个一组呈现二方连续的排列方式，整体图案规整有序又富有变化。菩萨下半身外着透明长裙，缘边同样为浅土红底色，图案为半破式二方连续结构。主体花型为半圆式联珠纹，纹样分为两层，外环为石青底色上绘白色联珠，联珠中间以竖线和横线相间隔，向内绘白色半圆，联珠环内为绿色圆瓣花朵，均呈一半式分布组合；宾花为绿色的对称式三叶纹样。主花与宾花上下交错，呈带状排列，整体配色简练，构成均衡有度。

（文：常青）

On the north side of the east wall in the main chamber of Cave 172 is Manjusri Bodhisattva tableau. Manjusri Bodhisattva sits on the lotus seat carried by the green lion. Although the skin and part of the clothes have oxidized and discolored, the trims of the transparent clothes on the outermost layer of the Bodhisattva are still clear and discernible, with detailed and exquisite patterns. Now the trim patterns of the Bodhisattva clothes are drawn and studied. The trim of this Manjusri Bodhisattva's upper body dress has light earth red background, and the main body of the pattern is rhombic pattern filled with ochre. The four sides and diagonal lines are white, and the dark green dots are dotted on the four sides and four corners. They are arranged two in a group repeated, and the overall pattern is in order and changeable. The Bodhisattva's lower body is covered with a transparent long skirt, the trim is also light earth red background, and the pattern is a semi-circular two in a group repeated structure. The main flower pattern is a semi-circular beads pattern, which has two layers. The outer ring is malachite green background, and white beads are painted on it. Inside the rings are divided by vertical lines and horizontal lines, and white semi roundels are painted inward. The inner part of the beads rings have green roundels; the secondary flower pattern is green symmetrical three leaves pattern. The main flowers and secondary flowers pattern are checkered up and down in banded arrangement. The overall color matching is concise and balanced.

(Written by: Chang Qing)

图：张博　Painted by: Zhang Bo

图：常青　Painted by: Chang Qing

Dunhuang Mogao Grottoes Cave

194 of the High Tang Dynasty

敦煌莫高窟盛唐

第194窟

第194窟是创建于盛唐时期的覆斗顶形窟，经晚唐、西夏重修，为唐代的代表洞窟之一。主室窟顶大部坍塌，仅北披残存头部。西壁开盝顶帐形龛，龛内彩塑一倚坐佛、二弟子、二菩萨、二天王，龛外南、北侧力士台上各塑一力士。龛沿残存云气纹及海石榴卷草边饰。龛下及力士台下西夏绘供养人数身。南壁绘维摩诘经变一铺。北壁绘观无量寿经变一铺。东壁门上存千佛，门南绘地藏、观世音各一身，门南侧下方唐绘女供养人一身。门北画千佛，南侧下方绘观世音一身、唐绘男供养人一身。前室及甬道存晚唐壁画。

此窟以西壁龛内外的彩塑精美著称。西壁龛内主尊佛像为弥勒佛，佛像神情庄严，一手抚膝，一手已残损，内着青绿锦缘僧祇支，腰部系带，外披深红团花袈裟，袈裟缘边有浅底小团花边饰。弟子阿难神色恭敬，面部丰润，双手交于腹前，上身着交领绿襦，衣服边缘有黑底小团花边饰。弟子迦叶双手合十，着田相袈裟。南北两侧的菩萨神情怡然，白皙丰润，朱唇绿须，娴静含蓄。南侧菩萨着圆领青绿散花纹上衣，外披天衣，下着长裙，长裙上绘有卷草和团花纹样。北侧菩萨斜披络腋，下服重裙。南侧天王浓眉细眼，嘴角含笑，上着绣铠，下着战裙。北侧天王怒目而视，头戴兜鍪，上着绣铠，下着战裙。龛外金刚力士雄壮健美，皆赤裸上身，下着青绿长裙，长裙上绘有卷草和团花。整窟彩塑一铺九身，人物主次分明，性格特征明显，服饰华丽，配色典雅。整窟人物服饰华丽，纹样细腻，将服饰质感表现得尤为出色，体现出作者的精巧细思。

此窟南壁绘维摩诘经变，画中文殊在西侧、维摩诘在东侧。维摩诘经变底下绘"帝王问疾图"。帝王身着冕服，袖口绘有卷草纹，下裳绘有龟背纹。文殊菩萨座下绘"各国王子问疾图"。王子们服饰各异，有袒露者，也有披裘者，展现出丝绸之路上各地的人物形象，也说明敦煌石窟是研究丝绸之路的各国人物形象的资料宝库。

（文：杨婧嫱）

Cave 194 is a truncated pyramidal ceiling cave built in the high Tang Dynasty, then repaired in the late Tang Dynasty and the Western Xia Dynasty. It is one of the representative caves of the Tang Dynasty. Most of the ceiling of the main chamber collapsed, with only few remaining on the north slope. The west wall has a tent shaped niche, and in the niche, there are painted sculptures of one sitting Buddha, two disciples, two Bodhisattvas and two Maharāja-devas. Outside the niche, the south and north platforms each has a Vīra sculpture. Along the niche edge are cloud pattern and sea pomegranate scrolling vine pattern decoration. Below the niche and Vīra platforms are many Western Xia donors. The south wall is painted with Vimalakirti Sutra illustration, and on the north wall is painted with Amitayurdhyana Sutra illustration. There are thousand Buddhas above the east door, a painted Ksitigarbha Bodhisattva and a painted Avalokitesvara Bodhisattva are on the south side of the door, and a female donor is painted on the south lower part of the door. Thousand Buddhas are painted on the north side of the door, a Avalokitesvara Bodhisattva and a Tang donor are painted in the lower part. In the front chamber and corridor preserved late Tang Dynasty murals.

This cave is famous for the exquisite painted sculptures inside and outside the west niche. The main Buddha sculpture in the west niche is Maitreya Buddha, and He looks solemn, with one hand rests on the knee and the other hand is broken. He wears cyan and green brocade trim Sankaksika, tied at waist. The outside covered with crimson kasaya with round flower pattern, and the trim of the kasaya is decorated with small round flowers with light background. Disciple Ananda looks humble, with plump and healthy face, two hands cross in front of belly, wears a green Ru on His upper body, which is decorated with small round flowers on black background at the trims. Disciple Kasyapa puts His hands together and wears field pattern kasaya, and the Bodhisattvas on both north and south sides look relaxed, white and plump, with red lips and green beard, quiet and implicit. The Bodhisattva on the south side wears a round collar green clothes with flower clusters, covered with silk scarf and wears long skirt on the lower body, which is painted with scrolling vine pattern and round flower pattern. The Bodhisattva on the north side diagonally covered by Luoye and wears skirt on the lower body. On the south side, the Maharāja-deva has thick eyebrows and thin eyes, smiling, the upper body wears embroidered armor and the lower body wears battle skirt. The Maharāja-deva on the north glares angrily, wearing helmet, embroidered armor on the upper body and battle skirt on the lower body. Outside the niche, the Vīras are magnificent, both bare their upper body, and wear cyan and green skirt on the lower body which painted with scrolling vine pattern and round flower pattern. This cave has a group of nine painted sculptures, with clear primary and secondary characters, obvious personalities, gorgeous clothes and elegant color matching. The clothes of the figures in the whole cave are gorgeous and the patterns are exquisite. The texture presenting of the clothes are particularly good, reflecting the artists' ingenuity.

The south wall of this cave is painted with Vimalakirti Sutra illustration, with Manjusri Bodhisattva on the west and Vimalakirti on the east. In the lower part of Vimalakirti Sutra illustration is Emperor Visiting Vimalakirti. The emperor wears Mian clothes, with scrolling vine pattern on the cuffs and turtle back pattern on the lower clothes. Below the seat of Manjusri Bodhisattva is princes from Various Countries Visiting Vimalakirti. The princes have different clothes, some people wear summer clothes and some people wear fur clothes, showing the images of people from different places along the Silk Road. This also means that Dunhuang Grottoes are a treasure house for studying the images of people from various countries on the Silk Road.

(Written by: Yang Jingqiang)

Painted sculpture Venerable
Ananda's clothes
on the south side of the west niche in the main
chamber of Cave 194 dated to the high Tang
Dynasty at Mogao Grottoes

彩塑阿难尊者服饰
莫高窟盛唐第194窟主室
西壁龛内南侧

盛唐第194窟主室西壁龛内南侧的彩塑阿难尊者是位少年比丘的长相，弯眉笑眼，嘴角上扬，喜庆欢愉，神情外聪内慧，双手交于腹前，谦恭虔敬站于莲花台之上。阿难身穿三衣袈裟（也称"三衣佛装"），内衣为绿色交领偏衫，领部镶嵌织锦花边，外着绿色宽袖中衣，领部和袖口也镶饰织锦花边；下着绿色锦裙，裙下摆处镶有贴边；最外层披着红色袈裟，在其领部和腰部翻出白色贴边，左胸处有带钩用于系结袈裟。整套法衣宽松而洒脱，更显其佛教文化的气息。

在画面中运用水彩的处理方法，集中表现佛装的造型特征和材料肌理，画面中没有出现勾勒的线条，而是色彩留白而产生的结构线条。这种处理方式进一步增强了画面的艺术审美价值。

（文：刘元风）

The painted sculpture Venerable Ananda in the south of the west niche of Cave 194 dated to the high Tang Dynasty, is a young Bhiksu with curved eyebrows and smiling eyes, raised mouth corners, looks jubilant and happy, intelligent outside and wise inside. His hands in front of His belly, looks humble and pious standing on the lotus platform. Ananda is wearing Sanyi kasaya (also known as three Buddha clothes). His underwear is a green cross collar Ru shirt, with brocade lace inlaid on the collar, green wide-sleeved Zhongyi outside, also with brocade lace inlaid on the collar and cuffs. The lower body wears green brocade Qun with welt at the hem. The outermost is covered by red shoulder-covering kasaya. The white welt turns out at the collar and waist, and a ring hook is set at the left chest to tie the kasaya. The whole set of the robe is loose and free, which shows the characteristic of Buddhist culture.

The watercolor processing method was used in the picture to focus on the modeling characteristics of Buddha clothes and the texture of materials. There are no outlines in the picture, but have the structural lines created by gaps between colors. This treatment further enhances the artistic aesthetic value of the picture.

(Written by: Liu Yuanfeng)

The painted sculpture right attendant Bodhisattva's clothes on the south side of the west niche in the main chamber of Cave 194 dated to the high Tang Dynasty at Mogao Grottoes

彩塑右胁侍菩萨 服饰 莫高窟盛唐第194窟主 室西壁龛内南侧

　　盛唐第194窟主室西壁龛内南侧的右胁侍菩萨造型生动传神，是盛唐时期敦煌莫高窟最具代表性的彩塑作品之一。其形象圆润丰腴，慈眉善目，头绾双鬟髻，神情温婉慈祥；身体轻盈且微倾重心移至左脚，左臂抬起，右臂自然下垂，五指纤细柔美；跣足立于莲花台之上。

　　胁侍菩萨上身穿绿色丝织碎花圆领无袖襦衫，领缘镶嵌织锦贴边，乳下有系带轻束。肩部天衣飘垂并回绕于左肘。下着绿色织锦长裙，其卷草纹样饱满而精致，裙下摆处镶饰贴边。黄色裙带自腰部经腹部打花结垂落身前。菩萨身上虽无多余的装饰品，但其优雅的姿态与华美的衣裙足以营造出整体服装的律动美感，也体现出盛唐服饰文化的审美特质。

（文：刘元风）

　　The attendant Bodhisattva on the south side of the west niche in the main chamber of Cave 194 dated to the high Tang Dynasty. His appearance is vivid, which is one of the most representative painted sculpture works in Dunhuang Mogao Grottoes of the high Tang Dynasty. This image is round and plump, with kind eyebrows and caring eyes, double rings hair bun, and the expression is gentle and kind. The body is light and slightly tilted, and the weight on the left foot, His left arm is raised, the right arm is naturally drooping and the five fingers are slender and soft, standing barefoot on the lotus platform.

　　The attendant Bodhisattva wears a green round collar sleeveless Ru silk shirt with brocade welt on the collar edge and a light tie under the breasts. The silk scarf on the shoulder hangs down and winds around the left elbow. The lower body wears a long green brocade skirt with full and delicate scrolling vine pattern, and the hem of the skirt is trimmed. The yellow skirt belt is knotted from the waist to abdomen and falls down in front of the body. Although there are no superfluous decorations on His body, the elegant posture and gorgeous clothes and skirts are sufficient to create a rhythmic beauty of the whole clothes. This also reflects the aesthetic characteristics of clothes culture of the high Tang Dynasty.

(Written by: Liu Yuanfeng)

The painted sculpture
Bodhisattva's Ru shirt pattern
and Venerable Kasyapa's skirt
trim pattern
in the west niche of the main chamber of Cave 194
dated to the high Tang Dynasty at Mogao Grottoes

彩塑菩萨襦衫图
案、迦叶尊者裙
边图案
莫高窟盛唐第194窟主室
西壁龛内

第194窟主室西壁龛内南侧彩塑右胁侍菩萨服饰上装饰着丰富的图案，这里选取其襦衫上的纹样进行整理绘制。襦衫以青绿色为底色，主体图案以十字形为骨架，装饰四出心形叶片。一行为深褐色叶片，点缀褐灰色花心，米黄色细线勾勒心形叶片轮廓；另一行为米黄色叶片，点缀褐色花心，土红色细线勾勒心形叶片轮廓。襦衫领口处的缘边以墨绿色为地，图案为半破式二方连续卷草纹，卷草式的花心，搭配双层花瓣，纹样流畅，色彩典雅。

第194窟主室西壁龛内的彩塑迦叶尊者身着袈裟、内衣、裙，此处选取迦叶尊者的裙子边缘进行整理绘制。在豆绿色的地上，两列不同样式的花纹交替排列。一列以淡黄色圆点为花心，墨绿色勾勒出六片花瓣，米黄色和土红色线条穿插勾勒花瓣轮廓；另一列以墨绿色圆点为花心，米黄色勾勒出六片花瓣。纹样错落有序，色彩庄重典雅。

（文：王可）

The clothes of the painted sculpture right attendant Bodhisattva in the west niche of Cave 194 is decorated with rich patterns. Here, the pattern on His Ru shirt is selected for studying. The Ru shirt takes turquoise as the background color, and the main pattern takes cross shape as the frame, and decorated four heart-shaped leaves. One raw is dark brown leaves, dotted with brown gray flower centers, and beige thin lines outline the heart-shaped leaves; the other raw is beige leaves and dotted with brown flower centers, and earth red thin lines outline the heart-shaped leaves. The neckline trim of the Ru shirt is dark green, and the pattern is semi two in a group repeated scrolling vine pattern, the scrolling vine style flower center matched with double-layer petals, which looks smooth and elegant.

The painted sculpture Kasyapa in the west niche of the main chamber in Cave 194 is dressed in kasaya, underwear and skirt. Here, the trim of His skirt is selected for studying. On the bean green background have two rows of different patterns arranged alternately. One row with light yellow dots as the center of the flowers, dark green fill the six petals, and beige and earth red lines intersperse to outline the petals; the other raw takes dark green dots as the flower center, and beige outlines six petals. This pattern is well arranged, and the colors are solemn and elegant.

(Written by: Wang Ke)

图：王可　Painted by: Wang Ke

The painted sculpture attendant
Bodhisattva's clothes
on the north side of the west niche in the main
chamber of Cave 194 dated to the high Tang
Dynasty at Mogao Grottoes

彩塑胁侍菩萨服饰
莫高窟盛唐第194窟主室
西壁龛内北侧

盛唐第194窟主室西壁龛内北侧胁侍菩萨彩塑，脸庞丰圆，翠眉朱唇，双目微垂，神态坦然。头梳高髻，发髻纹理清晰。左手下垂，右手轻举，纤纤玉指灵动而柔美。肌肤丰润莹洁，上身袒裸，斜披络腋，络腋的正面呈赭红色，反面呈蓝绿色。下身穿赭红色与蓝绿色相间的宽绰锦裙，锦裙的结构与褶皱随身体曲线而呈现出极具节奏感的线条和曲面效果。同时，锦裙上的卷草纹与团花纹布局疏密有致，体现了盛唐精湛的丝织技术与高超的制衣工艺。

画面采用水彩的表现方法，色彩丰富而典雅，用线生动而洒脱。从菩萨整体的艺术处理来看，形体美与服饰美相依共融，佛教艺术与彩塑艺术相结合，佛教文化与艺术审美相一致，呈现出盛唐时期社会的高度开放与文化的空前繁荣。

（文：刘元风）

The painted sculpture attendant Bodhisattva on the north side of the west niche in the main chamber of Cave 194 dated to the high Tang Dynasty who has a round face, green eyebrows and red lips, slightly drooping eyes and a calm look. His hair is in a high hair bun with clear details. The left hand droops and the right hand lifts gently, the slender jade like fingers are flexible and soft. His skin is supple and soft, the upper body is naked, diagonally covered with Luoye. The front of the Luoye is ochre red and the back is blue-green. The lower body wears a wide brocade skirt with ochre and blue-green, and the structure and folds of the brocade skirt show rhythmic lines and curved surface effect follow the body shape. At the same time, the scrolling vine pattern on the brocade skirt is consistent with the round flower pattern. This embodies the exquisite silk weaving technology and superb clothes making technique of the high Tang Dynasty.

This painting done by watercolor, the colors are rich and elegant, and the lines are vivid, free and easy. From the overall artistic treatment of this Bodhisattva, the body beauty and clothes beauty are interdependent and integrated, the Buddhist art and painted sculpture art are combined, and the Buddhist culture and artistic aesthetics are consistent. This shows the high-openness society and unprecedented prosperity culture of the high Tang Dynasty.

(Written by: Liu Yuanfeng)

图：刘元风　Painted by: Liu Yuanfeng

The painted sculpture
Vaishravana's clothes
on the north side of the west niche in the main
chamber of Cave 194 dated to the high Tang
Dynasty at Mogao Grottoes

服饰
彩塑毗沙门天王
莫高窟盛唐第194窟主室
西壁龛内北侧

盛唐第194窟主室西壁龛内北侧毗沙门天王彩塑，体型雄健魁岸，头戴耳护上翻的兜鍪（也称"胄"或"盔"，战将护首御兵之冠，秦汉时期命名"兜鍪"），圆头大耳，横眉怒目，肌肉紧绷，左手托塔，右手握拳，一副不可一世的神态，令人望而生畏。天王上身着铠甲（古代武将护身戎装，多用金属片、竹片、木片等制作而成），连体的身甲、胸甲和背甲以带扣束紧，胸部和腰部各束一带，腰带上半露金属光亮的护腹镜，肩覆披膊作兽头状。下身的战裙飘曳，缚裤束腿，脚蹬乌靴。

毗沙门天王的四肢粗壮，虎背熊腰，彰显其战将应有的强悍和威猛，肩臂的怒目兽头衔臂锦袖飘拂及战裙的飘扬更显其威风显赫，铠甲上蓝绿色精美的卷草花纹、团花，特别是腰裙上的主题雕花进一步体现出盛唐时期的军戎之盛及其战将的仪表之美，堪称其为莫高窟盛唐彩塑的杰作。

（文：刘元风）

The painted sculpture Vaishravana on the west niche of the main chamber in Cave 194 dated to the high Tang Dynasty who has a strong and wide body, wears an upturned ear covers helmet (also known as "Zhou" or "Kui", warrior's head armor in ancient time, was named as Doumou in the Qin and Han Dynasties). He has a round head and big ears, tightened eyebrows and stared eyes, and tight muscles. He holds a tower in the left hand and fists the right hand and looks pride and fearsome. This heavenly king wears body armor on the upper body (the ancient general's protective uniform was mostly made of metal, bamboo and wood chips). The conjoined body armor, chest armor and back armor are fastened by belt buckles, and the chest and waist are fastened separately. Above the waist belt is half exposed bright belly metal armor, and the shoulders are covered with shoulder armors in the shape of animal heads. The lower body's battle Qun is fluttering, legs are bound, and the feet in black boots.

This Vaishravana has strong limbs, tiger back and bear waist, which show the strength and ferocity. The angry beast heads on his shoulders and fluttering brocade sleeves around his arms and fluttering battle Qun show his majesty. The blue-green exquisite scrolling vine pattern and round flowers on his armor, especially the theme carvings on his waist wrap, further reflect the strength of the army and generals majesty of the high Tang Dynasty. This can be seen as a masterpiece painted sculpture of the high Tang Dynasty at Mogao Grottoes.

(Written by: Liu Yuanfeng)

这身彩塑天王昂首侧身，威风凛凛，所穿铠甲结构复杂、图案繁缛。此类铠甲并不是用铁或皮革制成用于实战的，而是一种仪仗甲，《唐六典》中称其为"绢甲"，它的出现可能是受到当时武官公服的帛制裲裆甲的启示，曾作为宫廷侍卫或武士的戎服。

这里整理出彩塑天王铠甲的局部图案。原图案位于天王上身勒甲索到革带之间，处于人物腹部中央的部位。半圆的护腹周围为饱满连续的卷草纹，花纹融合了牡丹、莲花、石榴等多种植物的造型特点，以石青、石绿为主色调，点缀些许白色和熟褐色，以土红色线勾勒而成，其翻卷连绵、密不透风的满铺式花叶呈现了盛唐装饰艺术特有的繁茂生命力。

这身彩塑天王所着铠甲下覆缚裤，塑师形象地表现出膝盖处系扎裤管而形成的褶皱，这样的装束轻便紧身、易于行动，是适合军旅、仪仗等人员穿着的服饰。裤子为淡黄底色，上面装饰着生动自然的散点式花叶纹。花纹呈自然生长的对称状，由利落饱满的五六片叶子簇拥着三个心形花苞，裤脚处还镶以半团花式缘边。比起上身铠甲的卷草纹装饰来说，裤子上的花叶纹显得疏朗别致，达到了彩塑装饰主次分明、层次多样的效果。

（文：崔岩）

The painted sculpture Maharāja-deva holds His head high and looks majestic. The armor He wears has complex structure and intricate patterns. This kind of armor was not made of iron or leather for actual combat, but a kind of honor armor. It is called "silk armor" in *Tang Liu Dian*. Its emergence may be inspired by the silk Liangdang armor of military officials uniform at that time, once used to be the military uniform of court guards or warrior's clothes.

Here we study a part of the painted sculpture Maharāja-deva armor's pattern. The original pattern is located between the armor cord and the leather belt on the Maharāja-deva's upper body, on the center of the belly. Around the semi-circular belly protection is surrounded by full and continuous scrolling vine pattern, which integrated the modeling characteristics of peony, lotus, pomegranate and other plants. The patterns are mainly in azurite and malachite green, dotted with a little white and dark brown, and outlined by earth red lines. This pattern is complex, continuous and flowers and leaves covered the whole area showing the unique vitality of the high Tang Dynasty decoration art.

This painted sculpture Maharāja-deva wears tied trousers under the armor, the sculptor vividly depicted the folds formed by tying trousers legs at the knee, this trousers are light, fit and convenient to move. It is suitable for military, honor guard and other personnel. This trousers have light yellow background, decorated with vivid and natural flower clusters and leaf pattern. The pattern is naturally growing in a symmetrical shape, five or six neat and full leaves around three heart-shaped flower buds, and the trousers cuffs are also inlaid with half round flower pattern trim. Compared with the scrolling vine pattern decoration of the upper body armor, the flower and leaf pattern on the trousers is sparse and unique, which is clear in priorities and full of layers.

(Written by: Cui Yan)

图：崔岩　Painted by: Cui Yan

116

The painted sculpture Vīra's skirt pattern
on the north side of the west niche in the main
chamber of Cave 194 dated to the high Tang
Dynasty at Mogao Grottoes

彩塑力士裙饰图案
莫高窟盛唐第194窟主室
西壁龛外北侧

盛唐第194窟主室西壁龛外的两身彩塑力士像造型准确生动，遒劲有力。北侧这身力士昂首阔步，张口怒吼，双手下压，裸露的上半身和小腿充分体现出肌肉凹凸起伏的体量感。力士下半身围裹半裙，裙摆随着身体的扭转翻折飘荡，形成强烈的动势。裙子边缘镶有宽阔的二方连续图案，一条为卷云纹，另一条为卷草纹，均具有涌动生长的效果，充分体现了盛唐时期大气磅礴的装饰风格。图案主色为石绿、石青、淡土红、深红和褐黑等色，以冷色调为主的配置符合人物的身份和气度。

（文：崔岩）

The two painted sculptures Vīra outside the west niche in the main chamber of Cave 194 dated to the high Tang Dynasty are vivid and muscular. The Vīra on the north side stands straight with His mouth open and two hands pressing down. The naked upper body and lower legs fully reflect the clear shape and volume of muscles. The lower body is wrapped in a skirt, and the skirt sways with the body, forming a strong momentum. The skirt trim is inlaid with wide two in a group repeated pattern; one is cirrus cloud pattern and the other is scrolling vine pattern, both of which have a effect of moving and growing, which fully reflect the magnificent decorative style of the high Tang Dynasty. The main colors of the pattern are malachite green, azurite, light earth red, crimson and brown black. The color configuration dominated by cold colors is in line with the figure's identity and character.

(Written by: Cui Yan)

图：崔岩　Painted by: Cui Yan

The painted sculpture
Buddha's kasaya pattern
on the west niche of the main chamber in Cave
194 dated to the high Tang Dynasty at Mogao
Grottoes

彩塑佛陀袈裟图案
莫高窟盛唐第194窟主室
西壁龛内

第194窟主室西壁龛内正中塑倚坐佛像一尊，主尊外披土红底色的田相袈裟，因为披着方式和倚坐姿态的缘故，袈裟的一角在双足间垂下，本图案择取此局部图案进行整理绘制。

袈裟缘边为二方连续式的卷草纹，这是盛唐时期的代表性图案之一。图案造型为波状的枝蔓上生长着繁密翻卷的叶片和花苞，花叶相间，连绵起伏，呈现出勃勃的生机。但是由于第194窟属于盛唐晚期洞窟，图案色彩上已显示出明显的转折态势。图案以石绿色为主，不再使用较多的对比色，配置方式上也舍却了最为经典的退晕法，而改为大面积平涂，导致色彩层次及华丽感降低，给人清冷秀丽之感。在田相格中装饰的大团花也不再像之前的宝相花那样层层叠叠，而变为单瓣花苞，显示出当时在造像装饰方面的审美变化。

（文：崔岩）

In the middle of the west niche of the main chamber in Cave 194 has a painted sculpture sitting Buddha. The Buddha is covered with field pattern kasaya in earth red background, and because of the way of dressing and siting posture, one corner of the kasaya hangs between the feet, here we choose this part for studying.

The trim of the kasaya is two in a group repeated scrolling vine pattern, which was one of the representative patterns during the high Tang Dynasty. The wavy vines are covered with dense and rolled leaves and flower buds, and the flowers and leaves are alternating and undulating, which showing vigorous vitality. However, as Cave 194 belongs to the late Tang Dynasty, the pattern color has shown an obvious changing trend. The pattern is mainly malachite green, no longer with many contrast colors. In terms of configuration, it also gave up the most classic color-gradation technique and changed to large-area flat coloring, which reduces the color layers and gorgeous feeling, and gives people a cool and clean feeling. The large round flowers decorated in the field pattern are no longer stacked like the previous Baoxiang flowers, but become single layer petal buds, showing the aesthetic change in sculpture decoration at that time.

(Written by: Cui Yan)

图：张博　Painted by: Zhang Bo

The emperor's Bixi and
sleeve trims pattern
on the south wall of the main chamber in
Cave 194 dated to the high Tang Dynasty at
Mogao Grottoes

帝王蔽膝、袖缘
图案
莫高窟盛唐第194窟主室
南壁

第194窟主室南壁绘维摩诘经变一铺，上部为文殊菩萨与维摩诘居士对坐辩法，下有帝王、各国使臣听法。其中，帝王头戴冕旒、身着衮服，这里选择帝王蔽膝和袖缘上的图案进行整理绘制。

帝王蔽膝上装饰着连续的龟背纹，这是一种边缘呈六边形、酷似龟甲的图案。因为龟甲是古代的占卜工具，能"兆吉凶"，且代表长寿和富贵，所以多使用在纺织品、建筑物和器物上。该图案骨架以联珠分割和构建，每个龟背框架内以石青、石绿两色相间配置，其间填饰深浅不同的六瓣朵花，形成规整、缜密的效果。

帝王上衣袖口处有宽缘边，装饰着二方连续式的卷草纹。唐代卷草纹有许多变化形式，其中一种是只保留波状线形结构和抽象花头的极简式，这里就是其中的一例。

（文：崔岩）

On the south wall of the main chamber in Cave 194 is painted with Vimalakirti Sutra illustration, in the upper part is Manjusri Bodhisattva and Vimalakirti debating, and below them are emperor and envoys of various countries listening to Dharma. Among them, the emperor wear Mianliu crown and Gun clothes. Here, the patterns on the emperor's Bixi and sleeve trims are selected for studying.

The emperor's Bixi are decorated with continuous turtle back pattern, which is a pattern with hexagonal edges and looks like tortoise shell. Because tortoise shells were used for divination in ancient times, which can indicate good or bad luck, and represent longevity and wealth, the pattern was mostly used in textiles, buildings and utensils. The pattern frame is divided and constructed by connecting beads, and each turtle back frame is configured with azurite and malachite green alternately, and filled with six petaled flowers of different shades to form a regular and dense effect.

The emperor's upper clothes cuffs have wide trims and are decorated with two in a group repeated scrolling vine pattern. There were many forms of scrolling vine pattern in the Tang Dynasty, one of them is the minimalist form that only retains the wavy linear structure and abstract flower heads, and here is an example.

(Written by: Cui Yan)

图": 张博　Painted by: Zhang Bo

The prince's clothes
on the south wall of the main chamber
in Cave 194 dated to the high Tang
Dynasty at Mogao Grottoes

王子服饰
莫高窟盛唐第194
窟主室南壁

盛唐开凿的莫高窟第194窟里，南壁维摩诘经变画中各国（各族）王子礼佛图的阵容极为强大。经历了魏晋二百余年的民族融合与初唐兼容并包的社会治理，进入鼎盛时期的唐王朝与各国、各民族的交流极为频繁，各国（各族）王子礼佛图中丰富的服饰形态成为研究当时服饰文化演进的重要图像资料。位列队列最前端的赤须王子是盛唐时期才开始出现的形象——红发梳髻、红须飘扬、体毛浓密，头戴带状头饰，上身袒裸，宽大的披帛前搭式穿着，下身着及膝短裤，披帛与短裤上均饰有绿蓝相间的伊卡特图案，戴圆形耳环、颈圈、手镯、足钏，赤足。

（文：李迎军）

In Cave 194 of Mogao Grottoes dated to the high Tang Dynasty, the princes of various countries (ethnics) worshiping Buddha in Vimalakīrti-Nirdeśa Sutra illustration on the south wall look great. After more than 200 years of national integration in the Wei and Jin Dynasties and inclusive social governance in the early Tang Dynasty, the Tang Dynasty entered its heyday and had extremely frequent exchanges with other countries and nationalities. The abundant dress images in princes of various countries (ethnics) worshiping Buddha have become important image materials for studying the evolution of dress culture at that time. The prince with red beard at the front of the queue is an image that began to appear in the high Tang Dynasty — with red hair in a hair bun, red beard fluttering, thick body hair, ribbon headdress, naked upper body, wide silk scarf draped in front of body, and knee length shorts on the lower body. Both silk scarf and shorts are decorated with cyan and green Icart pattern. He wears round earrings, neck ring, bracelets, foot bracelets and barefoot.

(Written by: Li Yingjun)

The prince's clothes
on the south wall of the main
chamber in Cave 194 dated to
the high Tang Dynasty at Mogao
Grottoes

王子服饰
莫高窟盛唐第194
窟主室南壁

初唐壁画中位列前茅的昆仑王子在194窟的听法图中退居次席，其体貌与着装特征和其他听法图基本统一，但服装结构与服饰图案更为清晰翔实。

这身昆仑王子体壮肤黑，头顶蓬松卷发，戴耳环、颈圈、臂钏、手镯、足钏，上身斜缠披帛，下身着及膝短裤（初唐时的缠裹式穿着方式已不明显），赤足。披帛与短裤上皆有伊卡特纹样。

（文：李迎军）

The Kunlun prince who stood in front in the early Tang Dynasty murals moved to back in Cave 194. His body feature and dress style are basically same in other Dharm listening painting, but his clothes structure and patterns are more clear and detailed.

This Kunlun prince is strong and dark, with fluffy curly hair on head. He wears earrings, neck ring, armlets, bracelets and foot bracelets, the upper body is wrapped with silk scarf, and the lower body is covered with knee length shorts (the wrapping style of wearing during the early Tang Dynasty is no longer obvious), barefoot. There are Ikat pattern both on silk scarf and shorts.

(Written by: Li Yingjun)

图：李迎军

Painted by: Li Yíngjūn

124

The prince's clothes
on the south wall of the main chamber
in Cave 194 dated to the high Tang
Dynasty at Mogao Grottoes

王子服饰图案
莫高窟盛唐第194窟主室
南壁

莫高窟第194窟这两位南亚、东南亚王子形象均穿着具有扎经染色工艺特征的织物。走在最前方的这位赤须王子上身所穿着的服饰图案以沙黄色为地，两种纹样交替排列。一种纹样呈现出石绿色的"S"形，两侧点缀蓝色的"Z"形，辅以排线手法绘制的白线；另一种以两个石绿色的扁平"菱形"上下排列，左右点缀"箭头"形，"箭头"形由内而外分别由深蓝色、蓝色和白色组成。走在其身后的昆仑王子上身所穿着的服饰图案以褐色为地，主体纹样为石绿色的"S"形，两侧点缀蓝色的"Z"形。这两组服饰图案都是在纹样的横向或用本色以排线的手法作延伸，或用白色排线增强纹样的模糊感，使两组图案呈现出参差、模糊、流动之感，与扎经染色工艺所呈现出来的视觉效果非常相似。

（文：王可）

In Cave 194 of Mogao Grottoes, the clothes of the two princes from south and southeast Asia have tie-dyeing characteristics. The red beard prince walking in front wears sandy yellow clothes with two patterns arranged alternately. One pattern has malachite green "S" shape, dotted with blue "Z" shape on both sides, supplemented by white line fence; the other pattern is two malachite green flat "Diamonds" arranged up and down, dotted with "arrows" on the left and right. The "arrow" shape is composed by dark blue, blue and white from the inside to the outside. The dress pattern on the upper body of the Kunlun prince walking behind is brown background, the main pattern is malachite green "S" shape, and the two sides are dotted with blue "Z" shape. The two groups of dress patterns are extended horizontally or use pattern color to draw line fence or white line fence to enhance the patterns' indistinct effect, so the two patterns have a sense of irregularity, indistinct and fluidity, which are very similar to the visual effect presented by tie-dyeing technique.

(Written by: Wang Ke)

图" 王可 Painted by: Wang Ke

The prince's clothes
on the south wall of the main chamber
in Cave 194 dated to the high Tang
Dynasty at Mogao Grottoes

王子服饰
莫高窟盛唐第194
窟主室南壁

与敦煌早期壁画相比较，唐以来的壁画人物形象更加生动写实，礼佛图中的各国（各族）王子不仅服饰造型各异，人物形象与体态的刻画也非常翔实生动，这为研究当时各国、各族的民族服饰文化提供了极其有价值的图像佐证。因此在绘画整理时，王子的面容、体态、服装、配饰都基本遵照壁画上的原始形象进行表现。位于队列中段外侧的这位王子体态丰腴、络腮胡须，头戴镂花金冠，身着圆领袍，系革带，内穿长襦、长裤、短靴。

（文：李迎军）

Compared with the early Dunhuang murals, the figures in the murals since the Tang Dynasty are more vivid and realistic. The princes of various countries (ethnics) in the Buddha worship painting not only have different clothes, but also have very detailed and vivid depiction of appearance and posture, which provides extremely valuable image materials for the study of the national dress culture of various countries and ethnic groups at that time. Therefore, when doing the painting, the prince's face, posture, clothes and accessory are basically expressed in accordance with the original image in the mural. The prince standing in the middle outside of the group looks plump, bearded, wearing a hollowed-out gold crown, round collar robe, leather belt, long Ru inside, trousers and short boots.

(Written by: Li Yingjun)

The prince's clothes
on the south wall of the main chamber
in Cave 194 dated to the high Tang
Dynasty at Mogao Grottoes

王子服饰
莫高窟盛唐第194
窟主室南壁

各国（各族）王子服饰中以窄袖长袍造型居多，位于队列中段外侧的这位王子穿着的宽袖上衣搭配下裳的服装别具特色。王子披发垂于脑后，头戴四股线型笼状金冠，着右衽大袖上衣，领口与袖口均有宽大的织锦边饰，下面搭配宽松肥大的浅色长裙，裙前饰有绿褐相间的蔽膝状饰物，足着尖头鞋（或靴）。

（文：李迎军）

The princes of various countries (ethnics) mostly wear narrow sleeved robes. The prince who stands in the middle outside the group wears a wide sleeved coat matched with Chang on the lower body which looks very special. The prince's hair hangs behind his head, wearing a four strand linear cage shaped gold crown and a large sleeved right lapel coat. There are wide brocade trims at the collar and cuffs. On the lower body is matched with a loose and wide light colored long skirt, and the front of the skirt is decorated with green and brown Bixi shaped accessory, and feet in pointed shoes (or boots).

(Written by: Li Yingjun)

图：李迎军 Painted by: Li Yingjun

The prince's clothes

on the south wall of the main

chamber in Cave 194 dated to

the high Tang Dynasty at Mogao

Grottoes

王子服饰

莫高窟盛唐第194

窟主室南壁

在这组庞大阵容中，至少有十几个国家或民族的王子（或使者）形象——头戴羽冠的东亚人、身着翻领袍的西域人、缠裹巾帛的南亚人等。他们来自世界各地，穿着各异的民族服装。这组壁画为研究世界民族服饰提供了极为丰富的图像资料，也成为唐代繁盛景象的真实反映。这位王子着窄袖绿色长袍，腰系革带，足蹬短靴，内搭上襦、长裤。头顶帽子高耸的钟形帽体与宽大的帽檐极具形式感，蓝红相间的图案与褐色皮毛边饰也繁简适度、相得益彰。

（文：李迎军）

In this group of people, there are at least a dozen images of princes (or envoys) — eastern Asians wearing feather crowns, western Asians wearing lapel robes, south Asians wrapped in scarves, etc. They came from all over the world and wore different national costumes. This mural provides extremely rich image materials for the study of national clothes in the world, and is also a true reflection of the Tang Dynasty prosperity. The prince wears a green robe with narrow sleeves, leather belt around his waist, feet in short boots, Ru shirt on the upper body and trousers on the lower body. The high bell shaped hat and wide brim have a great sense of form, and the blue-red pattern matched with brown fur trim looks just right and complement each other.

(Written by: Li Yingjun)

The prince's clothes

on the south wall of the main

chamber in Cave 194 dated to

the high Tang Dynasty at Mogao

Grottoes

王子服饰

莫高窟盛唐第194

窟主室南壁

在二十几个形象中，绝大多数王子都是四分之三侧面的造型，只有队列后端出现了唯一一位正面造型的王子形象，他所穿戴的服装结构与配饰细节也因此更加准确明了。这位王子头戴尖顶立檐帽，内穿圆领上襦、长裤、短靴，外罩窄袖翻领长袍，长袍的前衣襟开在前中心偏右的位置，腰间系革带，腰带前段垂配饰，从造型推断似是随身佩刀。

（文：李迎军）

Among the more than 20 images, most of princes have three-quarters profile, and only one prince image stands at the back of the group is a front portrait. Therefore, the clothing structure and accessories details are more accurate and clear. The prince wears a pointed hat with upturned brim, a round collar Ru shirt inside, long trousers and short boots, covered with a narrow sleeved lapel robe. The front opening of the robe is in the center slightly to right, leather belt around the waist and the front part of the belt has a accessory, which should be a knife according to the shape.

(Written by: Li Yingjun)

图：李迎军 Painted by: Li Yingjun

王子服饰

莫高窟盛唐第194窟主室

南壁

The princes' clothes

on the south wall of the main chamber in

Cave 194 dated to the high Tang Dynasty

at Mogao Grottoes

在队列中，绘于内侧的三子们只露出了胸与头，从显露的上半身服装形态看，有圆领、交领、翻领等多种领型，在交领服装中，除一位王子服装是左衽外，其余全是右衽。各位王子的肤色、服色与五官结构各异，帽饰差异尤为显著，每人戴的帽子从廓型、材质到图案、配色都个性鲜明，极大地凸显了盛唐时期世界各民族服饰文化的多样性特征。在绘画整理时，参照相关洞窟壁画上相对应的各国王子形象，补充了服装造型中被遮挡的部分结构，服装衣身的长短、袖子的肥瘦尚属推断，仍需进一步考证。

（文：李迎军）

In the group, the princes painted in the inner side only show their chest and head. From the upper body clothing form, there are many kinds of collar shapes, such as round collar, cross collar and lapel. About the cross collar clothes, except one prince's clothes is left collar, the rest are all right collar. The skin color, clothes color and facial features of the princes are different, and the differences of hat are particularly significant. The hats worn by the princes have distinctive personality from shape, material, pattern and color matching, which greatly highlight the diversity of the clothing culture of ethnic people in the world during the high Tang Dynasty. When doing the painting, based on the corresponding images of princes from various countries in the murals, the partially blocked parts in the mural are added. The length of the clothes and the width of sleeves are speculation, which still need further study.

(Written by: Li Yingjun)

图：李迎军　Painted by: Li Yingjun

Dunhuang Mogao Grottoes Cave
199 of the High Tang
Dynasty

敦 煌 莫 高 窟 盛 唐

第199窟

　　第199窟是创建于盛唐时期的覆斗顶形窟，经中唐、西夏重修。主室窟顶藻井为团花井心，四周绘垂幔。四披绘千佛。西壁开盝顶帐形龛，龛内唐塑、西夏修一趺坐佛，西夏移入一倚坐佛。龛顶中央绘棋格团花，四披绘药师佛立像及供养菩萨数身。龛内西壁西夏重修佛光，两侧上绘垂幔，下各绘一弟子。佛座两侧各绘一狮子。南、北壁上绘垂幔，下各绘三弟子。龛沿绘卷草及半团花边饰。龛下绘供器及男供养人像数身。龛外南侧盛唐绘一观世音菩萨，北侧中唐绘一大势至菩萨。南壁西起中唐画二观世音菩萨、一女供养人，中央中唐绘一观世音菩萨、一大势至菩萨、一供养比丘，东侧中唐绘六身千佛、八莲池菩萨、七坐佛。北壁中央中唐绘观无量寿经变一铺，西侧绘"十六观"，东侧绘"未生怨"。东壁存中唐壁画。前室存西夏壁画。

　　此窟人物造型灵动，姿态优美，尤其是手部动态丰富，或持物，或捻指，或合十。画师们充分发挥想象，结合现实人物，极具艺术性和创造性地绘制了宗教艺术中的形象。虽然人物肤色已变，但其服饰细节仍然清晰，能看出受外来艺术的影响。菩萨身披层层披帛，灵动飘逸，气质优雅。佛弟子袈裟衣褶流畅，图案精美，用三色五瓣花朵纹进行装饰，增添了服饰的质感。

（文：杨婧嫱）

Cave 199 is a truncated pyramidal ceiling cave built in the high Tang Dynasty, which was repaired in the middle Tang Dynasty and the Western Xia Dynasty. The caisson of the main chamber has round flower as the center, with valance painted around it, and the four slopes are covered with Thousand Buddhas. A tent shaped niche is in the west wall, and in the niche there is a painted sculpture sitting Buddha with two legs folded which was made in the Tang Dynasty and repaired in the Western Xia Dynasty, and in Western Xia Dynasty a painted sculpture sitting Buddha with two legs down was moved in. The niche's flat checks ceiling is filled with round flower pattern, and the four slopes are painted with a number of standing Bhaisajyaguru Buddha and Bodhisattvas. The west niche wall Buddha light was repaired in Western Xia and painted with valance on both sides, and a disciple is painted on the bottom of both sides. Both sides of the Buddha seat have painted a lion and the south and north walls are painted with valance on the upper parts, and the lower parts are painted with three disciples each. The niche is decorated with scrolling vine pattern and semi round flower pattern. Below the niche has painted offering utensils and several male donors. Outside the niche, a Avalokitesvara Bodhisattva is painted in the high Tang Dynasty on the south side and a Mahasthamaprapta Bodhisattva is painted in the middle Tang Dynasty on the north side. From the south wall to the west, there are two Avalokitesvara Bodhisattvas and a female donor, and one Avalokitesvara, one Mahasthamaprapta and one offering Bhiksu in the center, and six Thousand Buddhas, eight lotus pond Bodhisattvas and seven seated Buddhas in the east side all dated to the middle Tang Dynasty. In the center of the north wall is painted with Amitayurdhyana Sutra illustration dated to the middle Tang Dynasty, the Sixteen Visualizations in the west side and Ajatasattu's story in the east side. There are murals of the middle Tang Dynasty on the east wall and Western Xia murals in the front chamber.

The figures in this cave have flexible shapes and beautiful postures, especially the hands, either holding objects, or twiddling, or putting palms together. The painters fully used their imagination and combined reality to draw images, full of artistry and creativity to create religious art images. Although the skin color of the characters has changed, the details of their clothes are still clear, which can be seen that they were influenced by foreign art. The Bodhisattva wears layers of silk scarf, looks vivid and elegant. The Buddhist disciples' kasaya have smooth pleats and exquisite patterns, decorated with three-color five-petal flower pattern, which added the texture feeling of the dress.

(Written by: Yang Jingqiang)

The Bodhisattva's clothes
on the south outside the west niche in the main
chamber of Cave 199 dated to the high Tang
Dynasty at Mogao Grottoes

菩萨服饰
莫高窟盛唐第199窟主室
西壁龛外南侧

盛唐第199窟主室西壁龛外南侧的观世音菩萨形象端庄秀美，含情脉脉，眉间点缀白毫。左手托宝瓶，右手轻拈柳枝，跣足立于莲花座上。上身穿绿色右袒式僧祇支，边缘有白色半团花装饰，肩披蓝色丝质天衣。下着深红色织花长裙，裙摆处镶饰蓝色贴边，内佩绿色衬裙，其下摆也有贴边。腰部系有精美的长方形红蓝宝石腰带，并配有淡红色裙带在膝部打花结垂至身前。

菩萨头束高髻，佩戴化佛冠（观世音菩萨头上多佩戴的宝冠之一，冠中所呈现的化佛，即体现菩萨之本态），上饰有宝石镶嵌的火焰纹，身上佩戴的项链、手镯与璎珞浑然相连，自肩部垂下的双色彩带与冠缯延伸下来的圆环形细带一起上下穿插环绕，使整套服饰动感十足，飘飘欲仙。

诚然，从盛唐时期对于菩萨的精妙表达可以清楚地看出，佛教艺术向民族艺术的过渡，以及佛教绘画与民族绘画的有序融合，进而使菩萨服饰艺术体现出民族服饰艺术的审美内涵。

（文：刘元风）

The painted Bodhisattva on the south outside the west niche in the main chamber of Cave 199 dated to the high Tang Dynasty who looks dignified, beautiful and affectionate. There is a Urna between His eyebrows, and His left hand holds a precious bottle, the right hand twiddles a willow branch, and He stands barefoot on a lotus carpet. The upper body wears a green right-bared Sankaksika, the edge of the Sankaksika is decorated with white half round flowers, and the shoulders are covered with blue silk scarf. The lower body wears crimson floral dress with blue trim at the hem and a green petticoat inside. The waist is tied with an exquisite rectangular ruby sapphire belt, and a light red skirt belt is tied at the knee and hanging down in front of the body.

The Bodhisattva has a high hair bun and wears Buddha image crown (one of the most precious crowns worn by Avalokitesvara Bodhisattva. The Buddha image in the crown reflects the true state of Bodhisattva), which is decorated with flame pattern inlaid with gemstones. The necklace and bracelets worn on His body are connected with keyūra naturally. The double color ribbon hanging down from His shoulders is interspersed with the ring-shaped thin laces extending from the crown, making the whole dress full of movement and very holy.

Indeed, from the exquisite expression of the high Tang Dynasty Bodhisattva, it can be clearly seen that the transition from Buddhist art to national art and the orderly integration of Buddhist painting and national painting make the aesthetic connotation of national clothes art embodied in Bodhisattva clothes art.

(Written by: Liu Yuanfeng)

第199窟主室西壁龛内应有一佛塑像与二弟子画像，现在主尊佛塑像已遗失无存，佛光两侧壁面上的弟子像还保存较好，除了肤色变黑外，人物造型与服装细节还清晰可辨。绘于佛光北侧的弟子应是迦叶，在莫高窟壁画中，很多弟子像上的胡须都无法辨认，但这身画像中还可以相对清晰地分辨出胡须的造型，这也与迦叶的老者身份相符。与大多数洞窟中迦叶的历尽磨难苦行僧形象不同的是，莫高窟第199窟龛内的迦叶是一位饱读诗书的儒雅长者——这身迦叶双手持一卷经卷，神态虔诚、毕恭毕敬地肃立在覆瓣莲花台上，身披田相袈裟，上面装饰红、绿、蓝三色的五瓣花纹，这种形似梅花的圆形图案在初唐的弟子袈裟上就已经出现，花纹风格简洁、典雅庄重。

（文：李迎军）

There should be a Buddha sculpture and two painted disciples on the west niche wall in the main chamber of Cave 199. Now the main Buddha sculpture has lost, while the painted disciples on both sides of the Buddha light are still well preserved. In addition to the blacked skin color, the figures modeling and clothing details are still clear and recognizable. The disciple painted on the north side of the Buddha light should be Kasyapa. In Mogao Grottoes murals, the beard on many disciples can not be distinguished, but the shape of beard can be relatively clearly distinguished in this portrait, which is also consistent with the identity of Kasyapa's age. Different from the image of a suffering ascetic monk in most caves, Kasyapa in the niche of Cave 199 in Mogao Grottoes is a refined and Venerable elder who looks well educated—He holds a scroll of scripture by both hands, stands reverently and devoutly on a lotus platform, wears a field pattern kasaya which is decorated with five-petaled pattern of red, cyan and green, the plum blossoms like round patterns had appeared on disciple kasaya in the early Tang Dynasty. The pattern style is simple, elegant and solemn.

(Written by: Li Yingjun)

第199窟主室西壁龛内的这身弟子有着丰腴的体态，这在莫高窟诸多弟子像中并不常见。他手臂抬起，左手指下，右手指上，目视前方，神态虔诚，似张口欲言。这身弟子身披朱色田相袈裟，田相与袈裟底色的色相相同，只是明度有异，整件袈裟没有复杂的图案装饰，色调统一，简约但不单调。他采用盛唐最普遍的右祖式披法穿着袈裟，即将袈裟覆左肩，从后面络右腋，再从右腋下提起袈裟一角搭在左臂上。这种披法使袈裟里面（反面）也随着披挂的翻折而显露出来，袈裟里、面的颜色与图案随着穿着而交错显现，呈现出别具特色的韵味。

（文：李迎军）

This disciple on the west wall of the niche in the main chamber of Cave 199 has a plump body, which is not common in many disciples in Mogao Grottoes. He raises His arms, points down with His left hand and up with His right hand, eyes front, looks pious, and seems to open His mouth to speak. He wears a vermilion field pattern kasaya, although the whole body is red, the brightness is different. The whole kasaya has no complex pattern decoration, and the color is unified, simple but not monotonous. This disciple wears a kasaya in the most common right lapel style in the high Tang Dynasty, that is, covering the left shoulder with the kasaya, winding the right armpit from the back, and then lifting the corner of the kasaya from the right armpit to put it on the left arm. This wearing method makes the inside (reverse side) of the kasaya can be seen by the folding. The colors and patterns of the inside and surface of the kasaya appear alternately with the wearing, showing a special charm.

(Written by: Li Yingjun)

图：李迎军　Painted by: Li Yingjun

此为盛唐第199窟主室西壁龛顶西披北侧供养菩萨，侧立身，上身前倾，右手托举莲蕾，左手下垂持莲蕾，赤足站在双莲花座上。菩萨高鼻、深目、厚唇，脸庞丰圆，似西域人面相，神态前瞻。

菩萨短卷发，有头光，戴宝冠，有臂钏、手镯。其上身着条帛，从右肩部斜垂至左边肋下的细长带状布，也被称为"络腋"。此外，在右肩上还搭饰有长条披巾，披巾在右臂前绕成环形，随后一端垂于右臂后，另一端从身后穿过搭绕在左腕上。菩萨下着腰裙和长裙，长裙材质轻薄，可清晰透出菩萨的腿部，并有层层叠叠的裙纹，反映出当时纺织技术的成熟和画师技艺的高妙。

（文：赵茜、吴波）

This is the offering Bodhisattva in the west niche north side of the west slope in the main chamber of Cave 199 dated to the high Tang Dynasty. He stands in profile, leans forward, lifts the lotus bud with right hand, and the left hand hangs down holding another lotus bud, and barefoot on the double lotus seats. The Bodhisattva has a high nose, deep eyes and thick lips; His face is plump and round, looks like from Western Regions, with forward-looking.

This Bodhisattva has short curly hair, with head light and wears a crown. Armlets, bracelets, and the upper body wears silk scarf, which is a slender strip of cloth that hangs diagonally from the right shoulder to the left rib, also known as "Luoye". In addition, the right shoulder is also covered with a long silk scarf, which is wound in a ring in front of the right arm, then one end hangs behind the right arm, and one end past through from behind and wound on the left wrist. The Bodhisattva wears a waist wrap and a long skirt on the lower body. The material of the long skirt is light and thin, which we can clearly see the Bodhisattva's legs, and also have many folds, reflecting the maturity of textile technology and the skill of painters at that time.

(Written by: Zhao Xi, Wu Bo)

此为盛唐第199窟主室西壁龛顶西披南侧供养菩萨，与西披北侧菩萨遥遥相望。

菩萨束发，有头光，戴宝冠，从冠的形制来看，应属矮花蔓冠，短宝缯垂于脑后。菩萨左手托举盛开的莲花，右手持盛开的莲花垂于体侧，赤足站在异色的莲花座上。正反两面双色披巾在身前形成"U"形，两端从双肩搭至背后，左侧一端自然下垂，右侧一端从身后搭绕在胳膊上。菩萨下着围腰和长裙，围腰裹在长裙外，两端垂于体前。在围腰下，有垂带系结装饰于长裙之外。因龛顶位置没有阳光直射，菩萨像除肤色部分氧化变黑外，服饰色彩苍翠浓郁，以条帛、披巾、长裙的赭红色为主调，搭配绿色的围腰、蓝色的垂带，整体色彩雅致醇和。

（文：赵茜、吴波）

This is the offering Bodhisattva in the west niche south side of the west slope in the main chamber of Cave 199 dated to the high Tang Dynasty, facing to the Bodhisattva on the north side of the west slope.

The Bodhisattva's hair is tied, with head light and crown. According to the shape of the crown, it should be a short flower vine crown, with short crown laces hanging behind head. He holds a lotus in full bloom by His left hand, and another lotus in full bloom up side down in His right hand, and stands barefoot on two lotus platforms of different colors. The two-color silk scarf on both sides forms a U-shape in front of the body, with both ends draped from the shoulders to the back, the left end drooping naturally, and the right end draped around the arm from behind. The Bodhisattva wears waist wrap and long skirt on the lower body, the waist wrap is wrapped around the long skirt, and both ends hanging in front of the body. Below the waist wrap, there are tie pendants hanging in front to decorate the long skirt. Because there is no direct sunlight at the top of the niche, only the Bodhisattva's skin turns into black because of oxidation, and the colors of clothes are still green and fresh. The ochre red of ribbon, silk scarf and long skirt is the main color, matched with green waist wrap and blue vertical belt, and the overall color is elegant and mellow.

(Written by: Zhao Xi, Wu Bo)

The offering Bodhisattva's clothes in the west niche north side of the west slope in the main chamber of Cave 199 dated to the high Tang Dynasty at Mogao Grottoes

供养菩萨服饰
莫高窟盛唐第199窟主室西壁龛顶西披北侧

The offering Bodhisattva's clothes in the west niche south side of the west slope in the main chamber of Cave 199 dated to the high Tang Dynasty at Mogao Grottoes

供养菩萨服饰
莫高窟盛唐第199窟主室西壁龛顶西披南侧

图：吴波　Painted by: Wu Bo

此为盛唐第199窟主室西壁龛顶南披东侧供养菩萨。菩萨侧身单膝胡跪在莲花座上，眉目清秀，如祈愿状，双手交握放于胸前，听法似有所悟，整体氛围平和喜乐。

菩萨梳高髻，戴宝冠，有头光，余发覆肩，戴项饰，项饰的中央有圆形钿饰。双肩搭饰披帛，从左右肩部垂下遮覆背部。披帛与披巾相比，长度短于披巾，但宽度大于披巾。"披帛、披巾多以轻薄的纱罗为材料，披着的方式多种多样。"菩萨下着围腰和长裙，围腰系在长裙外，上边缘有波浪状起伏形成。在服饰色彩上，以红色、绿色、蓝色为主，红色长裙，绿色围腰，披巾正面为红色、反面为蓝色，与红长裙和蓝头发相呼应，绿色围腰与莲花座照应，整体色彩冷暖相间、搭配和谐。

（文：赵茜、吴波）

This is the offering Bodhisattva in the west niche east side of the south slope in the main chamber of Cave 199 dated to the high Tang Dynasty. The Bodhisattva kneels on the lotus seat with one knee, eyebrows and eyes are beautiful, like a prayer, and two hands in front of chest, seems like learned something from Dharma. The overall atmosphere is peaceful and happy.

The Bodhisattva has a high hair bun, with crown, head light, and the rest hair covering the shoulders, the necklace has a circular flower ornament in the center. The two shoulders are covered with silk shawl, hanging from the left and right shoulders to cover the back. Compared with the silk scarf, the length is shorter, but the width is wider. "Silk shawl and silk scarf are mostly made of light silk fabrics, which can be worn in a variety of ways." The lower body wears waist wrap and long skirt, the waist wrap is tied outside the long skirt, and the upper edge is wavy. In terms of clothing colors, red, cyan and green are the main colors. Red skirt. green waist wrap, and the silk scarf are red in front and blue in back, which echo with the red skirt and blue hair, the green waist wrap echoes with lotus seat. The overall color matching is harmonious, balanced in cold and warm.

(Written by: Zhao Xi, Wu Bo)

The offering Bodhisattva's clothes
in the west niche east side of the south slope in the main chamber of Cave 199 dated to the high Tang Dynasty at Mogao Grottoes
供养菩萨服饰
莫高窟盛唐第199窟主室西壁龛顶南披东侧

此为盛唐第199窟主室西壁龛顶东披南侧供养菩萨。菩萨侧立扭身，微微仰头，脸庞腴润，长眉入鬓，高鼻深目，厚唇，面相似有印度人特征，神情憨态可掬，别有动人之处。左手上举，右手微抬，赤足站在双莲花上。

菩萨戴宝冠，有头光，梳高髻，余发垂肩，戴手镯。上身着络腋衣，覆左肩、穿右腋。双臂在身前搭饰披巾，披巾两端自由垂落，加强了飘逸感。菩萨下着围腰和长裙，长裙波浪般的裙纹层层叠叠，充满韵律。在围腰和长裙之间还有一层长度至膝的短裙，层次丰富。在色彩搭配上，棕红色的络腋衣、披巾、长裙与绿色的围腰形成对比，蓝色的短裙起到了调和作用，与菩萨脚下的蓝色双莲花形成呼应，莲瓣外深内浅，颇具装饰美感。

（文：赵茜、吴波）

This is the offering Bodhisattva in the west niche south side of the east slope in the main chamber of Cave 199 dated to the high Tang Dynasty. The Bodhisattva stands in profile with body twisted, head slightly up, who has a plump face, long eyebrows reaching to temples, high nose, deep and bright eyes, thick lips, looks like an Indian, and the expression is happy and kind, very special. His left hand rises up, right hand slightly lifted, and stands barefoot on two lotuses.

This Bodhisattva wears a crown, and He has head light, combs a high hair bun, and wears bracelets. The rest hair covers on shoulders. The upper body wears Luoye, covering the left shoulder and through under the right armpit. The two arms hold silk scarf in front of the body, and the two ends fall freely to enhance the sense of elegance. The lower body wears waist wrap and long skirt, and the wavy skirt patterns of the long skirt are stacked and full of rhythm. There is also a knee length skirt between the waist wrap and the long skirt, with rich layers. In terms of color matching, the brown red Luoye, silk scarf and long skirt contrast with the green waist wrap, and the blue short skirt plays a blend role and echoes with the blue double lotus platforms under the Bodhisattva's feet. The lotus petals are dark outside and light inside, which has decorative beauty.

(Written by: Zhao Xi, Wu Bo)

The offering Bodhisattva's clothes
in the west niche south side of the east slope in the main chamber of Cave 199 dated to the high Tang Dynasty at Mogao Grottoes
供养菩萨服饰
莫高窟盛唐第199窟主室西壁龛顶东披南侧

图：吴波　Painted by: Wu Bo

Dunhuang Mogao Grottoes Cave

208 of the High Tang Dynasty

敦煌莫高窟盛唐

第208窟

第208窟是创建于盛唐时期的覆斗顶形窟，经五代重修。主室窟顶藻井为团花井心，四周绘垂幔，四披绘千佛。西壁开平顶敞口龛，龛内塑像已失。龛顶绘法华经"见宝塔品"，四周绘六飞天。龛内共画二菩萨、八弟子、六头光。龛沿口内侧画波状卷草，外侧画半团花边饰。龛下中央五代画供器及二供养菩萨，两侧及力士台下绘比丘及供养人数身。南壁中央绘观无量寿经变一铺，西侧绘"未生怨"，东侧绘"十六观"，北壁绘弥勒经变一铺。东壁门上绘千佛，门沿两侧五代各绘菩萨一身，门南绘二菩萨、盛唐绘一女供养人，门北绘二菩萨、十坐佛、一男供养人。前室及甬道存五代壁画。

此窟菩萨服饰上出现大量几何图案。几何纹的形式与当时提花织造技术有密切的联系。此窟内菩萨腰裙上绘有菱形纹，里面填充圆点、十字纹样等。菩萨的络腋上用工整排线的白线组成几何纹的骨架，应是模仿经线和纬线纺织的图案，从侧面反映出盛唐时期的纺织工艺。

（文：杨婧嫱）

Cave 208 is a truncated pyramidal ceiling cave built in the high Tang Dynasty and repaired in the Five Dynasties. The caisson of the main chamber has round flower as the center, with valance painted around it. Four slopes covered with Thousand Buddhas. The west wall has a flat ceiling niche and the sculptures in the niche have lost. The top of the niche is painted with Saddharmapundarika Sutra illustration, Stuupadarsanparivartah chapter, and six Flying Apsaras are painted around. There are two Bodhisattvas, eight disciples and six head lights painted in the niche. The inside of the niche edge is painted with wavy scrolling vine pattern, and the outside edge is painted with semi round flower pattern. In the center below the niche, there are offering utensils and two offering Bodhisattvas painting dated to the Five Dynasties. On both sides and below the Vīra platform, there are painted Bhiksu and a number of donors. In the center of the south wall there is Amitayurdhyana Sutra illustration; the Ajatasattu's story is on the west side, and the Sixteen Visualizations is on the east side. Maitreya Sutra illustration is painted on the north wall. Thousand Buddhas are painted on the east wall; each side above the door has a painted Bodhisattva dated to the Five Dynasties; the south side of the door is painted with two Bodhisattvas and a female donor dated to the high Tang Dynasty; the north side of the door is painted with two Bodhisattvas and ten seated Buddhas, and one male donor. There are Five Dynasties murals in the front chamber and corridor.

A large number of geometric patterns appear on the Bodhisattva clothes in this cave. The form of geometric pattern is closely related to the jacquard weaving technique at that time. There are diamond patterns painted on the Bodhisattva waist wrap in this cave, which are filled with dots, cross patterns, etc. On Bodhisattva's Luoye, the frame of geometric pattern is composed by neat white lines, which should be a imitation of warp and weft weaving pattern, reflecting the textile technology of the high Tang Dynasty in some point.

(Written by: Yang Jingqiang)

The Bodhisattva's clothes
on the south outside the west niche of the main
chamber in Cave 208 dated to the high Tang
Dynasty at Mogao Grottoes

菩萨服饰
莫高窟盛唐第208窟主室
西壁龛外南侧

　　盛唐第208窟主室西壁龛外南侧供养菩萨，容貌丰润甜美，楚楚动人。左手托着花瓶，右手轻拈柳枝。上身斜披络腋（此处络腋的披法有所不同，一般均从左肩落下，而此款络腋是从右肩落下）。下身着赭石色丝质绣花罗裙，其下摆镶蓝色贴边。蓝色的腰裙上装饰精致的菱形纹样，宽宽的双面条带围在腰间，条带的正面呈绿色，背面是点缀几何纹的赭石色，条带缠绕在从腰部垂下来的蓝色绳带上折返而垂落在身前。另有绿色彩绦自腰部垂于裙子两侧。

　　菩萨头束高髻，余发披肩，佩戴化佛冠，正中上部和两侧装饰有日月图形，从冠缯延伸下来的彩带绕臂飘落。尤为鲜见的是身上的璎珞，其材质、工艺及"X"形佩戴方式均独具特色，彰显其在共性倾向中的个性化审美风格。

（文：刘元风）

　　The offering Bodhisattva on the south side of the west niche in the main chamber of Cave 208 dated to the high Tang Dynasty, who has a plump, sweet and moving appearance. He holds a vase by left hand and twiddles a willow branch by right hand. The upper body is diagonally covered by Luoye (the cover method of Luoye here is different; the common method is from left shoulder down, while this one falls from the right shoulder). The lower body is wearing an ochre silk Luo skirt embroidered flower pattern, with blue welt at the bottom, and the blue waist wrap decorated with exquisite rhombus pattern. The wide double-faces strip is around the waist, and the front side of the strip is green, and the back dotted with ochre geometric pattern. The strip is wrapped around the blue cord hanging from the waist, turned back and dropped in front. The other two green ribbons hang down from the waist on both sides of the skirt.

　　The Bodhisattva's head has a high hair bun, the rest hair covers the shoulders, and He wears a Buddha image crown, the upper part of the middle and both sides are decorated with sun-moon pattern, and the colored ribbons extending from the crown fall around His arms. What is particularly rare is the keyūra on the body, its material, technique and "X" wearing style are unique, highlighting a personalized aesthetic style in the common tendency.

(Written by: Liu Yuanfeng)

The Bodhisattva's
waist wrap pattern
on the south outside the west niche in the
main chamber of Cave 208 dated to the
high Tang Dynasty at Mogao Grottoes

菩萨腰裙图案
莫高窟盛唐第208窟主室
西壁龛外南侧

第208窟主室西壁龛外南侧的菩萨下身外裹腰裙，腰裙底色为石青色，整体图案从上到下可分为三段：第一段为赭褐色勾勒的联珠纹；第二段为主体纹样，以赭褐色与浅绿色相间排布的菱形为骨架进行连缀排列，三种不同构成的几何纹样填饰其中，错落有序，呈现四方连续的构成形式；第三段为赭褐色勾勒的弓字纹与联珠纹。整体图案为疏密相间的几何纹样构成，秩序统一又富有变化。绘制过程中参考了常沙娜主编的《中国敦煌历代服饰图案》一书的整理临摹稿。

（文：常青）

The Bodhisattva's lower body on the south outside the west niche of the main chamber in Cave 208 is wrapped with a waist wrap. The main color of the waist wrap is azurite, and the overall pattern can be divided into three sections from top to bottom: the first section is the beads pattern outlined in ochre brown; the second section is the main pattern, rhombic lattice arranged alternately in ochre brown and light green is the frame for continuous arrangement, three different geometric patterns are filled and decorated in, which are checkered and orderly, showing a four in a group continuous form; the third section is ochre brown outlined bow shaped pattern and beads pattern. The whole pattern is composed in dense and sparse balanced geometric patterns, which is unified and changeable. When doing the illustration, reference was made to the book *Clothing Patterns of China Dunhuang Mural* edited by Chang Shana.

(Written by: Chang Qing)

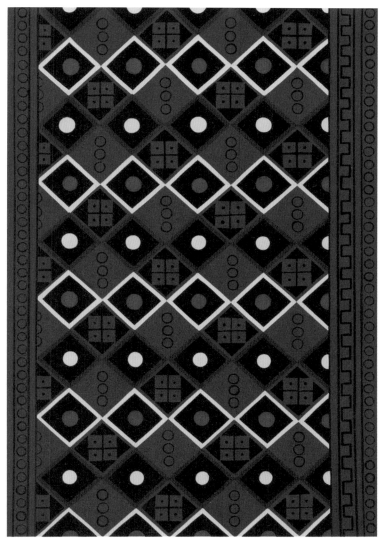

图'：常青　Painted by: Chang Qing

The Bodhisattva
waist wrap pattern
on the south side of the west niche in the
main chamber of Cave 208 dated to the high
Tang Dynasty at Mogao Grottoes

菩萨腰裙图案
莫高窟盛唐第208窟主室
西壁龛内南侧

第208窟主室西壁龛内南侧的菩萨，虽然肤色已经氧化变色，但其服饰依旧色彩鲜艳，纹样清晰。此菩萨面容丰腴，神态安详，头戴镶嵌宝珠的日月冠，身佩璎珞，双手持莲花，站立于莲花台之上。上身斜披土红色与石绿色双面络腋，正面有规整灵巧的菱形纹样，下半身着朱色真丝印花长裙，点缀十字小花，外穿双色几何纹拼接腰裙，上半段图案与络腋图案相同，外裹石绿色腰襻，另有彩绦系于腰间并垂于身前和两侧，服饰华美，别具特色。现将腰裙图案进行整理绘制。两幅图案的主体纹样均为菱形，菱形骨架的内部填充与其空间相适应的几何纹样，大小、疏密变化有致，白线勾勒的弓字纹和联珠纹条带作为边饰。整体图案色彩和谐，造型细腻，对比变化中不失统一。绘制过程中参考了常沙娜主编的《中国敦煌历代服饰图案》一书的整理临摹稿。

（文：常青）

The Bodhisattva is in the south side of the west niche in the main chamber of Cave 208; although His skin color has oxidized and discolored, His clothes colors are still bright and the patterns are clear. The Bodhisattva has a plump face and a serene look, wearing a sun and moon crown which is inlaid with jewels, keyūra on body and holding a lotus by both hands. He stands on a lotus platform, the upper body is diagonally covered with earth red and malachite green double-color Luoye, with regularly and skillfully diamond patterns on the front. The lower body is covered with a vermilion silk skirt with printed flower pattern, dotted with cross flower pattern, and a two-color geometric stitched waist wrap. The pattern of the upper part is the same as that of the Luoye, wrapped with malachite green waist band, and a colorful cord is tied around the waist hanging in front and both sides of the body, looks gorgeous and unique. Now the waist wrap pattern is studied. The main pattern of the two patterns are rhombic, the interior of the rhombic frames are filled with geometric patterns corresponding to its space, changing in size and density. The bow pattern and beads pattern stripes outlined by white lines are used as edge decorations. The overall pattern is harmonious in color, exquisite in shape, and unified in change. When doing the illustration, reference was made to the book *Clothing Patterns of China Dunhuang Mural* edited by Chang Shana.

(Written by: Chang Qing)

图：常青　Painted by: Chang Qing

菩萨络腋图案

莫高窟盛唐第208窟主室

西壁龛内北侧

The Bodhisattva's
Luoye pattern
on the north side of the west niche in the
main chamber of Cave 208 dated to the
high Tang Dynasty at Mogao Grottoes

第208窟主室西壁龛内北侧的菩萨上半身披络腋，搭左手腕悬挂下垂，底色为土红色，图案以菱形为骨架交错连缀排列。现将此菩萨络腋的图案进行整理绘制。图案主体纹样是石青色和石绿色箭头相背组成的菱形纹样，菱形内部依空间填饰相应的白色圆点，呈四方连续的构成方式排列，剩余空间按箭头的方向规整排列白色竖线。整体图案疏密有致，均衡灵巧，并呈现出伊卡特织物的视觉特征，展现出中国古代服饰艺术的精美，以及染织工艺技术的精湛。绘制过程中参考了常沙娜主编的《中国敦煌历代服饰图案》一书的整理临摹稿。

（文：常青）

The Bodhisattva on the north side of the west niche in the main chamber of Cave 208 who's upper body covered with Luoye and draped over His left wrist, the background color is red soil, and the pattern is diamond as the frame checkered arranged. The pattern of this Bodhisattva's Luoye is now studied. The main body of this pattern is rhombuses composed by azurite and malachite green arrows opposite each other. The interior of the rhombuses are filled with corresponding white dots according to the space, which are arranged in four in a group repeated. The remaining space is regularly arranged with white vertical lines according to the direction of the arrow. The overall pattern is dense and sparse balanced, which presents the visual characteristics of Ikat fabrics. It shows the exquisite ancient Chinese clothing art and developed dyeing and weaving technology. When doing the illustration, reference was made from the book *Clothing Patterns of China Dunhuang Mural* edited by Chang Shana.

(Written by: Chang Qing)

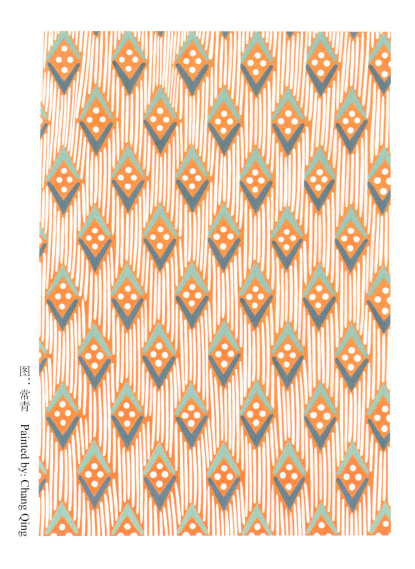

图：常青　Painted by: Chang Qing

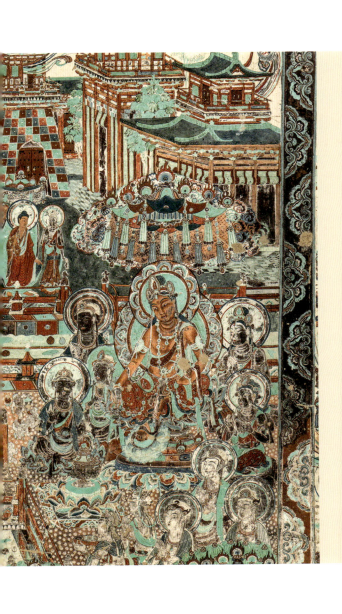

　　第217窟是创建于盛唐时期的覆斗顶形窟，经晚唐、五代、清重修。主室窟顶藻井为团花井心，周围绘卷草、垂幔，四披绘千佛。西壁开平顶敞口龛，龛内盛唐彩塑、清修跌坐佛一身，其余塑像已失。龛顶绘说法图一铺。龛内西壁浮塑团花火焰纹佛光。龛内共绘四菩萨、八弟子、六头光。龛沿口内侧绘小团花边饰，外侧绘菱形纹边饰。龛下绘供器及供养人。龛外南、北侧分别为大势至菩萨和观世音菩萨。南壁绘法华经变一铺。北壁绘观无量寿经变，西侧及下侧绘"未生怨"，东侧绘"十六观"。东壁绘法华经变"观音普门品"一铺，门北沿五代画沙门洪认供养像。前室及甬道存晚唐壁画，前室西壁门上存盛唐画供养人。

　　第217窟为敦煌豪门阴家所开凿的洞窟。整窟壁画保存完好，线条流畅细腻，色彩青绿交辉，呈现出富丽的大唐气象。西壁龛外大势至菩萨，面容恬静，体态优美，头戴宝瓶冠，遍身绮罗，锦裙纱帔，衣饰以红绿色为主调，棋格纹样作为点缀，整体造型圆润秀雅、雍容华贵。西壁龛外观世音菩萨，面庞圆润，头戴化佛冠，一手持净瓶，另一手持莲花，衣饰华丽，造型稳重端庄。大势至菩萨上身着僧祇支，图案使用几何格纹框架，主体以深蓝为底色，格子内有白色十字花纹、散点花或圆形散点进行点缀，整体方正有序。观世音菩萨下裙以深蓝色为底色，用紫、白、绿色渐变的线条及三个圆圈一组的白色联珠共同组成四方连续的纹样，二者错落排列，使图案有序又充满动感。

（文：杨婧嫱）

Cave 217 is a truncated pyramidal ceiling cave built in the high Tang Dynasty, which was repaired in the late Tang Dynasty, the Five Dynasties and the Qing Dynasty. The caisson of the main chamber has round flower pattern as the center, surrounded by scrolling vine pattern, valance and Thousand Buddhas. There is a flat ceiling niche in the west wall; in the niche, there is a painted sculpture of one sitting Buddha dated to the high Tang Dynasty and repaired in the Qing Dynasty. The rest of the sculptures have lost. A Dharma assembly is painted on the top of the niche. On the west niche wall there are round flower pattern, flame pattern, and Buddha light. Four Bodhisattvas, eight disciples and six head lights are painted in the niche. The niche is decorated with small round flowers on the inner side of the edge and rhombic patterns on the outer side, below the niche is painted with offering utensil and donors. The south and north sides outside the niche are Mahasthamaprapta Bodhisattva and Avalokitesvara Bodhisattva respectively. The south wall is painted with Saddharmapundarika Sutra illustration, and on the north wall is painted with Amitayurdhyana Sutra illustration, Ajatasattu's story on the west and lower part, and Sixteen Visualizations on the east. The east wall is painted with Samantamukhaparivartah of Saddharmapundarika Sutra, and the north edge of the door is painted with the image of Buddhist Hongren dated to the Five Dynasties. Murals of the late Tang Dynasty are preserved in the front chamber and corridor, and donor images of the high Tang Dynasty are remained above the west door of the front chamber.

Cave 217 was excavated by the Yin family, a powerful family in Dunhuang. The murals in the whole cave are well preserved, with smooth and delicate lines and azurite and green colors, showing a rich Tang Dynasty atmosphere. Outside the west niche, there is Mahasthamaprapta Bodhisattva with a quiet face and beautiful posture, wearing a bottle crown, Qi and Luo all around body, brocade skirt and silk scarf. His clothes are mainly red and green, decorated with chess patterns; the overall shape is plump and elegant. Outside the west niche, Avalokitesvara Bodhisattva has a round face and wears a Buddha image crown whose one hand holds a water bottle and the other hand holds a lotus, richly dressed and dignified. The Bodhisattva wears Sankaksika, the pattern has a geometric frame, the main body is dark blue, and the frame is decorated with white cross pattern, flower clusters or dot clusters, the whole design is square and orderly. The lower skirt of Avalokitesvara Bodhisattva takes dark blue as the background color, and uses purple, white and green gradual changing lines and white beads in a group of three circles to form four in a group repeated patterns. The two are well-arranged, making the pattern look orderly and dynamically.

(Written by: Yang Jingqiang)

Mahasthamaprapta
Bodhisattva's clothes
on the south outside the west niche of the
main chamber in Cave 217 dated to the
high Tang Dynasty at Mogao Grottoes

大势至菩萨服饰
莫高窟盛唐第217窟主室
西壁龛外南侧

盛唐第217窟主室西壁龛外南侧大势至菩萨服饰（佛经说："以智慧光，普照一切，令离三涂，得无上力。"故称此菩萨为大势至，又为《七佛药师经》中八大菩萨之一）是莫高窟盛唐时期极具代表性的壁画作品。其面相俊美，神态庄严，双目垂视，留有胡须。双手在腹部翻腕交叉，跣足立于莲花之上。上身穿织锦僧祇支，上面的几何纹样细腻而精致，且镶饰红色织花贴边。下身着淡绿色碎花罗裙，裙缘和下摆镶饰红色织花贴边，腰部系棕色腰裙，且有蓝色贴边。肩披透明天衣绕臂上下飘落。菩萨头戴莲花宝瓶冠，冠的两侧有火焰珠宝纹装饰。冠缯飘带和耳饰一起飘垂，自冠缯延伸下的彩带绕肘下落。莲花坠颈饰、臂钏、手镯绚丽多彩，璎珞自肩部在身前与丝带、彩绳交相辉映。

在画面的艺术处理上，菩萨的造型比例匀称，姿态优美，服饰华丽，层次丰富而有序，用线挺拔而洒脱，色彩富丽而厚重，在一定程度上代表了盛唐时期壁画绘制的最高艺术水平。

（文：刘元风）

The clothes of Mahasthamaprapta Bodhisattva on the south outside the west niche of the main chamber in Cave 217 dated to the high Tang Dynasty (the Buddhist Scripture says: "Shine on everything with the light of wisdom, make them leave sufferings, and get supreme power." Therefore, this Bodhisattva is called Mahasthamaprapta, and one of the eight Bodhisattvas in the *Seven Buddha Bhaisajyaguru Sutra*) is a very representative mural work of the high Tang Dynasty at Mogao Grottoes. He has a handsome face, a solemn look, eyes drooping and bearded. His two hands crossed outwardly in front of abdomen and stands barefoot on a lotus. The upper body wears brocade Sankaksika, the geometric patterns on it are delicate and exquisite, also inlaid with red woven flowers welt. The lower body is wearing a light green floral Luo skirt, the skirt edge and bottom hem are decorated with red woven welt, and the waist is covered by brown waist wrap with blue welt. His shoulders are covered with transparent ribbons, which fly up and down around arms. The Bodhisattva wears a lotus vase crown with flame jewels pattern on both sides. The crown laces and earrings hang together, and the ribbons extending from the crown laces fall around elbows. The lotus-pendant neck ornament, armlets and bracelets are colorful, and the keyūra from shoulders in front of the body shines with the ribbons and color ropes.

In the artistic treatment of the picture, the Bodhisattva's modeling proportion is well-balanced, the posture is beautiful, the clothes are gorgeous, the layers are rich and orderly, the lines are straight and free, and the colors are rich and thick. To a certain extent, this represents the highest artistic level of mural painting of the high Tang Dynasty.

(Written by: Liu Yuanfeng)

图：刘元凤　Painted by: Liu Yuanfēng

大势至菩萨僧祇支
图案
莫高窟盛唐第217窟主室
西壁龛外南侧

Bodhisattva
Mahasthamaprapta's
Sankaksika pattern
on the south outside the west niche of the
main chamber in Cave 217 dated to the high
Tang Dynasty at Mogao Grottoes

　　盛唐第217窟主室西壁龛外南侧大势至菩萨所着僧祇支纹样精美繁复，图案主体以深蓝色为底色，上绘有墨绿色、深红色方格纹，格子内有白色十字花纹、绿色花心白色点饰的小花以及白点绘制的方形中间饰红点的三种花纹，三者错落排列，色彩稳重典雅，整体结构严谨，同时充满着节奏感。缘边以海棠红为底色，半破式二方连续的团花纹样首尾相连，造型丰腴，地部疏朗。缘边纹样简洁大气，主体纹样方正有度。

（文：王可）

　　Bodhisattva Mahasthamaprapta's Sankaksika pattern on the south outside the west niche of the main chamber in Cave 217 dated to the high Tang Dynasty is exquisite and complex. The main body of the pattern is dark blue, painted with dark green and crimson checkered pattern, with white cross pattern, green flower centers decorated with white dots and white dots square decorated with red dots in the middle. The three patterns are arranged in a checkered manner, with stable and elegant colors, the overall structure is rigorous and full of rhythm. The edge is red begonia as the background color, and the semi two in a group repeated flower pattern connected end to end. The shape is plump and the ground is spacial. The edge pattern is simple but generous, and the main pattern is square and moderate.

(Written by: Wang Ke)

图：王可　Painted by: Wang Ke

Avalokitesvara
Bodhisattva's clothes
on the north outside the west niche of the
main chamber in Cave 217 dated to the
high Tang Dynasty at Mogao Grottoes

观世音菩萨服饰
莫高窟盛唐第217窟主室
西壁龛外北侧

盛唐第217窟主室西壁龛外北侧观世音菩萨，面形圆润丰满，与众菩萨不同的是，额上多生一只竖眼，此种形式被认为是佛教禅宗深为尊崇的准提观世音，意为"清净"，这在盛唐壁画中是较为少见的。

准提观世音左手提净瓶，右手持青莲花，莲叶舒卷，上身披络腋，络腋正面为红色，背面为绿色，下身穿五彩缤纷的织锦长裙，三段式几何纹样瑰丽多姿，下摆处镶饰深灰色贴边和绿色的滚边。腰部系红绿色的彩带和棕色的彩绦，彩带绕彩绦折返垂落。菩萨头束高髻、佩戴化佛冠，两侧镶嵌绿色宝石，并有日月纹饰点缀其上。红绿色冠缯系结在两侧。臂钏为粉红色玛瑙镶嵌，别具特色。璎珞由莲花纹宝珠的短璎珞和斜拄式长璎珞构成，项圈式短璎珞中镶嵌四颗绿宝石，长璎珞中部间隔有莲花纹宝珠，长短璎珞在菩萨右肩处相连接。薄纱天衣自肩部绕臂且在身体的前面和左右飘拂，并与脚踩的莲花相呼应。整套菩萨服饰色彩浓重而艳丽，虚实相兼，动静结合，别具风格。

（文：刘元风）

Avalokitesvara Bodhisattva on the north outside of the west niche in Cave 217 dated to the high Tang Dynasty has a round and plump face. Different from other Bodhisattvas, there is an additional vertical eye in His forehead. This form is considered to be Zhunti Guanyin deeply respected by Zen Buddhism, which means "purity". This is relatively rare in murals of the high Tang Dynasty.

Zhunti Bodhisattva carries a water bottle by left hand and holds a green lotus leaf by right hand, and the lotus leaf is rolled. His upper body is covered with Luoye, of which the front side is red and the back is green. The lower body is wearing a colorful brocade skirt, with the magnificent three-section geometric patterns, and the bottom hem is decorated with dark gray trim and green binding. The waist is tied with red and green ribbons and brown cords and the ribbons turn back and fall around the cords. The Bodhisattva's hair is tied in a high hair bun, wearing a Buddha image crown, inlaid with green gemstones on both sides, and decorated with sun and moon pattern, red and green crown laces on both sides. The armlets are inlaid with pink agate, which is unique. The keyūra is composed of a short keyūra with lotus pattern beads and an inclined long keyūra. The collar short keyūra is inlaid with four emeralds, the middle of the long keyūra has lotus pattern beads, and the long and short keyūra are connected at the right shoulder of the Bodhisattva. The tulle ribbon winds around the arm from the shoulder and flutters in front of the body, left and right, and echoes with the lotus stepped by feet. The whole set of Bodhisattva clothes has strong and gorgeous colors, virtual and real, dynamic and static, which has a unique style.

(Written by: Liu Yuanfeng)

图：刘元风　Painted by: Liu Yuanfeng

Avalokitesvara Bodhisattva's skirt pattern
on the north outside the west niche of the main chamber in Cave 217 dated to the high Tang Dynasty at Mogao Grottoes

观世音菩萨裙子图案
莫高窟盛唐第217窟主室
西壁龛外北侧

第217窟主室西壁龛外北侧的观世音菩萨，下半身着三段式几何纹织锦长裙，色彩纹样均保存得非常完整。

第一段图案为石青底色，主体纹样为三圆联珠纹及红白绿三色相间排线构成的矩形纹样，两种纹样交错呈四方连续的构成方式排布，弓字形和连续的"S"形曲线纹构成带状边饰，整体图案规整细腻，风格别具一格，充满节奏感。

第二段图案以四方连续菱格纹样为主，红地上饰有蓝绿菱形纹饰，搭配白色圆形纹样，不仅提升了画面中色彩的明暗关系，也使纹样造型更加丰富。

第三段图案为石绿底色，赭褐色菱纹与棋格纹相交构成主体纹样骨架，其间错落有致点缀竖线及蓝白圆点组成的小花，配色简练，联珠纹与卷云纹组成边饰，整体图案对称均衡，错落有序。此身菩萨服饰华丽精美，图案异彩纷呈，将中国古代高超的染织技艺展现得淋漓尽致。绘制过程中参考了常沙娜主编的《中国敦煌历代服饰图案》一书的整理临摹稿。

（文：常青、姚志薇）

The Avalokitesvara Bodhisattva on the north outside the west niche of the main chamber in Cave 217 wears a three bands geometric patterns brocade skirt on the lower body, and the colors and patterns are well preserved.

The first section of the pattern is malachite green as background, and the main pattern is a rectangular pattern composed by three circular beads and alternating lines of red, white and green. The two patterns are checkered and arranged in four in a group repeated way. The bow shape and continuous "S" shape curve pattern form a ribbon edge decoration. The overall pattern is neat and delicate, unique and full of rhythm.

The second section is mainly composed by four in a group repeated rhombic pattern, with blue-green diamond pattern on the red ground and white round pattern, which not only improves the light and dark relationship of colors in the painting, but also enriches the shape of patterns.

The third section of the pattern is malachite green as background, the ochre brown rhombic pattern intersects with the checks pattern to form the main pattern frame, which is interspersed with small flowers composed by vertical lines and blue and white dots. The color matching is concise, and the combined beads pattern and cirrus cloud pattern form the edge decoration. The overall pattern is symmetrical and balanced, checkered and orderly. This Bodhisattva has gorgeous and exquisite clothes and colorful patterns, which vividly shows the superb dyeing and weaving skills of ancient China. When doing the illustration, reference was made to the book *Clothing Patterns of China Dunhuang Mural* edited by Chang Shana.

(Written by: Chang Qing, Yao Zhiwei)

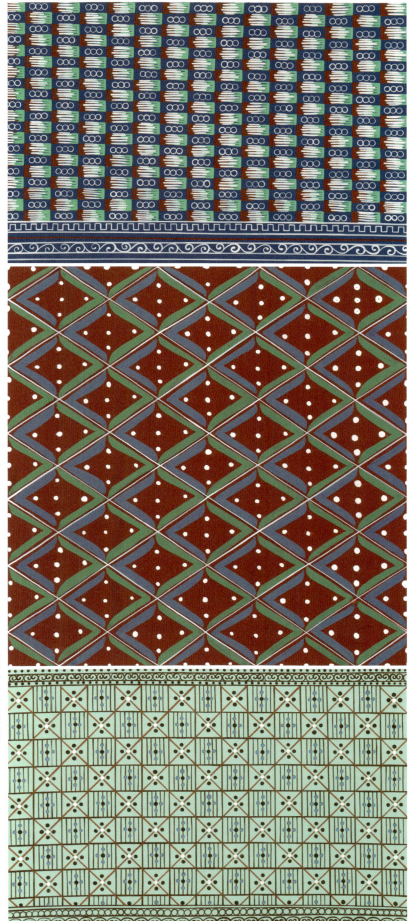

图：常青、姚志薇　Painted by: Chang Qing, Yao Zhiwei

The Dharma listening
Bodhisattva's clothes
on the south above the east door in the main
chamber of Cave 217 dated to the high Tang
Dynasty at Mogao Grottoes

听法菩萨服饰
莫高窟盛唐第217窟主室
东壁门上南侧

盛唐第217窟主室东壁门上南侧听法菩萨，其形象有一定的个性，高鼻秀目，神情专注，跏趺坐于莲花上，身体略向前倾，表现出对法华经的虔敬。菩萨头束高髻，余发披肩，头上佩戴绿松石镶嵌的三珠宝冠，冠体是红绿相间锯齿形装饰形式，其项链、耳环、臂钏、手镯等装饰品中也都镶嵌有绿松石，体现了装饰品的整体统一性风格。菩萨身披黑褐色绣花络腋，下穿赭褐色织锦长裙，锦裙上有精美的几何形纹样装饰，裙摆镶饰蓝色贴边，肩披褐色绣花天衣。

在其艺术处理和表达上，对菩萨的神态和细节把握上颇为精到，绘制手法基本上是淡彩的绘画形式，用线简练而概括，设色以平涂为主，略加晕染，整体上呈现出一定的装饰性和盛唐绘画中所特有的人文情怀。

（文：刘元风）

The Dharma listening Bodhisattva on the south side above the east door of the main chamber in Cave 217 dated to the high Tang Dynasty, His image has a certain personality, a high nose and beautiful eyes, and looks focused. He sits on lotus seat with legs folded, and leans forward slightly, showing His devotion to Lotus Sutra. He combs a high hair bun and hair covers shoulders, a three jewels crown inlaid with turquoise on His head, and the crown body has red and green sawtooth decorative design. Turquoise is also inlaid in His necklace, earrings, armlets, bracelets and other accessories, reflecting the overall unified style of the accessory. His upper body wears dark brown Luoye embroidered with flowers and ochre brown brocade skirt on the lower body. The brocade skirt is decorated with exquisite geometric patterns, and the skirt hem decorated with blue welt, and His shoulders are covered with brown silk scarf embroidered with flowers.

In its artistic treatment and expression, this painting has a good grasp of the Bodhisattva's appearance and details. The painting method is basically light color painting form and the lines are concise and summarized. The colors are mainly flat painting, slightly shading, showing a certain degree of decorative effect and the special humanistic feelings in the paintings of the high Tang Dynasty as a whole.

(Written by: Liu Yuanfeng)

图：刘元风

Painted by: Liu Yuanfeng

听法菩萨裙子
图案

莫高窟盛唐第217窟
主室东壁门上南侧

The Dharma listening
Bodhisattva's skirt pattern
on the south side above the east door of the
main chamber in Cave 217 dated to the high
Tang Dynasty at Mogao Grottoes

该图案位于莫高窟第217窟主室东壁门上南侧的听法菩萨裙摆处，以土红、石青为主要色调，画家在作画时巧妙使用主色与过渡色，在布料裙式上勾画出晕染效果。后饰白色线条与点状图案，不仅丰富了颜色种类、增加了图案描绘手法，且图案本身也显得俏皮灵动。

（文：姚志薇）

This pattern is located at the skirt trim of the Dharma listening Bodhisattva on the south side above the east door of the main chamber in Cave 217 at Mogao Grottoes, with earth red and azurite as the main colors. When doing the painting, the painter skillfully used the main color and transition color to do the color shading effect on the fabric skirt, then added white lines and dots, which not only enriched the color types and increase the pattern depicting techniques, but also made the pattern itself attractive and flexible.

(Written by: Yao Zhiwei)

菩萨裙子图案

莫高窟盛唐第217
窟主室南壁西侧

The Bodhisattva's
skirt pattern
on the west side of the south wall in the main
chamber of Cave 217 dated to the high Tang
Dynasty at Mogao Grottoes

该图案位于莫高窟第217窟主室南壁西侧的菩萨衣饰上，以红地蓝绿色六瓣小花造型为主，呈现出简洁、乖巧的造型特质，与盛唐时期花枝繁复的图案风格形成鲜明对比，丰富了盛唐时期图案纹样的品类。

（文：姚志薇）

This pattern is located on the Bodhisattva's clothes on the west side of the south wall in the main chamber of Cave 217 at Mogao Grottoes. It is mainly shaped by six petaled red, cyan and green small flowers, showing a simple and clever design characteristics, which in sharp contrast to the complex patterns of flowers and branches in the high Tang Dynasty, this enriched the pattern categories during the high Tang Dynasty.

(Written by: Yao Zhiwei)

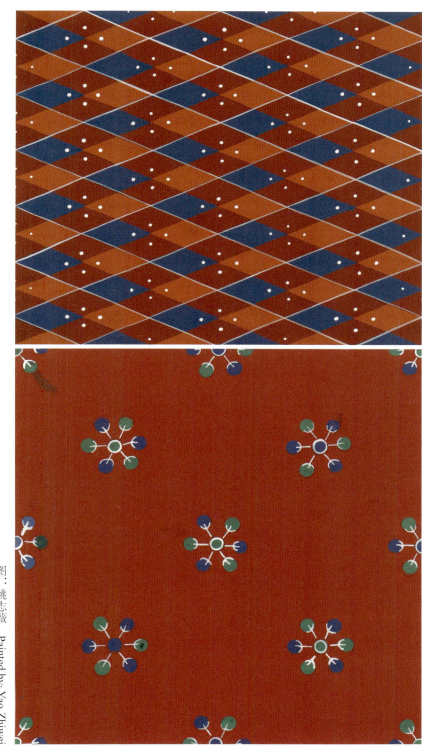

图：姚志薇　Painted by: Yao Zhiwei

The Bodhisattva's clothes on the west side of the south wall in the main chamber of Cave 217 dated to the high Tang Dynasty at Mogao Grottoes

菩萨服饰
莫高窟盛唐第217窟主室
南壁西侧

　　盛唐第217窟主室南壁西侧的菩萨神情恬静安详地跏趺坐于莲花台上，左手轻托璎珞串珠，右手手指翘起，似受佛法启迪而再作思量之状态。菩萨形象俊美，弯眉秀目，朱唇饱满，头束高髻，发辫披肩。菩萨头上佩戴摩尼珠镶嵌的莲花纹宝冠（"摩尼"者，梵语作"mani"，为"离垢"之意），三颗摩尼珠下都配有小的绿松石，并且这种摩尼珠在臂钏上也同时出现。

　　菩萨上身斜披深红色络腋，络腋上有四瓣花纹饰。下身穿深红色长裙，裙下摆处有蓝色贴边，裙子上有六瓣花纹饰。自头冠两侧垂下的长带绕肘落于腿上，与肩披薄纱天衣交相呼应。特别是"X"形长璎珞，由串珠连接而成，自颈部项圈两侧向下延伸，在腹部连接圆形装饰物后继续向左后垂至腿部。菩萨整体服饰的色彩配置以暖色调为主，以绿色为点缀，包括菩萨的头光装饰，与菩萨的整体造型一样，静中有动，于和谐中寻求变化。

（文：刘元风）

The Bodhisattva on the west side of the south wall in the main chamber of Cave 217 dated to the high Tang Dynasty sits with legs folded on the lotus seat with a quiet and serene look, holding the keyūra beads by left hand and right hand fingers up, which seems to be in a state of contemplation inspired by Buddha. This Bodhisattva has a well made appearance, curved eyebrows, beautiful eyes, full red lips and high hair bun. His braided hair covers the shoulders, wearing a lotus pattern crown inlaid with Mani orbs ("Mani" is Sanskrit, meaning "leaving dirt"), and the three Mani orbs are equipped with small turquoises, and this kind of Mani orb also appears on the armlets.

The Bodhisattva's upper body is diagonally covered with dark red Luoye, which is decorated with four-petal flower pattern. The lower body wears a long crimson skirt with blue trim at the hem and six-petal pattern decoration on the skirt. The long bands hanging from both sides of the crown fall on the legs around the elbows and echo with the gauze ribbons on the shoulders. In particular, the "X" shaped long keyūra is connected by beads, extending downward from both sides of the neck collar, and continuing to the left and back then to the legs after connecting the circular ornament at the abdomen. The color configuration of the Bodhisattva's overall dress is mainly warm tone and decorated with green, including the Bodhisattva's head light decoration, which is like the Bodhisattva's overall shape, movement in stillness, seeking change in harmony.

(Written by: Liu Yuanfeng)

The Bodhisattva's clothes on the west side of the south wall in the main chamber of Cave 217 dated to the high Tang Dynasty at Mogao Grottoes

菩萨服饰 莫高窟盛唐第217窟主室 南壁西侧

盛唐第217窟主室南壁西侧的菩萨仪态从容，沉静跏趺坐于莲花台之上，双目微垂，点唇丰润饱满（唐代时期盛行"点唇"装饰，用于点唇的唇脂是从天然的红花中提纯出来的。最早是匈奴妇女的化妆用品，后通过丝绸之路传入中原地区，由于唇脂具有较强的覆盖特性，可用以改变口唇的形状，将原有的口唇覆盖而重新点画出完美的唇形）。

菩萨头束高髻，余发垂肩，内穿僧祇支，外披绿色袈裟，其领缘和袖口处镶有红色贴边，腰系红色贡带。下穿翠绿色长裙，裙子下摆处也镶有红色贴边。最外层是朱红色的袈裟，其左胸部有圆形的钩纽，袈裟底部翻卷处露出绿色的内里。

（文：刘元风）

The Bodhisattva on the west side of the south wall in the main chamber of Cave 217 dated to the high Tang Dynasty looks peaceful, sitting quietly with both legs folded on the lotus seat, slightly drooping eyes and full lips (The "Lip Pointing" make-up was popular in the Tang Dynasty, and the lip grease used for lip pointing was purified from natural red flowers. It was first used by Hun women as cosmetics, and then introduced to Central Plains through Silk Road, because lip grease has strong covering feature, it can be used to change the shape of lips, to cover the original lip shape and draw a perfect lip shape).

The Bodhisattva has a high hair bun, and the rest hair covers shoulders. He wears Sankaksika inside and green kasaya outside, the collar edge and cuffs are inlaid with red welts, and a red band is tied around waist. The lower body wears a long emerald skirt with red welt at the hem, and the outermost wears shoulders-covering kasaya, with a round hook button on the left chest, and the green inner lining is exposed at the bottom of the kasaya.

(Written by: Liu Yuanfeng)

The Bodhisattva's clothes
on the west side of the south wall in the main
chamber of Cave 217 dated to the high Tang
Dynasty at Mogao Grottoes

菩萨服饰
莫高窟盛唐第217窟主室
南壁西侧

盛唐第217窟主室南壁西侧的菩萨五官雅致，启唇微笑，双手持琉璃花盘，双腿跪于圆毯之上。上身披络腋，络腋正面为深红色，上面点缀四瓣花纹饰，背面为褐色，络腋前面绕臂、后面搭背。下穿深红色阔腿裤，上有与络腋同样的四瓣花纹点缀其间，同时在大腿部位有条状围合的莲花纹装饰，腰部系带状式腰带，臀部有绿色彩带系结垂落。菩萨头发束髻后护肩，头上佩戴莲花纹发带，发带正中有圆形宝石点缀，耳环、手镯均为绿色串珠构成，并有透明的薄纱在身前上下缠绕。

在画面的绘制处理上，菩萨形体比例匀称，姿态优雅，色彩采用对比色配置，艳丽明快，材料质感及纹样表现细腻精致，线条有粗细、浓淡、虚实变化。从整体菩萨服饰来看，既有佛教服饰的内涵，同时又有盛唐世俗服饰的婉约之美。

（文：刘元风）

The Bodhisattva on the west side of the south wall in Cave 217 dated to the high Tang Dynasty has elegant facial features. His mouth opens and smiles, holding a glass flower plate by both hands, and kneels on a round carpet. The upper body is covered by Luoye, and the front side is dark red, decorated with four-petal flower pattern, and the back is brown. The Luoye in front part is wrapped around the arms and the back part is carried on the back. The lower body wears dark red wide-leg pants with the same four-petal pattern on Luoye. At the same time, there is a lotus pattern decoration around the thighs, belt around the waist, and a green ribbon at hips. The Bodhisattva's hair is tied in a hair bun and shoulders are covered, the hair band has lotus pattern, and the middle of the hair band is decorated with round gemstone. Earrings and bracelets are made of green beads, and transparent tulle is wound up and down in front of the body.

In the painting aspect, the Bodhisattva's body proportion is well-balanced, the posture is elegant, which used contrast colors configuration, looking gorgeous and lively; the material texture and pattern performance are delicate and exquisite, and the lines have thickness and thinness, heavy and light, solid and transparent changes. From the perspective of the overall Bodhisattva clothes, it is not only has the connotation of Buddhist clothes, but also has the graceful beauty of secular clothes of the high Tang Dynasty.

(Written by: Liu Yuanfeng)

图：刘元风

Painted by: Liu Yuanfeng

The Bodhisattva's skirt pattern
on the west side of the south wall in the main
chamber of Cave 217 dated to the high Tang
Dynasty at Mogao Grottoes

菩萨裙子图案
莫高窟盛唐第217窟主室
南壁西侧

此处选择敦煌莫高窟第217窟主室南壁西侧菩萨所着的清晰、精美的裙子图案进行整理绘制。裙饰主体为深红色，图案以十字形为骨架，蓝色和绿色圆点作为花瓣，白线勾勒出十字骨架和花萼，四角装饰白色小圆点，花型小巧精致，生动活泼，呈四方连续规律排列。以白、绿两色色条分隔，在大腿处清晰可见宝相花花纹装饰。裙中缘边以褐色为底色，图案为半破式二方连续的宝相花，使用蓝色、绿色以层层退晕的方法描绘花瓣的递进关系，既可以与裤装蓝绿色十字小朵花相呼应，又增添了服饰的华贵之美。

这种半破式二方连续的宝相花纹样应该是专门分段织花再加上色条过渡有利于裁边的织锦，这种织物在新疆吐鲁番出土的红地中窠宝花锦中就可得见，也更加证明了壁画中绘制的纺织品的真实性。

（文：王可）

Here, the clear and exquisite skirt pattern of the Bodhisattva on the west side of the south wall in the main chamber of Cave 217 in Dunhuang Mogao Grottoes is selected for studying. The main body of the skirt is dark red, and the pattern takes the cross shape as the frame, the blue and green dots as the petals, the white line outlines the cross frame and calyx, and the four corners are decorated with small white dots. The flower shape is small, exquisite, lively and arranged in four in a group repeated regular manner. They are separated by white and green color stripes, Baoxiang flower pattern decoration can be clearly seen at the thigh. The trim of the skirt is brown as the background color, and the pattern is a semi Baoxiang flower pattern two in a group repeated. The progressive relationship of the petals is depicted by layer by layer of color-gradation technique in blue and green, which not only echoes with the small blue-green cross flower of the trousers, but also added the gorgeous beauty of the clothes.

This semi Baoxiang flower pattern two in a group repeated should be brocade with special segmented weaving flowers and added color stripes for transition, which is convenient to cut at the edges. This kind of fabric can be seen in flower brocade with red background unearthed in Turpan, Xinjiang, and this further proves the authenticity of the textiles drawn in the murals.

(Written by: Wang Ke)

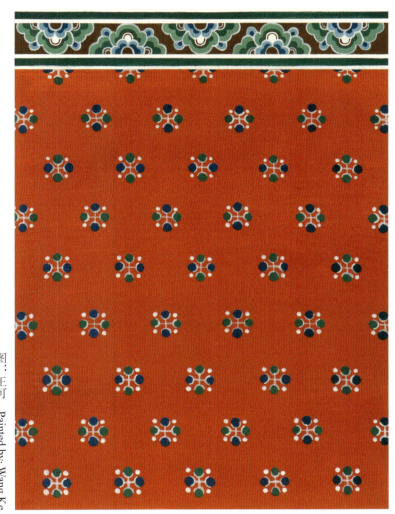

图：王可　Painted by: Wang Ke

The disciple's clothes
in the west niche of Cave 217 dated
to the high Tang Dynasty at Mogao
Grottoes

弟子服饰
莫高窟盛唐第217窟西壁
龛内

第217窟西壁龛内共有浮塑一佛光、六头光，壁画四菩萨、八弟子。壁画中的人物形象绘于浮塑的后面，身体与服装或多或少被浮塑遮挡。这身弟子像绘于主尊佛北侧，他手持香炉、身披红绿灰三色相间的山水纹田相袈裟肃立在莲花台上，身体左右两侧手臂的肢体动作与袈裟的披挂方式被前面的浮塑佛光与头光挡住。在绘画整理时，笔者按照唐时期袈裟披挂的惯用方式，并参照莫高窟第127窟南壁弟子像、第420窟主室西壁龛内弟子像的造型绘制出被遮挡部分的人物形态及服装结构。

（文：李迎军）

In the west niche of Cave 217, there are one Buddha light and six head lights relief, and four painted Bodhisattvas and eight disciples. The figures are painted behind the reliefs, and the body and clothes are more or less covered by the reliefs. This disciple is painted on the north side of the main Buddha. He stands on the lotus platform and holds a incense burner, wears a red, green and gray landscape field pattern kasaya. The body movements of the two arms and the way of wearing the kasaya are blocked by the Buddha light and head light reliefs. When doing the painting, they were restored according to the usual way of wearing kasaya in the Tang Dynasty, and referred to the shapes of the disciples on the south wall of Cave 127 and the disciples in the west niche of the main chamber in Cave 420 in Mogao Grottoes to paint the blocked part of figure and clothing structure.

(Written by: Li Yingjun)

The Maharāja-deva's clothes
on the south wall of the main chamber in Cave
217 dated to the high Tang Dynasty at Mogao
Grottoes

天王服饰
莫高窟盛唐第217窟主室
南壁

学术界对莫高窟第217窟主室南壁画面内容的解读尚无定论，先有"法华经变说"将南壁东侧的这幅图像解释为"八王子礼佛图"，后有学者提出"佛顶尊胜陀罗尼经变说"，将这幅图像解释为"四天王请佛说法图"。无论将这一形象解读为王子还是天王，这身戎装形象对于研究盛唐时期的甲胄造型都有重要的参考价值。

这身戎装造型头饰宝珠，身穿披膊、身甲、胫甲、战靴，甲衣的甲片呈细条状并列成排组合，甲衣之下露出内衬袍服宽大的袖子与衣摆。在总体造型中，右肘下方的一块长橄榄状棕色图形所表达的服装造型尚不明了，古时武将有在腰间佩虎尾、豹尾的习惯，但此处是不是豹尾尚不确定。笔者在绘画整理时参照其他人物甲胄结构，将这一棕色色块画成了衣袖。

（文：李迎军）

The academic interpretation of the south wall mural in the main chamber of Cave 217 at Mogao Grottoes is still inconclusive. Previously, scholars interpreted the mural as "Lotus Sutra Illustration". The picture on the east side is "Eight Princes Worship Buddha". Later, some scholars believed that the mural is "The Theory of Usnisa Vijaya Dharani Sutra Illustration", and interpreted the picture as "The Four Heavenly Kings Invite Buddha to Preach". Whether this figure is a prince or Maharāja-deva, the military uniform has important reference value for the study of armor in the high Tang Dynasty.

The Maharāja-deva wears a jewel on his head and wears shoulder covers, body armor, shin armor and battle boots. The armor pieces are in thin strips and arranged in rows. The wide sleeves and hem of the robe under the armor can be seen. In the overall shape, the clothing shape expressed by a long olive shaped brown part below the right elbow is still unknown. In ancient times, military generals had the habit of wearing tiger and leopard tail around their waist, but it is uncertain whether this is a leopard tail here. When doing the painting, the painter referred to the structure of other armors to draw the brown color area into sleeves.

(Written by: Li Yingjun)

图：李迎军　Painted by: Li Yingjun

Queen Vaidehi's clothes
on the east side of the north wall in Cave
217 dated to the high Tang Dynasty at
Mogao Grottoes

壁东侧

莫高窟盛唐第217窟北

韦提希夫人服饰

此图位于第217窟北壁东侧的"十六观"中，韦提希夫人面前有一棵装饰华丽的宝树，应是"宝树观"经变故事。

韦提希夫人头梳惊鹄髻，身着襦裙外加半袖，袖有深蓝色的袖祛，手肘以下袖袂部位下垂，形似垂胡袖。东汉刘熙《释名疏证补》卷五："禅衣之无胡者也，言袖夹直，形如沟也……"先谦曰："胡，牛颔垂也。"《汉书·郊祀志》有"龙垂胡"，颜注："胡，谓颈下垂肉也。"《释名》释形体第八："胡，互也，在咽下垂，能敛互物也。"《礼记·深衣》记载："袂圆以应规。"在《释名疏证补》中释文："下垂曰胡。"盖胡是颈咽皮肉下垂之义，因引申为衣物下垂者之称，古人衣袖广大，其臂肘以下袖之下垂者，亦谓之胡，即垂胡袖。

（文：董昳云、吴波）

This painting is located in the Sixteen Visualizations on the east side of the north wall in Cave 217. In front of Queen Vaidehi, there is a richly decorated treasure tree, which should be the story of "Visualization treasure tree" illustration.

Queen Vaidehi wears a startled swan hair bun and a Ru skirt with half-sleeved coat. The sleeves have dark blue cuffs, and the sleeves below her elbows are like drooping Hu sleeves. Volume V of Liu Xi's book *Shi Ming Shu Zheng Bu* (explanation of Buddhist names): "The Buddhist clothes without Hu means the sleeves bend like valley shape ..." Predecessors once said that: "Hu, cattle's hanging chin." In *Han Shu · Jiao Si Zhi*: "Dragon has hanging Hu." Yan noted: "Hu means neck has drooping meat." In *Shi Ming the Interpretation of Forms the Eighth*: "Hu is the part that can store food after swallow." In *Li Ji · Shen Yi*: "The sleeves are round so they droop." *Shi Ming Shu Zheng Bu* explains: "drooping is called Hu", because Hu means the meat under neck, so people call the drooping clothes as Hu. The ancients had broad sleeves, and the drooping sleeves below their arms and elbows are also called Hu, that is, drooping Hu sleeves.

(Written by: Dong Yiyun, Wu Bo)

Queen Vaidehi's clothes
on the east side of the north wall in Cave
217 dated to the high Tang Dynasty at
Mogao Grottoes

壁东侧

莫高窟盛唐第217窟北

韦提希夫人服饰

此图位于第217窟北壁东侧的"十六观"中，韦提希夫人跪于一池水塘旁，应是"宝池观"经变故事。

韦提希夫人头戴宝冠，似祥云又似蜷曲盛放的菊花，且与同窟菩萨所戴冠型类似，一方面展现出繁复精致的造物之美，另一方面也表现出菩萨服饰与世俗服饰之间相互借鉴的关联性。韦提希夫人柳叶眉，朱红唇，神态庄重虔诚。内着曲领中单，外着深色大袖对襟袍服，领缘、衣摆底缘、袖祛为深蓝色。服饰形制简单、配色沉稳，更加突出冠饰的别致。

（文：董昳云、吴波）

This painting is located in the Sixteen Visualizations on the east side of the north wall in Cave 217. In front of Queen Vaidehi, there is a pond, which should be "Visualization treasure pond" illustration.

Queen Vaidehi wears a treasure crown, which looks like auspicious clouds and curling chrysanthemums, and is similar to Bodhisattva crown in the same cave. On the one hand, it shows the complex and exquisite beauty of creation; on the other hand, it also shows the correlation between Bodhisattva clothes and secular clothes. Queen Vaidehi has willow eyebrows, red lips and a solemn and pious look. She wears a curved collar Zhongdan inside, and a dark large sleeves Duijin robe outside. The collar edge, hem edge and cuffs are dark blue. The dress has simple shape and stable color matching, which highlights the uniqueness of crown decoration.

(Written by: Dong Yiyun, Wu Bo)

图" 吴波　Painted by: Wu Bo

The secular women's clothes on the north side of the east wall in the main chamber of Cave 217 dated to the high Tang Dynasty at Mogao Grottoes

世俗女子服饰 莫高窟盛唐第217窟主室 东壁北侧

此图为第217窟主室东壁北侧"观音普门品"描绘观世音救诸苦难中的一对相互依偎的年轻女子，身旁有一位青年男子正向她们作揖求爱。"观音普门品"中说：如果有人陷于情欲，念一声观世音菩萨，便得离情欲。两位年轻女子亭亭玉立，一位双手合十，似乎口中正在默念观世音名号祈求戒除情欲，另一位女子右臂挽住同伴，左臂环于脑后，似嬉戏状，为庄严的宗教壁画增添了几许世俗谐趣的气氛。

两位女子均梳抛家髻，穿着半袖襦裙。唐代杜佑《通典·卷一百八·礼六十八·开元礼纂》记载皇后王妃内外命妇服的制度，其中有"女史则半袖裙襦"。从右侧女子的半袖看，为黄色对襟半袖，左侧女子绿色半袖仅显腰背局部。两件半袖衣长均短至腰上，接近乳之下缘，或在门襟下摆处系结，或于门襟中部系结。女子内穿小袖曳地长裙，由小花朵装饰，右侧绛红底白色花朵三瓣，左侧赭石底白色花朵四瓣。右侧女子足穿云头履，左侧女子仅显现鞋跟部。

（文：董昳云、吴波）

This painting shows two young women snuggling up to each other from Saddharmapundarika Sutra the chapter of Samantamukhaparivartah illustration, Avalokitesvara Bodhisattva saves all sufferings on the north side of the east wall in the main chamber of Cave 217. Beside them, a young man is bowing and courting them. The chapter of Samantamukhaparivartah says that if someone is trapped in lust, he or she recites Avalokitesvara Bodhisattva will be free from lust. The two young women stand tall and graceful, one holds palms together and seems to be silently reciting the name of Avalokitesvara to pray for abstinence from lust. The other woman holds her companion in her right arm and puts her left arm behind her head, which seems to be playful, adding a little secular and humorous atmosphere to the solemn religious murals.

The two women both comb Paojia hair bun and wear half sleeved Ru skirt. The Tang Dynasty Duyou's book *Tongdian* volume one hundred and eight, Li sixty-eight, Kaiyuanlizuan recorded women's clothing system of the queen and princess and female officials, which has "female officials wear half sleeved Ru skirt". Seeing the woman's half sleeves on the right, it is a yellow half sleeves with parallel lapels, while the green half sleeves on the left woman only shows part of the waist and back. The length of the two half sleeved clothes are short to waist, close to lower edge of breasts, tied at the lower hem of the opening, or in the middle of the opening. The two women wear small sleeves long skirt with small flowers pattern, on the right is three-petal white flowers on crimson ground and on the left is four-petal white flowers on ochre ground. The woman on right whose feet in cloud head shoes, and the woman on left only shows the heel of the shoes.

(Written by: Dong Yiyun, Wu Bo)

图：吴波　Painted by: Wu Bo

The secular man's clothes
on the east wall of the main chamber in
Cave 217 dated to the high Tang Dynasty
at Mogao Grottoes

世俗男子服饰
莫高窟盛唐第217
窟主室东壁

此图为第217窟主室东壁法华经变"观音普门品"中的一位世俗男子，似乎正在叱责跪在身旁的人，呈愤怒状。这是画匠在表现经文"三毒"中的"嗔恚"，与其余两组画面一同组成"贪、嗔、痴"的内容。敦煌壁画通过生动具体的形象将抽象的教义表现出来，寓教于像，使信众在潜移默化中受到影响。

男子头戴璞头，后垂两脚，身穿翻领襕袍，此领口外翻的样式明显受到胡服的影响，袖口加长，遮蔽双手。腰束革带，足蹬乌皮靴。

（文：董昳云、吴波）

This painting shows a man on the east wall of the main chamber in Cave 217, in which Saddharmapundarika Sutra illustration the chapter of Samantamukhaparivartah. He seemed to be scolding the person kneeling beside him in anger. This is the painter's depiction of "anger" in the "three poisons" of the scripture, which together with the other two groups of pictures constitute the content of "greed, anger and ignorance". Dunhuang murals express abstract doctrines through vivid and concrete images, which make believers imperceptibly affected.

This man wears a Fu hat, with the two ends hanging back, and a lapel Lan robe. The neckline turned out is obviously affected by foreign clothes, and the cuffs are lengthened to cover hands. Leather belt at the waist and black leather boots on feet.

(Written by: Dong Yiyun, Wu Bo)

The secular man's clothes
on the east wall of the main chamber in
Cave 217 dated to the high Tang Dynasty
at Mogao Grottoes

世俗男子服饰
莫高窟盛唐第217
窟主室东壁

此图为第217窟主室东壁法华经变"观音普门品"描绘观世音救诸苦难中的一位世俗男子。此男子敞胸露怀，一手高举，题旁漫漶不清。盛唐第45窟法华经变"观音普门品"中也有一处男子同为敞胸露怀，此处榜题云："若多愚痴常念恭敬观世音菩萨便□难处。"二者对比来看，第217窟此男子应同样在表现观世音"解三毒"的情景。

男子头戴褐色幞头，足蹬褐色皮靴，身穿绛色翻绿领襕袍。男子袒露右臂和胸怀，右袖由后背向前环系于腰部。袍的外层面料为绛红色，在翻开的衣领和衣摆处、袖口处，均能看到石绿色内衬。

（文：董昳云、吴波）

This painting shows a man on the east wall of the main chamber in Cave 217, in which Saddharmapundarika Sutra illustration the chapter of Samantamukhaparivartah, Avalokitesvara Bodhisattva saves all difficulties. In Cave 45 dated to the high Tang Dynasty, in which Saddharmapundarika Sutra illustration the chapter of Samantamukhaparivartah also has a man opens his clothes, which has an inscription: if someone is fool who can call Avalokitesvara Bodhisattva and his difficulties will be solved. In comparison, the man in Cave 217 should also show "Avalokitesvara eliminates three poisons".

This man wears brown Fu hat, brown leather boots, and a crimson green collar Lan robe. He exposes his right arm and chests, and the right sleeve is tied around the waist from the back to the front. The outer side of the robe is crimson, and the malachite green lining can be seen at the turned out collar, hem and cuffs.

(Written by: Dong Yiyun, Wu Bo)

图：吴波　Painted by: Wu Bo

佛陀波利服饰
莫高窟盛唐第217窟主室
南壁

此图出自第217窟主室南壁佛说法图西侧。学术界对该壁画内容存有争议，有"法华经变说"与"佛顶尊胜陀罗尼经变说"两种观点。本图以"数字敦煌"相关解说和日本下野玲子学者的观点为依据，以"佛顶尊胜陀罗尼经变说"为准。

此为说法图中佛陀波利骑行返西土取经的场景。佛陀波利手执马鞭，罩绛红饰蓝边袍，着绿色镶边大口袴。有关帷帽，原名"幂䍦"，也有写作"幂帷"或"幂罗"，后发展成"帷帽"。《旧唐书·舆服志》曾叙述："武德、贞观之时，宫人骑马者，依齐、隋旧制，多着幂䍦，虽发自戎夷，而全身障蔽，不欲途路窥之。王公之家，亦同此制。永徽之后，皆用帷帽，拖裙到颈，渐为浅露。……则天之后，帷帽大行，幂䍦渐息。"

（文：赵茜、吴波）

This figure is located at the west side of the south wall in the main chamber of Cave 217. The academic circles have disputes over the content of the mural, including "the theory of Saddharmapundarika Sutra illustration" and "The Theory of Usnisa Vijaya Dharani Sutra Illustration". This figure is based on the relevant explanations from digital Dunhuang and the views of Japanese scholar Akatsuki, and used "The Theory of Usnisa Vijaya Dharani Sutra Illustration".

In the painting, Buddhapalita is riding back to the west to get scriptures, he holds a whip, wearing a veil hat, a crimson robe with blue edges, and a big mouth trousers with green edges. About veil hat, the original name was "Mili", or "Miwei" or "Miluo", which later developed into "Weimao". In *Jiu Tang Shu·Yu Fu Zhi* recorded "During Wude and Zhenguan period, court people ride horses follow the Qi and Sui tradition, usually wear Mili. Although it originated from foreign places, it covers the whole body and people can't see, and the nobles favored this. After Yonghui period, the cloak is neck high, and gradually covers lesser. After Wuzhou period, veil hat became popular and Mili gradually disappeared."

(Written by: Zhao Xi, Wu Bo)

图：吴波　Painted by: Wu Bo

The Bhiksu and servant's clothes on the south wall of the main chamber in Cave 217 dated to the high Tang Dynasty at Mogao Grottoes

比丘与侍从服饰 莫高窟盛唐第217窟主室 南壁

这两张图为第217窟主室南壁 "佛顶尊胜陀罗尼经变说" 中的人物形象，一为骑行在后方的比丘，一为走在最前方的婆罗门引导人物。

图中比丘身穿胡衫，"胡衫本指胡服，后泛指源于西域少数民族的服饰。其典型形制为锦绣浑脱帽、翻领窄袖袍和透空软锦靴。盛行于初唐至盛唐时期。唐刘言史《王中丞宅夜观舞胡腾》诗：'织成蕃帽虚顶尖，细氎胡衫双袖小'。"

图中作为二比丘的引导侍从为婆罗门形人物，即 "婆罗门僧" 的佛陀波利从故乡带来的随从者，其典型形象为深目高鼻，葛布缠头，上身祖裸，披长巾，下着花短裤或裙，系围腰，赤足，戴足钏，有的还戴珥珠。此图中侍从头裹石绿色葛布；双色长巾从右肩斜挎，于背后缠绕至左臂下垂；着绛红色短裙，长度及膝。

（文：赵茜、吴波）

These two pictures are also the characters in "The Theory of Usnisa Vijaya Dharani Sutra Illustration" on the south wall of the main chamber in Cave 217. One is the Bhiksu riding in the rear and the other is the Brahman guiding figure walking in the front.

The riding Bhiksu in the painting wears a Hu shirt. The Hu shirt originally refers to the Hu clothes, and later generally refers to the clothes originated from ethnic minority groups in the Western Regions. The typical match is brocade embroidery Huntuo hat, narrow sleeved lapel robe, and soft hollow brocade boots, this was popular from the early Tang Dynasty to the high Tang Dynasty. The poem of *Wang Zhongcheng Ye Guan Wu Hu Teng* (Wang Zhongcheng watches Hu Teng dance at night) by Liu Yanshi of the Tang Dynasty:"Woven into a foreign hat with a hollow pointed top, and a thin Hu shirt with small sleeves."

The guide in the painting is a Brahman servant who is brought by Buddhaplita. The typical profile is deep eyes and high nose, Ge cloth wrapped around head, naked upper body just hanging a long scarf, lower body wears flower pattern shorts or skirt wrapped in waist wrap, barefoot with foot bracelets, and some wear earrings. In this painting, the servant's head is wrapped in malachite green Ge cloth; the two-color long silk scarf is covered from the right shoulder and wrapped around the back and drooping on the left arm; wearing a crimson skirt with knee length.

(Written by: Zhao Xi, Wu Bo)

图：吴波　Painted by: Wu Bo

　　第219窟是创建于盛唐时期的覆斗顶形窟。主室窟顶藻井存一半团花井心，周围残存一些垂幔，四披绘千佛。西壁开斜顶敞口龛，龛内西壁佛光两侧画弟子；南壁绘一菩萨、一化佛、二弟子；北壁绘一化佛。龛下绘供器及二菩萨。龛外南侧力士台下存女供养人三身。南、北壁绘千佛。

　　此窟虽然内容较少，但龛下及力士台下仍有几身精彩的供养菩萨及供养人。其中两身女性供养人顾盼生姿，穿交领襦裙，着披帛，身姿修长而优雅。供养菩萨半跪在莲花台上，上身环绕着披帛，下着长裙，姿态优美。此窟画面清晰，人物生动，对盛唐服饰的研究有一定的价值。

（文：杨婧嫱）

Cave 219 is a truncated pyramidal ceiling cave built in the high Tang Dynasty. The caisson on the top of the main chamber has semi round flower pattern as the center, and remains some valance and Thousand Buddhas around. The west wall has a niche with a sloping ceiling, in which has painted disciples on both sides of the Buddha light on the west wall; the south wall is painted with a Bodhisattva, a Buddha and two disciples; the north wall is painted with a Buddha. Below the niche is painted with offering utensils and two Bodhisattvas. There are three female donors below the Vīra stage on the south outside the niche. Thousand Buddhas are painted on the south and north walls.

Although there are few contents in this cave, still some wonderful attendant Bodhisattvas and donor images painted below the niche and Vīra stages. Two of the female donors look forward, wearing cross collar Ru skirt and silk scarf, with slender body and elegant posture. The attendant Bodhisattva is half kneeling on a lotus platform, the upper body is surrounded by silk scarf, and the lower body wears long skirt, looking graceful. This painting is clear and the characters are vivid, which has certain value to study the high Tang Dynasty clothes.

(Written by: Yang Jingqiang)

The offering
Bodhisattva's clothes
on the north side of the west niche in the main
chamber of Cave 219 dated to the high Tang
Dynasty at Mogao Grottoes

供养菩萨服饰
莫高窟盛唐第219窟主室
西壁龛下北侧

此图为第219窟主室西壁龛下北侧的供养菩萨。菩萨左侧身，跪坐于莲花座上，双臂上举略高于头顶，双手所持之物因壁画漫漶不清，推测可能为香炉，眉眼低垂，面部表情虔诚肃穆。头戴宝冠，宝冠中央饰有宝珠，宝珠四周有花瓣状装饰，冠座为空心圆环戴于头顶，冠缯从两侧耳后垂下并似在后颈部搭绕。宝缯为"敦煌艺术中菩萨宝冠两侧的丝带。其物象因时代不同而异，或飘举向上，或平展伸出，或垂至于肩"。菩萨戴手镯，双臂搭饰披巾飘落，腰部束围腰，围腰上边缘外翻呈波浪状，有璎珞绕身，围腰下着长裙。从服饰色调上看，冠缯、披巾、围腰均为绿色，长裙为绛红色，红绿相得益彰。

（文：赵茜、吴波）

　　This painting is the Bodhisattva on the north side of the west niche in Cave 219. From the perspective of the left side, the Bodhisattva kneels down on the lotus seat, His arms raised slightly above His head, and the objects held by His hands are unclear which is speculated as an incense burner. He has drooping eyebrows and eyes, with pious and solemn facial expression. His head wears a treasure crown, and the center of the treasure crown is decorated with a treasure jewel which has petal shaped decoration around the treasure bead. The crown base is a hollow ring, which is worn on the top of the head. The crown laces hanging from behind ears on both sides and seems to be wrapped behind neck. Crown laces are "the ribbon on both sides of the Bodhisattva's crown in Dunhuang art. The image varies from time to time, either flying upward, spreading out, or hanging down to the shoulders." He wears bracelets, silk scarf, waist wrap, and the upper edge of the waist wrap has formed into a wavy shape, decorated with keyūra, and a long skirt under the waist wrap. From the perspective of dress color, the crown laces, silk scarf and waist wrap are green, and the long skirt is crimson, which complement each other.

(Written by: Zhao Xi, Wu Bo)

图：吴波　Painted by: Wu Bo

The female donor's clothes on the west niche of the main chamber in Cave 219 dated to the high Tang Dynasty at Mogao Grottoes

女供养人服饰

莫高窟盛唐第219窟主室西壁

此图为第219窟主室西壁龛外南侧力士台下女供养人，梳双髻，身穿襦裙，上身为窄袖襦，下穿橘色曳地长裙，足蹬岐头履。此身襦裙样式沿袭了隋代裙襦的风格，裙身瘦长，较为合体。外披石绿色的"帔"，学界基本将"帔"称为"披帛"。"披帛"最早出现于五代的文献中，如五代后梁马缟的《中华古今注》。在唐朝的文献中将此形制服饰称为"帔"，韩愈《韩昌黎诗集编年笺注》卷一中，刘熙释名："帔，披也，披之肩背，不及下也。"在唐代，帔的披挂方式有多种，此身帔表现为一端掖入左侧裙腰之中，其余的帔绕过左肩，披盖后背，于右肩往前，搭于左臂之上后垂下。女供养人执礼如仪，表现出虔诚的姿态。

（文：董昳云、吴波）

This painting is the female donor below Vīra stage on the south outside the west niche of the main chamber in Cave 219. She combs two hair buns, wearing a Ru skirt with narrow sleeves on the upper body, an orange long trained skirt on the lower body, and her feet in split head shoes. This skirt style follows the Sui Dynasty tradition, which is thin and fit. The shoulders are covered with malachite green "Pei", scholars generally call "Pei" as "Pibo". Pibo first appeared in the documents of the Five Dynasties, such as *Zhong Hua Gu Jin Zhu* (Chinese ancient and modern notes) by Ma Gao in later Liang of the Five Dynasties. In the documents of the Tang Dynasty, this clothes was called "Pei". In Volume 1 of Han Yu's *Han Chang Li Shi Ji Bian Nian Jian Zhu* (Notes on the chronology of Han Changli's poetry collection), Liu Xi interprets the name: "Pei, covering the shoulders and back not reach to the lower body." In the Tang Dynasty, there were many ways to wear Pei. This Pei has one end tucked into the left waistband, and the rest bypasses the left shoulder then covers the back, over the right shoulder and drapes on the left arm, then hangs down. This female looks graceful and has a pious attitude.

(Written by: Dong Yiyun, Wu Bo)

The female donor's clothes on the west niche of the main chamber in Cave 219 dated to the high Tang Dynasty at Mogao Grottoes

女供养人服饰

莫高窟盛唐第219窟主室西壁

此图为第219窟主室西壁龛外南侧力士台下女供养人，头梳高髻，身穿襦裙，上身为窄袖襦，呈浓郁的绛红色，双手藏于袖袂之中。外披棕黄色的帔，在靠近颈侧有绿色缘边，帔的一端掖入左侧裙腰之中，其余的帔绕过左肩，披盖后背，于右肩往前，盖过双手后垂下。供养人下着深色曳地长裙（或为氧化变色所致），足蹬尖头履。此身襦裙样式沿袭了隋代裙襦的风格，裙身瘦长，较为合体。

（文：董昳云、吴波）

This painting is the female donor below Vīra stage on the south outside the west niche of the main chamber in Cave 219. She has a high hair bun and wears a Ru skirt. Her upper body wears a narrow sleeved Ru, which is in deep crimson, the two hands hold together and hidden in sleeves. The shoulders are covered by a brownish-orange silk shawl, the edge near the neck is green, one end of the silk scarf is tucked into the left waistband. The rest of the silk shawl goes around the left shoulder, covers the back and over the right shoulder, then covers both hands and hangs down. The donor wears dark long skirt (or caused by oxidation and discoloration) and pointed shoes. This skirt style follows the Sui Dynasty skirt style, which is thin and fit.

(Written by: Dong Yiyun, Wu Bo)

图：吴波　Painted by: Wu Bo

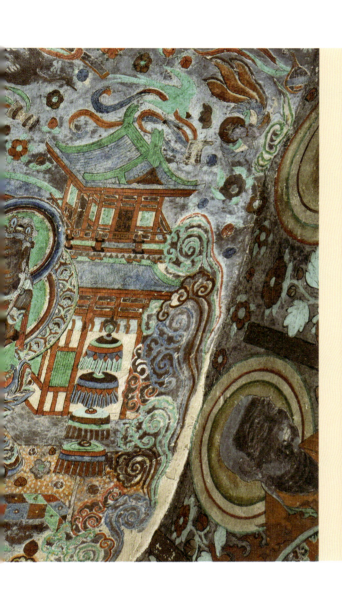

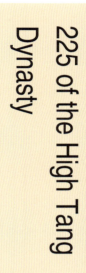

Dunhuang Mogao Grottoes Cave
225 of the High Tang
Dynasty

敦煌莫高窟盛唐

第225窟

　　第225窟是创建于盛唐时期的覆斗顶形窟，南、西、北壁各开一龛，经中唐、五代、清重修。主室窟顶藻井为团花井心，周围东、北、西三披绘卷草、璎珞帷幔，四披绘千佛。西壁开平顶敞口龛，龛内盛唐彩塑一倚坐佛、二弟子，清修一菩萨。龛顶绘说法图。龛壁浮塑佛光，两侧共绘八弟子、六头光。龛沿绘卷草纹及半团花边饰。龛外南、北侧各绘一观世音菩萨。南壁开平顶敞口龛，龛内存一塑像底座。龛顶绘说法图一铺。龛壁浮塑佛光，两侧共绘八弟子、六头光。龛沿盛唐绘百花蔓草纹边饰。龛外南、北两侧中唐分别绘观世音、地藏一身。北壁开斜顶敞口龛，龛内彩塑释迦牟尼涅槃像一身，身后弟子及天人数身。龛壁绘双树，中唐绘灵鸟卷草纹火焰背光。东壁门上中唐绘供养人及千佛。门南、北五代绘壁画。前室及甬道存五代壁画。

　　此窟主室西壁龛外南侧菩萨的披帛较有特色，其幅宽较宽，披在肩上，形似披风，尾端缠绕双臂，随风飘逸。随着唐代女性着披帛已然成为一种风尚，反映出此时菩萨形象逐渐世俗化、女性化。

（文：杨婧嫱）

Cave 225 is a truncated pyramidal ceiling cave built in the high Tang Dynasty. There is a niche on the south, west and north walls respectively, which has been repaired in the middle Tang Dynasty, the Five Dynasties and the Qing Dynasty. The caisson on the top of the main chamber has round flower pattern as the center, surrounded by painted scrolling vine pattern and keyūra valance on the east, north and west slopes, and the four slopes covered by Thousand Buddhas. There is a flat ceiling niche in the west wall, in the niche which has painted sculpture of one siting Buddha and two disciples dated to the high Tang Dynasty, and a Bodhisattva made in the Qing Dynasty. The top of the niche is painted with a Dharma assembly, Buddha light relief on the niche wall, and eight disciples and six head lights are painted on both sides, the niche edge is decorated with flower and leaf pattern in the high Tang Dynasty. A Avalokitesvara Bodhisattva is painted on each the south and north sides of the niche. The south wall has a niche with a flat ceiling, in which there is a sculpture base. A Dharma assembly is painted on the top of the niche. Buddha light relief is on the niche wall, and eight disciples and six head lights are painted on both sides. The niche edge is decorated with flowers and vines dated to the high Tang Dynasty. Outside the niche, a Avalokitesvara Bodhisattva and Ksitigarbha Bodhisattva are painted on the south and north side dated to the middle Tang Dynasty. The north wall has a niche with sloping ceiling. In the niche, there are painted sculptures of Sakyamuni nirvana, several disciples and heavenly beings behind. The niche wall is painted with double trees, and in the middle Tang Dynasty painted holy bird scrolling vine pattern flame backlight. Above the east door has painted donors and Thousand Buddhas in the middle Tang Dynasty. On the south and north side of the door have Five Dynasties murals. There are Five Dynasties murals in the front chamber and corridor.

The Bodhisattva's silk scarf on the south side outside the west niche of the main chamber in this cave is very distinctive, which is wide and drapes over the shoulders just like a cloak. The ends of the silk scarf are wrapped around both arms and flying with the wind. Because women wearing silk scarf was a fashion in the Tang Dynasty, this reflecting the gradual secularization and feminization of Bodhisattva image during this time.

(Written by: Yang Jingqiang)

Avalokitesvara Bodhisattva's clothes on the south side of the west niche in the main chamber of Cave 225 dated to the high Tang Dynasty at Mogao Grottoes

观世音菩萨服饰
莫高窟盛唐第225窟主室
西壁龛外南侧

盛唐第225窟主室西壁龛外南侧观世音菩萨素面如玉，留有胡须，双目凝视，似有所思。右手持香炉，左手食指和中指翘起，肩披绿色天衣，下身穿土红色曳地波浪裙（盛唐时期女性的裙子一般为多褶，由于纺织技术的提高，织物的幅宽增加且轻薄柔软，出现了百褶裙、波浪裙和间色裙。百褶裙少则数十个，多则近百个褶；波浪裙是运用织物的横竖幅和垂感而形成的视觉效果；间色裙又称"破裥裙"，是由两种或多种颜色的织物拼接而制成的裙子）。裙子分为内裙和外裙双层，内裙有蓝色的贴边，外裙的纵向贴边和横向贴边均为赭红色织锦。腰部系绿色的腰带和腰裙，腰裙的贴边为土黄色，与主体裙子的颜色相一致，同时，裙子的侧面有裙带垂落。

菩萨头上佩戴莲花冠，并有蓝宝石镶嵌在冠的正中与两侧，花冠两侧点缀有珠串垂坠，"X"形的长璎珞自颈部两侧垂至腹部，连接于严身轮上，由严身轮垂下两条珠宝串珠落于两侧膝部。

（文：刘元风）

The Avalokitesvara Bodhisattva on the south outside the west niche of the main chamber in Cave 225 dated to the high Tang Dynasty is as clean as jade, with beard and staring eyes, which seems like contemplating. His right hand is holding a censer, the index finger and middle finger of the left hand are up, the shoulders are covered with a green shawl, and the lower body is wearing an earth red wavy skirt (During the high Tang Dynasty, women's skirts were generally multi pleated. Due to the improvement of textile technology, the width of the fabric increased, also light, thin and soft, then people have pleated skirt, wavy skirt and color stripe skirt. Pleated skirt had dozens or more than 100 pleats; wavy skirt had the visual effect formed by using the horizontal and vertical lines; color stripe skirt, also known as broken pleats skirt, was made of two or more colors fabrics stitched together). The skirt is divided into an inner skirt and an outer skirt. The inner skirt has blue welt, and the longitudinal and transverse welts of the outer skirt are ochre brocade. The waist is tied by a green belt and waist wrap, and the welt of the waist wrap is earth yellow, which is consistent with the color of the main skirt. At the same time, there are skirt ribbons hanging on the sides of the skirt.

The Bodhisattva wears a lotus crown with sapphire inlaid in the middle and both sides of the crown, beads strings hanging on both sides. The "X" shaped long keyūra hangs from both sides of the neck to abdomen and connected to the Yanshenlun (jade ring). Two beads jewelry are hung from the Yanshenlun and fall on both knees sides.

(Written by: Liu Yuanfeng)

The Dharma listening
Bodhisattva's clothes
on the south side of the west niche ceiling in
the main chamber of Cave 225 dated to the
high Tang Dynasty at Mogao Grottoes

听法菩萨服饰
莫高窟盛唐第225窟主室
西壁龛顶南侧

此图为盛唐第225窟主室西壁龛顶南侧说法图中的听法菩萨。

菩萨右侧身，修眉俊目，目光下视，上身后挺，双手捧莲，双脚踩在莲花座上，体态优美；梳低髻，头戴璎珞，形制类似于现今的发带；戴臂钏、手镯，臂钏中央饰蓝色宝珠；身穿天衣，天衣从后背穿过右臂腋下环绕至右肩，又从右肩垂于身后。菩萨双臂缠绕细条带至身后形成多环"U"形，条带末端有形如燕尾的装饰，下着围腰与长裙，外裹的围腰因紧扎而边缘形成有韵律的折叠波浪形裙纹，流畅的衣纹表现出面料悬垂的质感。服饰以绿、红对比为主，并以蓝色调和。

（文：赵茜、吴波）

This painting is the Dharma listening Bodhisattva on the south side of the west niche ceiling in the main chamber of Cave 225 dated to the high Tang Dynasty.

The Bodhisattva is on His right side perspective, with slender eyebrows and handsome eyes. He looks down, upper body upright, both hands hold lotus, and feet step on the lotus seat, in a beautiful posture. He combs a flat hair bun, and keyūra on head, the shape and function is similar to today's hair band. Armlets, bracelets and blue jewels in the center of armlets. He wears heavenly clothes, the heavenly clothes pass through the right armpit from back to right shoulder, and then hang behind. The Bodhisattva's arms are wrapped around by thin color cord and fall behind to form a multi ring U-shape. The ends of the color cord are shaped like swallow tail. The lower body wears a waist wrap and a long skirt, the waist wrap forms a rhythmic folding wavy skirt pattern at the edge due to tight tying. The smooth clothing pattern shows the texture of the fabrics. The clothes are mainly green and red, and balanced with blue.

(Written by: Zhao Xi, Wu Bo)

The disciple's clothes
on the south niche of the main chamber in
Cave 225 dated to the high Tang Dynasty
at Mogao Grottoes

弟子服饰
莫高窟盛唐第225窟主室
南壁龛内

主室的南、西、北三壁皆开龛，南壁开平顶敞口龛，龛壁有浮塑佛光，佛光两侧各绘有四弟子、三头光。这身位于南壁龛西侧的弟子双手合十，披田相袈裟，赤脚站于莲花台上。

由于头光的遮挡，这身弟子右侧的服装结构没能在壁画中绘制完整，但根据袈裟与衣袖、手臂的总体动势可以推断出人体造型与服装的结构。该身弟子采取将袈裟覆左肩、络右腋的穿着方式，这是在敦煌莫高窟中常见的右袒式披法，但与右袒式通常采用的袒右臂、斜披穿着的方式有所区别。这身弟子原本绕在后背的袈裟边缘搭在他的右肩上，从而形成覆双肩、斜披穿着的造型，该穿着方法与莫高窟第217窟西壁龛内迦叶的穿法相同。

（文：李迎军）

The south, west and north walls of the main chamber all have a niche. The south wall has a niche with flat ceiling, which has Buddha light relief on the wall, and four disciples and three head lights are painted each on both sides of the Buddha light. This disciple, who is located in the west side of the south niche, is standing on the lotus platform barefoot with two palms together, covered with field pattern kasaya.

Because the head light blocked some parts, the clothing structure on the right side of the disciple is not complete in the mural, but the human body shape and clothing structure can be inferred from the overall shape of the kasaya, sleeves and arms. This disciple wears a kasaya covering the left shoulder and wrapping the right armpit, which is a common right shoulder bared style in Dunhuang Mogao Grottoes, but it is different from the traditional style; the edge of the kasaya supposed to wrap around the back is put on His right shoulder now, so as to form the shape of covering both shoulders, this way of wearing is the same as Kasyapa in the west niche of Cave 217 in Mogao Grottoes.

(Written by: Li Yingjun)

图: 李迎军   Painted by: Li Yingjun

Dunhuang Mogao Grottoes Cave

319 of the High Tang Dynasty

敦煌莫高窟盛唐

第319窟

　　第319窟是创建于盛唐时期的盝形顶窟。主室窟顶藻井为三团花井心，西、南、北披绘千佛。西壁马蹄形佛坛上彩塑一佛、二弟子、二菩萨、二天王，西壁浮塑火焰纹佛光。东壁与窟顶东披已毁。南、北壁绘千佛，西端各绘一弟子、二菩萨、一头光。

　　此窟彩塑虽已变色，但神韵犹存。主尊佛像结跏趺坐，着通肩袈裟，神情庄严。弟子阿难面容圆润，双手拢袖交叠于腹前，上着青绿交领上襦，下着长裙，外披红色袈裟。弟子迦叶沉稳从容，双手合十，外披田相袈裟。两侧菩萨"游戏坐"于莲花台之上，上身半裸，着披帛，项饰璎珞，穿长裙。两侧天王气势威武，身着铠甲，下着战裙，脚着长靴。整铺彩塑构图均衡，造型生动，衣纹流畅，为莫高窟保存较好的一铺盛唐彩塑。

（文：杨婧嫱）

Cave 319 is a cave with flat ceiling, which was built in the high Tang Dynasty. The caisson on the top of the main chamber has three round flowers as the center, with Thousand Buddhas painted on the west, south and north slopes. On the horseshoe shaped Buddha altar in the west wall, there are painted sculptures of one Buddha, two disciples, two Bodhisattvas and two Maharāja-devas, and the Buddha light relief with flame pattern on the west wall. The east wall and east slope have collapsed. Thousand Buddhas are painted on the south and north walls, and one disciple, two Bodhisattvas and one head light are painted on the two west ends respectively.

Although the painted sculptures' color in this cave has changed, their charm still exists. The main Buddha sculpture sits with two legs folded, wears two shoulders covered kasaya and looks solemn. Disciple Ananda has a round face, folded His sleeves in front of belly, wears a dark green cross lapel Ru on the upper body, long skirt on the lower body and covered with red kasaya. Disciple Kasyapa looks calm and peaceful, with His palms together and covered with field pattern kasaya. Two Bodhisattvas on both sides "Casual Sit" on the lotus platforms, their upper body is naked, covered with silk scarf, wears keyūra on neck and long skirt on the lower body. The two Maharāja-devas on both sides look powerful, wearing armor, battle skirt and boots. The whole painted sculptures have balanced composition, vivid shape and smooth clothing lines. They are a group of well-preserved painted sculptures of the high Tang Dynasty in Mogao Grottoes.

(Written by: Yang Jingqiang)

The painted sculpture
Bodhisattva's clothes
on the north side of the west niche in the
main chamber of Cave 319 dated to the high
Tang Dynasty at Mogao Grottoes

彩塑菩萨服饰
莫高窟盛唐第319窟主室
西壁龛内北侧

盛唐第319窟主室西壁龛内北侧彩塑菩萨头束高髻，目光向龛外凝视，眉间有白毫，双耳垂肩。右手抬起，与左手做同样的手印。右腿盘屈，左腿垂下作"游戏坐"式坐于莲花台上，左脚踩莲花。

菩萨上身袒露，斜披红色络腋并在胸部打结。下身穿红黄色的镶饰金边的织锦长裙，有散点式的卷曲纹装饰其间，与菩萨头光的缠枝纹有异曲同工之妙。腰间系深褐色波浪纹腰带，肩披红绿相间的天衣，绕臂垂落。莲花纹项链和臂钏、手镯相映成趣。

本尊菩萨彩塑造型精准，比例适中，四肢修长，轮廓生动。菩萨的小腹微微隆起，彰显女性特有的美感，彩塑线条遒劲流畅，色彩含蓄深沉，变化有序的曲线将丰腴的肢体透过丝质长裙隐约显现其形态的起伏与律动，自然而舒展。

（文：刘元风）

In the west niche of the main chamber in Cave 319 dated to the high Tang Dynasty, the painted sculpture Bodhisattva on the north side has a high hair bun and looks out of the niche, a Urna between the eyebrows and long earlobes. His right hand raised and made the same gesture as the left hand, the right leg bend and the left leg down which forms the "Casual Sit (one leg bent sit)" posture. He sits on the lotus seat and steps on the lotus with left foot.

The Bodhisattva's upper body is naked, with red Luoye diagonally draped and tied at chest. The lower body is wearing a long red and yellow brocade skirt inlaid with gold lines, which is decorated with winding twig pattern, this is similar to the tangled vine pattern of Bodhisattva's head light. The waist is tied with a dark brown wavy belt, and the shoulder is covered with a red and green silk scarf, which falls around the arms. Lotus pattern necklace, armlets and bracelets complement with each other.

This painted sculpture Bodhisattva has accurate modeling, moderate proportion, slender limbs and vivid outline. The Bodhisattva's belly is slightly raised, showing the unique beauty of motherhood. This painted sculpture has strong and smooth lines, implicit and dark colors, and orderly changing curves manifest plump limbs which can be seen vaguely ups and downs shapes and rhythms through the silk skirt, looks natural and free.

(Written by: Liu Yuanfeng)

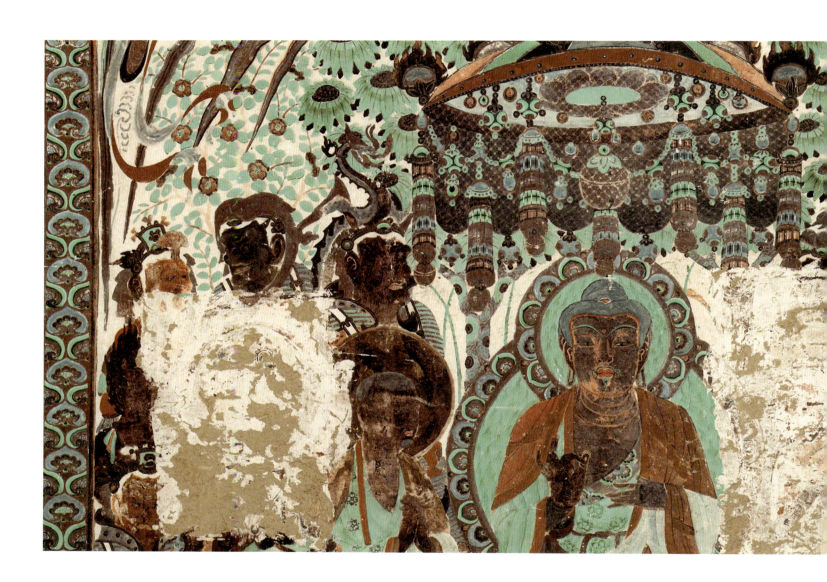

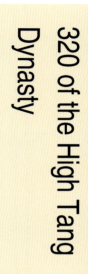

Dunhuang Mogao Grottoes Cave
320 of the High Tang
Dynasty

敦煌莫高窟盛唐

第320窟

　　第320窟是创建于盛唐时期的覆斗顶形窟，经中唐、宋、元重修。主室窟顶藻井为云头牡丹团花井心，周围绘垂角彩铃，四披绘千佛。西壁开平顶敞口龛，龛内存彩塑一倚坐佛、一弟子、二菩萨。龛顶绘弥勒说法图。龛壁浮塑佛光，两侧共绘八弟子、二菩萨。龛沿绘半团花边饰。龛外南、北侧各绘观世音。龛下表层宋绘供养人数身及狮子，底层盛唐绘供器。南壁绘千佛，中央绘释迦说法图一铺，其中缺失的两幅画面于1924年被盗，下宋绘男供养人数身。北壁西起中唐绘菩萨一身；中央盛唐绘观无量寿经变，东侧绘"未生怨"，西侧绘"十六观"；东侧中唐绘供养菩萨一身及供养比丘一身；下宋绘女供养人数身。东壁宋及元绘壁画。甬道存宋代壁画。

　　莫高窟第320窟也是盛唐代表洞窟之一。西壁龛内佛、弟子、菩萨仍是盛唐原塑，整窟壁画色彩浓艳、保存如初。西壁龛内左胁侍菩萨头戴宝冠，身姿曼妙，上身半裸，着红绿两色络腋，长裙紧贴身体，衣饰处理丰富多彩，彰显出菩萨身姿修长、造型庄重的形象。菩萨圆润的脸庞、微突的腹部、宽大的胯部，体现出盛唐丰肌秀骨、珠圆玉润的审美倾向。彩塑菩萨的腰裙使用宝相花纹作为主体装饰，腰裙下方缘边图案为条带式二方连续的半破式宝相花。宝相花是从自然花卉概括出的花瓣、花苞、叶片的变形，经过艺术加工形成平面化的纹样。整体图案配色简练，以青绿色和棕色为主色，用层层退晕的方式体现出花瓣的层次关系。腰裙图案细腻繁复，从侧面反映出盛唐纺织技术的工艺提高。

（文：杨婧嫱）

Cave 320 is a truncated pyramidal ceiling cave built in the high Tang Dynasty, which was repaired in the middle Tang Dynasty, Song Dynasty and Yuan Dynasty. The caisson on the top of the main chamber has cirrus cloud peony round flower as center, surrounded by hanging triangle color bells and Thousand Buddhas. There is a flat ceiling niche in the west wall which has painted sculptures of one siting Buddha, one disciple and two Bodhisattvas. Maitreya Buddha is painted on the top of the niche, and the niche wall has Buddha light relief, and eight disciples and two Bodhisattvas are painted on both sides. The niche edge is painted with semi round flower decoration. On the south and north outside the niche are painted with Avalokitesvara. Below the niche, the surface layer is painted with a number of donors and lions dated to the Song Dynasty, and the bottom layer is painted with offering utensils dated to the high Tang Dynasty. Thousand Buddhas are painted on the south wall, and Sakyamuni Buddha Dharma assembly is painted in the center. Two paintings are missing, and they were stolen in 1924, and a number of male donors on the lower part were painted in the Song Dynasty. From the west side of the north wall, a Bodhisattva was painted in the middle Tang Dynasty; Amitayurdhyana Sutra illustration in the center was painted in the high Tang Dynasty, the east side is Ajatasattu's story and Sixteen Visualizations on the west side; on the east side has a offering Bodhisattva and a Bhiksu painted in the middle Tang Dynasty; a number of female donors in the lower part painted in the Song Dynasty. The east wall has Song and Yuan Dynasty murals, and in the corridor is the Song Dynasty murals.

Cave 320 of Mogao Grottoes is also one of the representative caves of the high Tang Dynasty. The Buddha, disciples and Bodhisattvas in the west niche are still the original sculptures of the high Tang Dynasty. The murals in the whole cave are colorful and preserved in good condition. In the west niche, the left attendant Bodhisattva wears a crown, with graceful posture, naked upper body, red and green two-color Luoye, long skirt fit to the body, with rich and colorful clothing decoration, showing the slender body and solemn character of the Bodhisattva. The Bodhisattva has round face, slightly protruding belly and wide hips, which reflect the aesthetic tendency of plump body, thin bones, round body shape and jade like skin in the high Tang Dynasty. The waist wrap of the painted Bodhisattva has Baoxing flower pattern as the main decoration, and the lower edge pattern is a strip of two in group repeated semi Baoxiang flower pattern. Baoxiang flower pattern is the deformation of petals, bracts and leaves abstracted from natural flowers; after artistic processing, it becomes into a planar pattern. The overall pattern color matching is concise, with turquoise and brown as the main colors, reflecting the layer relationship of petals in the way of layer by layer color-gradation technique. The waist wrap pattern is delicate and complex, which reflects the improvement of textile technology in the high Tang Dynasty.

(Written by: Yang Jingqiang)

The Contemplating
Bodhisattva's clothes
on the north wall of the main chamber
in Cave 320 dated to the high Tang
Dynasty at Mogao Grottoes

思惟菩萨服饰

莫高窟盛唐第320窟主室

北壁

盛唐第320窟主室北壁思惟菩萨头束盛唐式高髻，余发披肩，莲花纹绿宝石镶嵌在正中位置，面容丰腴秀美，妩媚动人，肌肤洁净如玉，左手自然放于右小腿上，右手托腮，头微侧作沉思状。略显慵散随意地坐于阁内床上。其右腿半跏，左腿下垂。菩萨上身赤裸，下着土红色长裙，外披宽而长的天衣，天衣的正面为绿色，背面为蓝色。值得注意的是，思惟菩萨的头上没有光环，脚下也没有莲花，看来应该是安居于净土世界的智者。

同时，唐代由于社会文化、艺术空前繁荣，在艺术作品中反映出的人物形体的审美倾向上多以胖为美，特别是盛唐时期，脸型趋于圆润，虽然少数菩萨的嘴唇上留有蝌蚪式的胡须，但总体上更具盛唐世俗女性的特征，尽显"S"形的曲线美。从这种角度来看，思惟菩萨丰满的脸型和体型恰恰契合了这种特征，呈现出雍容华贵之美感。

（文：刘元风）

The Contemplating Bodhisattva on the north wall of the main chamber in Cave 320 dates to the high Tang Dynasty, who has a high hair bun of the high Tang Dynasty style, and the rest of His hair covers shoulders, and a lotus shape emerald is embedded in the middle. His face is plump and beautiful, charming and moving, and skin as clean as jade, the left hand naturally places on right leg, and the right hand holds His cheek, head slightly turned in a meditative state. He sits on the bed in the pavilion with right leg half crossed and left leg drooping, the upper body is naked and an earth red skirt on the lower body. A wide and long silk scarf around the body, which the front side of the silk scarf is green and the back is blue. It is worth noting that the contemplating Bodhisattva has no halo behind head and no lotus under feet. It seems that He should be a wise man who lives in the Pure Land World.

At the same time, due to the unprecedented prosperity of social culture and art in the Tang Dynasty, the aesthetic tendency of figures reflected in art works mostly were fat. Especially during the high Tang Dynasty, faces tended to be round. Although a few Bodhisattvas have tadpole beards on their lips, they generally have the characteristics of secular women of the high Tang Dynasty, showing the beauty of "S" shaped curves. From this point of view, the plump face and body shape of this Contemplating Bodhisattva just fit this feature and present the elegant beauty.

(Written by: Liu Yuanfeng)

图：刘元风　Painted by: Liu Yuanfeng

The dancer's clothes
on the north wall of the main chamber in Cave
320 dated to the high Tang Dynasty at Mogao
Grottoes

舞伎服饰
莫高窟盛唐第320窟主室
北壁

　　盛唐第320窟主室北壁舞伎身姿修长，五官俊俏，弯眉秀目，头束高髻，佩戴镶嵌录宝石的莲花纹发带，余发披肩；四肢灵动，左腿挺直，赤足蹬地，右腿盘靠左膝，右脚外翻朝天。

　　舞伎上身袒露，颈部佩戴华丽的项饰，有一颗大的莲花纹宝石镶嵌其中，间隔有四颗依次排列的宝石串珠。其下身穿的长裙基本形制为上紧下松，长至脚踝，衣纹线条流畅，裙摆处有用褶皱塑型而织成的主体旋涡纹装饰，其材料为垂感强的弹性丝织物。舞伎双手执长长的双色（正面为绿色，反面为灰色）帛带，作类似"顺风旗"姿而起舞，舞姿热烈而曼妙，体现出舞裙的飘逸灵动。舞伎的身体伴随着帛带的飞扬而激情舞动，飞舞的帛带在身体的四周和上下急速翻飞，构成了若干条富于张力的弧线，波动的圆弧身姿与帛带之间相互借力，营造出绚烂多彩的视觉美感。

（文：刘元风）

On the north wall of the main chamber in Cave 320 dated to the high Tang Dynasty, he dancer has a slender posture, handsome facial features, curved eyebrows, beautiful eyes, a high hair bun, a lotus pattern hair band inlaid with emeralds and hair overs shoulders. Her limbs are flexible, the left leg is straight, barefoot stomps ground, the right leg rests on the left knee, and the right foot turn outward.

The upper body of the dancer is naked, around the neck wearing a gorgeous necklace which inlaid a large lotus shape gem in the middle, and four gems arranged separately in sequence. The shape of the long skirt she wears is basically tight at the top and loose at the bottom, long to the ankle, and the lines of the dress are smooth. The hem of the skirt is decorated with the main vortex pattern shaped by pleating, and the material is elastic silk fabric with strong draping effect. The dancer holds a long two-color silk band by both hands (green on the front and gray on the back), and dances in a manner similar to "downwind flag". The dance is warm and graceful, reflecting the elegant and dynamic of the dancing dress. The body of the dancer moves passionately with the flying silk band. The flying silk band flutters around up and down the body, forming a number of undulating arcs between the body posture and the silk band to create a dazzling and colorful visual beauty of clothing.

(Written by: Liu Yuanfeng)

The Flying Apsaras' clothes on the south wall of the main chamber in Cave 320 dated to the high Tang Dynasty at Mogao Grottoes

飞天服饰
莫高窟盛唐第320窟主室
南壁

第320窟是唐四期洞窟，主室南壁中央的释迦说法图上部分布有四身飞天，中间两身相背，姿态为横向飞舞，两侧的两身飞天纵向飘举，面向中央。辅以流云整体呈对称形态分布于画面顶部。本图为左侧第一身飞天，双手上举，屈左腿，右腿伸开，身体饱满而舒展，富有一定的力量感。颈部佩戴璎珞，裸上身，下着长裙，腰部系扎，腰带外翻下垂。长裙上的图案与同时期盛唐图案一致，都是十字结构的小团花，疑为画家仿照当时的纺织品印染工艺所绘。如果参照新疆出土的唐代纺织品，会发现类似的花朵图案的工艺多为印花。飘带围绕在两臂与周身，并且画家为了考虑画面效果有意夸张飘带下端的长度和曲线效果，以使飞天刚好与旁侧的云气共同装饰画面的左上角，形成适合图案式的整体造型。

（文：张春佳）

Cave 320 is the fourth period cave in the early Tang Dynasty. There are four bodies Flying Apsaras in the upper part of the Sakyamuni Dharma assembly in the center of the south wall of the main chamber. The two bodies in the middle are back to each other, and the posture is horizontal flying. The two bodies Flying Apsaras on both sides flying vertically and face the center, supported by flowing clouds and the whole picture is symmetrically distributed at the top of the painting. This picture is the first body Flying Apsaras on the left, lifting both hands, bending the left leg and stretching the right leg. The body is full and stretched, full of a certain sense of strength, wearing a keyura on the neck, naked upper body, a long skirt on the lower body, tied at the waist, and a sagging waistband. The patterns on the long skirt are consistent with those in the high Tang Dynasty of the same period. They are all small round flowers with cross structure. It is suspected that the painter painted them in imitation of the printing and dyeing textile at that time. If we refer to the Tang Dynasty textiles unearthed in Xinjiang, we will find that most of the similar flower patterns are printed. The ribbon surrounds both arms and the whole body, and the painter deliberately exaggerated the length and curve effect at the lower end of the ribbon in order to enhance the picture effect, so that the Flying Apsaras is just enough to decorate the upper left corner of the picture together with the clouds on the side, forming an overall decoration effect.

(Written by: Zhang Chunjia)

图：张春佳　Painted by: Zhang Chunjia

The Flying Apsaras' clothes
on the south wall of the main chamber in Cave
320 dated to the high Tang Dynasty at Mogao
Grottoes

飞天服饰
莫高窟盛唐第320窟主室
南壁

第320窟第四身飞天位于主室南壁释迦说法图上部右侧，此身飞天与中央右侧飞天在姿态上互相呼应，以流云衔接整体。双手做散花状，大体形态与四身飞天中最左侧基本对称。飞天也是袒露上身，以飘带穿插在手臂外侧。仔细观察会发现，这四身飞天除了发型以外，最大的区别就是裙腰的样式——画家力图在整体中寻求一些细节变化。此身飞天腰部的缠裹方式与唐四期洞窟第172窟洞壁上部南侧菩萨立像有相似之处，都是裙腰向外翻出异色部分，并且在腰部再系扎，垂下双带。这四身飞天裙子上的图案基本一致，都是十字结构的小团花，推测或为印花工艺。飘带在表现飞天姿态时起到重要的辅助作用，通过飘带飞舞的方向，可以更完整地呈现飞天的动势，与云气一同构成整体画面的流动曲线。

（文：张春佳）

The fourth Flying Apsaras in Cave 320 is located on the right upper part of Sakyamuni Dharma assembly on the south wall in the main chamber. This Flying Apsaras echoes with the Flying Apsaras on the right side of the center, connected by flowing clouds as a whole. Her hands are scattering flowers, and the general shape is basically symmetrical with the leftmost Flying Apsaras. This Flying Apsaras is also with naked upper body, ribbons over the shoulders. Careful observation will reveal that apart from the hairstyle, the biggest difference between these four bodies is the style of waistband — the painter tried to give some differences in the whole. The waist wrapping method of this Flying Apsaras is similar to the standing Bodhisattva on the south side upper part of the cave wall in Cave 172 dated to the fourth period of the Tang Dynasty. They all turned out waistband and have different colors, and tied again at the waist, then hang down two ends. The patterns on these four Flying Apsaras' skirts are basically the same, they are all small flowers with cross structure, which maybe an imitation of printing technique. The ribbon plays an important auxiliary role in the performance of flying posture. Through the flying direction of the ribbon, the momentum of flying can be presented more completely, and together with clouds, it forms the flow curve of the overall picture.

(Written by: Zhang Chunjia)

图：张春佳

Painted by: Zhang Chunjia

The Flying Apsaras' clothes
on the south wall of the main chamber in Cave
320 dated to the high Tang Dynasty at Mogao
Grottoes

飞天服饰

莫高窟盛唐第320窟主室

南壁

第320窟的第二身飞天位于主室南壁释迦说法图上部中央左侧。与前面左侧的第一身飞天形成呼应，姿态上有互相追逐之态，并以流云穿插其间，从而形成一个动态的组合，这样的动势也符合盛唐追求动感的人物造型审美倾向。从壁画上依稀可见飞天梳双丫髻，手臂上扬，手姿轻松舒展。上身袒露，下身的长裙包裹着横向飘舞的下半身，腰裙部有外翻的层次，同时上部系有腰带，并垂双带，这两条短小腰带飞扬的姿态恰好与飞天周身缠绕的大飘带形成有效补充。整体色彩以土红和石绿色调为主，但是氧化部分依据周围环境颜色和洞窟整体用色推断亦为红色调。

第320窟第三身飞天位于主室南壁释迦说法图上部中央右侧，姿态大体对称。这样的排布使四身飞天各有呼应，较为强调交流感。双丫髻是释迦说法图中央两身飞天的发型，与外侧有区别变化。周身的璎珞较为简洁，裙子的缠裹方式和上身的赤裸也保留了印度此类形象的着衣风格。和与其相背飞天的腰裙部分相比，没有向外翻出的部分，只是腰带系双环结并垂下。敦煌的飞天与古印度飞天的造型有着非常显著的区别，在肢体形态上更为纤瘦修长，与飘带和云纹一同强调轻盈飞举之态。而印度石窟中保留的诸多壁画或浮雕飞天则更多展现肌体的饱满健硕之感，似乎如何乘云飞翔并不是表现的重点。这是两种艺术风格、文化背景影响作用下，艺术家对于人体表现呈现出的巨大差异。印度的飞天到了中国，在人体造型上发生本土化转变的同时，服饰的款式却在一定程度上保留了印度特征，但是服饰纹样同时也本土化了。这是一种艺术选择的过程——敦煌地区进行创作的艺术家将更多的生活经验和审美观念带入洞窟壁画表现，飞天是其中的典型案例之一。

（文：张春佳）

The second Flying Apsaras in Cave 320 is located on the left side upper part of Sakyamuni Dharma assembly on the south wall of the main chamber, echoing with the first Flying Apsaras on the left; they are arranged in chasing each other, connected by cirrus cloud, to form a dynamic combination. Such momentum feature is also in line with the aesthetic tendency of pursuing dynamic character modeling in the high Tang Dynasty. From the mural we can see the Flying Apsaras combs hair in double Ya hair buns, raises her arms and stretches her hands. The upper body is naked, and the long skirt is wrapped around the horizontal flying lower body. The waistband turned out and tied the upper part with belt and two ends hanging. These two short belts are just complement to the large band wrapped around the body. The main colors are earth red and malachite green, but the oxidized part was also red according to the surrounding color and the overall color of the cave.

The third Flying Apsaras in Cave 320 is located on the right side upper part of the Sakyamuni Dharma assembly on the south wall of the main chamber, with a roughly symmetrical arrangement. This arrangement makes the four bodies Flying Apsaras echo with each other, more emphasis on connection. Double Ya hair bun is the hairstyle of the two Flying Apsaras in the middle, which is different from the other two, their keyūra around the body are relatively simple, and the wrapping way of skirt and the naked upper body also retain the clothing style of this kind of image in India. Compared with the other two waistbands, there are no turned out part, just the belts are tied into a double ring knot and hung down. There are significant differences between Dunhuang Flying Apsaras and India Flying Apsaras. In terms of body shape, Dunhuang Flying Apsaras is more slender, with ribbons and clouds to emphasize the state of flying. While many murals or reliefs of Flying Apsaras preserved in Indian grottoes show more sense of fullness and strength of the body, it seems like how to fly by clouds is not the focus. Under the influence of the two artistic styles and cultural backgrounds, artists showed great differences in the performance of the human body. When Flying Apsaras from India came to China, the localization made the body shape changed, the clothing style retained the Indian characteristics to a certain extent, but the clothing pattern was localized at the same time. This is artistic choice—artists who worked at Dunhuang brought more life experience and local aesthetic concepts into the cave murals, and Flying Apsaras is one of the typical cases.

(Written by: Zhang Chunjia)

图＂张春佳 Painted by: Zhang Chunjia

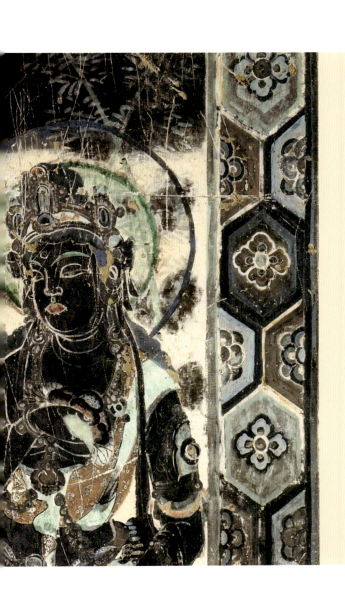

Dunhuang Mogao Grottoes Cave 444 of the High Tang Dynasty

敦煌莫高窟盛唐

第444窟

　　第444窟是创建于盛唐时期的覆斗顶形窟，经宋、清重修。西壁开斜顶敞口龛，龛内存彩塑二弟子、二菩萨、一天王。龛顶绘团花，龛内西壁绘佛光，南、北壁共绘六头光、六弟子。龛沿绘卷草、一整二半团花边饰。龛外南、北侧各绘宝盖、头光及供养童子。龛下存宋绘供养人数身。南、北壁中央绘说法图各一铺，四周绘千佛。东壁门上绘多宝塔，门南、北绘"观音普门品"，门沿两侧宋绘菩萨各一身。前室及甬道存宋代壁画。

　　此窟壁画风格成熟，壁画上的菩萨身姿秀丽，遍身绮罗，装饰华丽；天王雄壮有力，身着甲胄，全副武装，气势威严，极具装饰意义。服饰色彩以朱红、石绿对比色为主调，色调丰富热烈，整体呈现出辉煌灿烂的盛唐风格。

（文：杨婧嫱）

Cave 444 is a truncated pyramidal ceiling cave built in the high Tang Dynasty, which was repaired in the Song and Qing Dynasties. The west wall has a niche with a sloping ceiling, in which there are painted sculptures of two disciples, two Bodhisattvas and one Maharāja-deva. The top of the niche is painted with round flower pattern, and Buddha light relief on the west niche wall, and six head lights and six disciples are painted on the south and north walls. The niche edge is decorated with scrolling vine pattern and a whole and two halves round flower pattern. The south and north outside the niche are painted with canopies, head lights and offering children. A number of donors are painted below the niche dated to the Song Dynasty. In the center of the south wall and the north wall each are painted a Dharma assembly, and surrounded by Thousand Buddhas. Above the east door is a painted pagoda, Samantamukhaparivartah illustration is painted on the south and north side of the door, and a Song Dynasty Bodhisattva is painted on both sides of the door. There are murals of Song Dynasty in the front chamber and corridor.

The murals in this cave have mature style, the Bodhisattvas on the murals are beautiful, colorful and richly decorated. The Maharāja-devas are majestic, fully armed, powerful and of great decorative significance. Taking the contrasting dress colors vermilion and malachite green as the main tone, the colors are rich and warm, showing a brilliant style of the high Tang Dynasty.

(Written by: Yang Jingqiang)

The Bodhisattva clothes
on the east side of the south wall in the
main chamber of Cave 444 dated to the
high Tang Dynasty at Mogao Grottoes

菩萨服饰
莫高窟盛唐第444窟主室
南壁东侧

盛唐第444窟主室南壁东侧菩萨在主尊的右侧，有一副丰润秀丽的面孔，目光凝视，额上画白毫。左手持莲花，右手轻拈璎珞串珠，跣足立于莲花之上。头束云髻，余发披肩，佩戴化佛宝冠，冠体中部有红宝石镶饰其上，两侧有双层镶嵌绿宝石的莲花纹装饰，宝缯下垂贴耳，璎珞自项圈中间下垂至腹部一分为二，又分别绕在左、右前臂垂落。菩萨上身披赭石色络腋，上有细小的三瓣花朵点缀其间。下身穿赭红色长裙，裙上有精致的四瓣花朵装饰，裙摆处镶蓝色贴边，臀部有织锦绣花腰裙，并有双色（正面为赭红色，背面为绿色）宽带围裹，且在腰下打结两端波浪状飘垂。自冠缯两侧延伸的长带绕左右肘自然下垂，腰部的彩绦双层环绕，其两端在身体两侧贴裙垂落。

在画面的处理上，菩萨的整体造型内秀安静，用色古雅，大面积的暖色与小面积的冷色形成对比。注重菩萨五官和手部的细致描绘，使其婉约柔美，超凡脱俗。

（文：刘元风）

The Bodhisattva on the east side of the south wall who is on the right side of the main Buddha in the main chamber of Cave 444 dated to the high Tang Dynasty, who has a plump and beautiful face, staring eyes, and a round Urna on forehead. He holds a lotus in left hand and gently twiddles keyūra beads by right hand, barefoot stands on lotus. His hair is tied in a cloud hair bun, the rest covers shoulders, and wears a Buddha image crown. The middle of the crown body is decorated with ruby, and the two sides are decorated with double-layer lotus pattern inlaid with emeralds. The crown laces are hanging close to ears. The keyūra hangs from the middle of the collar to abdomen, which is divided into two, and then fall around the left and right forearms respectively. The Bodhisattva upper body is covered with ochre Luoye, dotted with small three-petal flowers; the lower body is wearing an ochre red skirt, which is decorated with exquisite four-petal flowers, the skirt is inlaid with blue welt at the hem, and the hips are covered by brocade waist wrap embroidered with flowers, which is wrapped by two-color band (ochre red on the front and green on the back), knotted below the waist, and the two ends are wavy and fluttering. The long ribbons extending from both sides of the crown laces naturally droop around the left and right elbows, and the color cords from waist formed two circles and then hanging on both sides of the body.

In picture processing, the overall shape of the Bodhisattva is quiet with inner peace that colors are quaint, and the large areas warm colors in contrast to the cold colors in small areas. The painter payed attention to the detailed description of Bodhisattva's facial features and hands, so as to make it graceful, soft and extraordinary.

(Written by: Liu Yuanfeng)

The Bodhisattva's clothes
on the west side of the south wall in the
main chamber of Cave 444 dated to the high
Tang Dynasty at Mogao Grottoes

菩萨服饰
莫高窟盛唐第444窟主室
南壁西侧

盛唐第444窟主室南壁菩萨在主尊的左侧，与右侧菩萨对应，其面容丰满、眉间有白毫。左手提净瓶，右手轻托莲叶和莲花。其服饰与右侧菩萨相似，上身披红绿两色络腋，下身穿赭石色及脚面的长裙，四瓣花朵点缀其间，裙摆镶饰蓝色贴边。臀部穿有蓝色织锦腰裙，腰裙外围套双色（正面为绿色，背面为赭石色）丝质宽带，在腰以下打结后自然垂落。腰带的中间和两侧有绿宝石镶嵌。另有彩绦在腰部多层环绕，并在两侧下垂。

菩萨鬓发绕耳，余发披肩，头上佩戴化佛宝冠，冠体正中和两侧有五颗莲花纹绿宝石镶嵌其上，冠缯从头后两侧垂落。臂钏为莲花纹红宝石镶嵌，自冠缯延伸的长带与璎珞一起绕左右臂下落。

值得提出的是，盛唐时期菩萨的服饰色彩极为丰富而典雅，与当时的造型艺术相关联，其色彩更多地体现了中国传统的"五色之变"配置规律（其中"五色"即五方正色），而且多运用对比色的配置方式，但由于颜料的矿物和植物的物理属性使然，在整体色彩上依然呈现出天然和谐的视觉美感。

（文：刘元风）

The Bodhisattva on the south wall who is on the left side of the main Buddha in the main chamber in Cave 444 dated to the high Tang Dynasty, which corresponds to the Bodhisattva on the right side. His face is plump and a Urna between eyebrows. The left hand carries a water bottle, and the right hand gently holds a lotus leaf and a lotus. The dress is similar to the Bodhisattva on the right. The upper body is covered with red and green Luoye, and the lower body is dressed in a long ochre skirt to feet, dotted with four-petal flowers, and the skirt hem is decorated with blue welt. The hips are covered by blue brocade waist wrap, the waist wrap is covered by two-color (green on the front and ochre on the back) wide silk band, which is knotted below the waist and falls naturally. The middle and sides of the belt are inlaid with emeralds. In addition, the colorful cord surround the waist twice and droops on both sides.

The Bodhisattva's sideburns around ears and hair covers shoulders. He wears a Buddha image crown on head, and there are five lotus pattern emeralds inlaid on the middle and both sides of the crown body. The crown laces hang from the back of head, and the armlets are inlaid with lotus pattern ruby. The long band is extending from the crown laces and the keyūra falls around His left and right arms.

It is worth mentioning that the clothes colors of Bodhisattvas during the high Tang Dynasty were extremely rich and elegant, which were related to the plastic arts at that time. Their colors reflected the Chinese traditional "five colors" configuration law (in which "five colors" were the Five Directions Orthodox colors), and usually used the contrast colors configuration. However, due to the mineral and vegetal pigments physical property, the overall color still presents a natural and harmonious visual beauty.

(Written by: Liu Yuanfeng)

The Maharāja-deva's
clothes
on the east wall of the main chamber
in Cave 444 dated to the high Tang
Dynasty at Mogao Grottoes
天王服饰
莫高窟盛唐第444窟主室
东壁

《法华经》"观音普门品"中有观世音菩萨现三十三种身为众生说法，使其得度之说，这身天王表现的就是"应以毗沙门身得度者，即现毗沙门身而为说法"的情景。壁画上的毗沙门天王身着甲衣，左手托宝塔，伸右臂扬掌为信众说法。

毗沙门天王身着的甲衣包括：披膊、护臂、明光甲、束甲带、护腹、腿裙、胫甲、皮靴，与极具实战防护功能的全套甲胄不同的是，这身毗沙门天王腰带上还缠绕着披帛、头上戴着宝珠、脖子上围系豹皮领。宝缯飞扬的头饰与披帛标示着穿着者佛国天将的身份，豹皮领则在毗沙门天王像中较少出现，这一材质独特的服饰品也使得这身造型在诸多天王像中独树一帜。同时，这身天王像也体现了壁画绘制中甲衣装饰化的趋势，由于天王颈上围的豹皮领替代了甲衣的护项，所以原本系结在护项上、勒紧明光胸甲的束甲带失去了受力点，于是画面上的束甲带隐在了明光胸甲的下面，从而失去了实用功能。

（文：李迎军）

In Saddharmapundarika Sutra the chapter of Samantamukhaparivartah, Avalokitesvara Bodhisattva has 33 incarnations to save all sentiment beings. This Maharāja-deva shows the scene of "those who can be saved by Vaiśravaṇa, then Avalokitesvara Bodhisattva will become into Vaiśravaṇa and gives Dharma teaching". In the mural, Vaiśravaṇa is dressed in armor, holding a pagoda in his left hand, stretching his right arm and raising the palm to give Dharma teaching.

The armor worn by Vaiśravaṇa includes: shoulder covers, arm covers, Mingguang armor, armor fasten belt, belly protection, battle skirt, shin armor and leather boots. Different from the full set of armor with practical protection function, this Vaiśravaṇa armor belt is also wrapped with silk scarf, jewel on head and leopard leather collar around neck. The flying headdress and silk scarf indicate the Buddhist world general identity of the wearer, and the leopard skin collar is rarely seen in the image of Vaiśravaṇa. This unique dress also makes this figure unique among many other Maharāja-deva images. At the same time, the image of the Maharāja-deva reflects the trend of decorative armor in mural painting. Because the leopard skin collar around the Maharāja-deva's neck replaced the neck armor, the armor belts originally tied on the neck armor to fasten the Mingguang armor lost the force bearing points; so the armor belts in the painting are hidden under the Mingguang armor, thus they have lost the practical function.

(Written by: Li Yingjun)

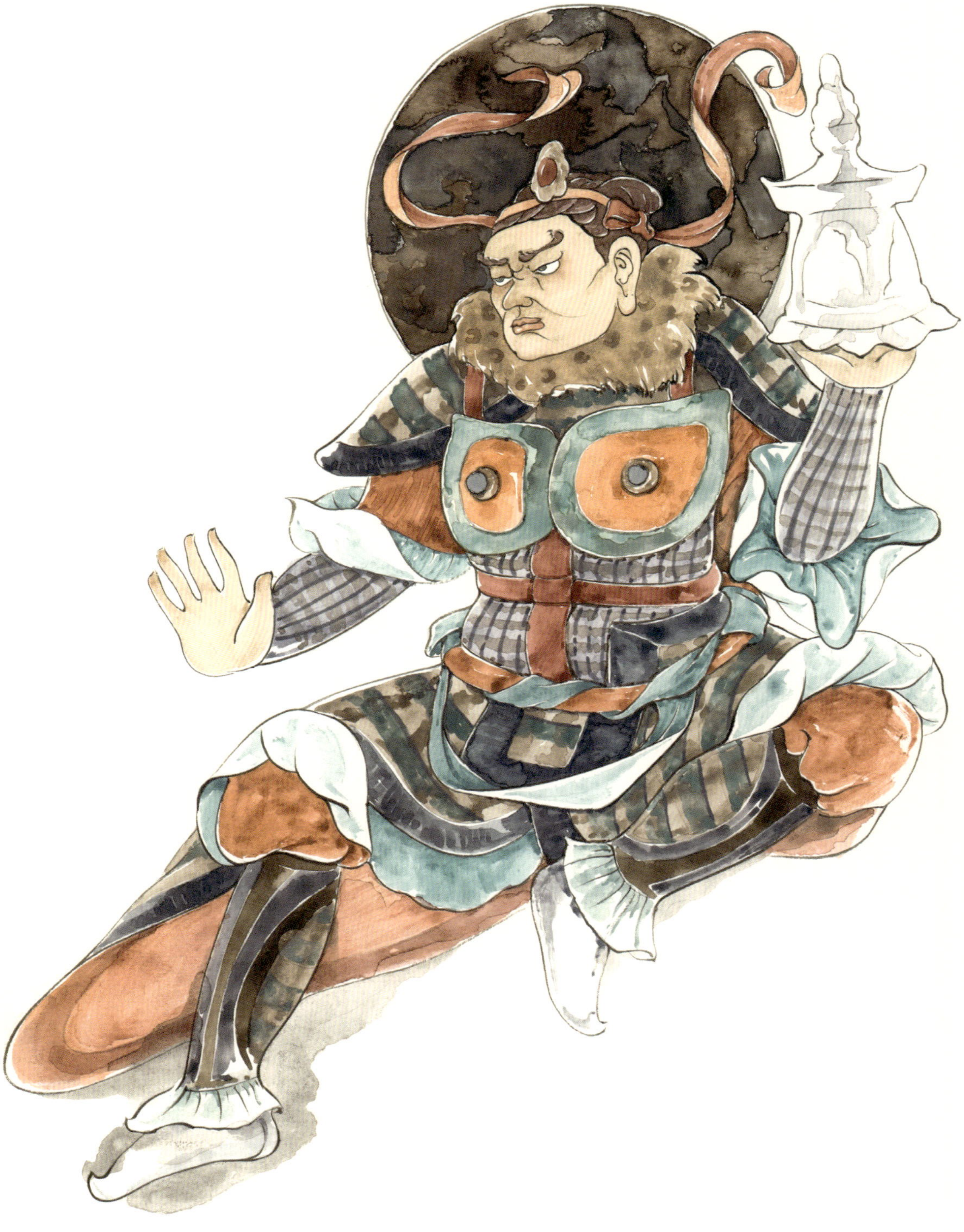

图：李迎军 Painted by: Li Yingjun

The horse rider's clothes
on the east wall of the main chamber
in Cave 444 dated to the high Tang
Dynasty at Mogao Grottoes

骑士服饰
莫高窟盛唐第444窟主室
东壁

在第444窟主室东壁，画师通过沉稳的色块与粗犷的笔触，将两身顶盔掼甲的骑士与肥健彪悍的骏马表现得威风凛凛、活灵活现。画面外侧手持短剑、纵马飞奔的骑士头戴兜鍪、盔缨高耸，身着披膊、护臂、身甲、腿裙、胫甲，腰系皮带，脚穿皮靴。从壁画线条中可以判断甲衣是通过无数细小的甲片串缀起来的，并且甲衣的整体造型紧窄适体，便于肢体灵活地运动。在这幅纵马出巡图中，骑士几乎全身都被甲胄严密防护起来，仅露出面部与双手，但马身却未着甲，人与马的装备形成了强烈的反差。同样的搭配还出现在莫高窟第156窟《张议潮统军出行图》的士兵卫队中、新疆吉木萨尔北庭古城佛寺壁画的出行图骑兵中，以及新疆吐鲁番出土的彩绘骑马武士俑上。

（文：李迎军）

On the east wall of the main chamber in Cave 444, the painter used dark color blocks and rough strokes to depict the two riders who wear helmets and ride on strong horses, looking confident and lively. The rider on the outer side is holding a short sword and running fast who wears a helmet which has high tassel, and shoulder covers, arm covers, body armor, waist belt, battle skirt, shin armor and leather boots. From the mural lines, it can be judged that the armor is made up of many small armor pieces strung up together, and the overall shape of the armor is tight and fit, which is convenient for limbs movement. In this painting, the rider is almost fully covered by armor, with only his face and hands being exposed, but the horse is not wearing armor. The equipments of the man and horse form a strong contrast, the same match also appears in the *Zhang Yichao Honor March* in Cave 156 of Mogao Grottoes, and the honor march cavalry in the Beiting ancient city Buddhist temple mural in Jimusar, Xinjiang, and the painted terracotta riders unearthed in Turpan, Xinjiang.

(Written by: Li Yingjun)

图：李迎军　Painted by: Li Yingjun

The painted sculpture
Bodhisattva's skirt pattern
on the south side of the west niche in Cave
444 dated to the high Tang Dynasty at
Mogao Grottoes

彩塑菩萨腰裙图案
莫高窟盛唐第444窟主室
西壁龛内南侧

彩塑菩萨的腰裙以蓝、绿、金三色大块面装饰，将这条图案装饰其间，红底呼应裙身色调，花纹由内而外节奏鲜明有绽放之美，外层的蓝色云头花瓣是莫高窟盛唐花纹的独特创造，不仅表现在服饰染织图案中，于洞窟藻井、壁面边饰中也常见这种造型，呈现出富丽、饱满的装饰效果。

第444窟这身彩塑菩萨的裙身部分，左右各有一竖列的截金图案作装饰，内部空间以小菱形装饰于每一个单元中，并与裙身上相邻的装饰图案之间以色带间隔，视觉效果疏密有致。描金、截金都是敦煌壁画中常用的装饰手法，点缀于色彩鲜明的菩萨服饰上，更显织物的华美。

（文：高雪）

The waist wrap of the painted sculpture Bodhisattva is decorated with three colors of blue, green and gold. This pattern decoration has red background which echoes with the skirt body, and the pattern has a distinct rhythm from the inside to the outside, with blooming beauty. The blue cloud head petals on the outer layer is a unique creation of the high Tang Dynasty pattern in Mogao Grottoes, which is not only reflected in the dyeing and weaving patterns of clothes, but also common in the caisson and wall decoration in caves; it presents a rich and full decorative effect.

The skirt of the painted Bodhisattva in Cave 444 is decorated with a vertical row of gold-cutting pattern on the left and right sides, and the internal spaces are decorated with small diamonds, which are separated from the adjacent decorative pattern on the skirt by color bands, with balanced visual effect. Gold tracing and gold cutting were commonly used decorative techniques in Dunhuang murals, and they were used on the brightly colored Bodhisattva clothes, showing the beauty of the fabrics.

(Written by: Gao Xue)

图二 高雪　Painted by: Gao Xue

莫高窟第444窟彩塑菩萨多用金色装饰，在这幅边饰图案中也采用金色勾线，花瓣层次感鲜明，以繁丽动人。作为边饰单元纹样的半花式花型较为单纯，以反复、连续的节奏表现边饰图案整体的美感。

中间这条图案是彩塑菩萨裙缘的石榴卷草，写意的石榴果实生长在叶片饱满的波状连续缠枝上，茎叶流畅饱满有张力，石榴卷草填满空间，作正反排列，与枝蔓上饱满的卷叶共呈风动摇曳之姿，色彩以青、绿、朱、褐、白构成，统一协调，节奏鲜明。

（文：高雪）

The painted sculpture Bodhisattva in Cave 444 of Mogao Grottoes used a lot of gold decoration. Gold lines are also used in this edge decoration. The petal layers are clear which looks complex and beautiful. The semi flower as the edge decoration unit is relatively simple, which expressed in a repeated and continuous way to show the overall beauty.

The pattern in the middle is the pomegranate scrolling vine pattern on the skirt trim of the painted sculpture Bodhisattva. The freehand pomegranate fruits grow on the wavy and continuous tangled branches with full leaves, and the stems and leaves are smooth, full and with tension. A cluster of pomegranate scrolling vine fills one space and is arranged in positive and negative way, which echoes with the full scrolling leaves on the branches. The colors are composed by blue, green, red, brown and white, which are unified, coordinated and rhythmic.

(Written by: Gao Xue)

彩塑佛弟子袖缘边饰，由单侧瓣叶片的造型作变化有序排列，图案起伏较小，排列规整，配色上不失唐代锦绣般的富丽感，冷暖相映，是严肃与美观并存的佛弟子服饰边饰图案。

（文：高雪）

The painted sculpture disciple's sleeve edge decoration is composed by orderly arranged single half leaves. The pattern curve range is small and the arrangement is regular, the color matching does not lose the rich feeling of the Tang Dynasty, with cold and warm colors complementing each other, which is a serious and beautiful disciple clothing edge decoration pattern.

(Written by: Gao Xue)

彩塑菩萨裙缘图案
莫高窟盛唐第444窟主室
西壁龛内南侧

The painted sculpture
Bodhisattva's skirt edge pattern
on the south side of the west niche in Cave 444
dated to the high Tang Dynasty at Mogao Grottoes

彩塑佛弟子袖缘
图案
莫高窟盛唐第444窟主
室西壁龛内南侧

The painted sculpture
disciple' sleeve edge
pattern
on the south side of the west niche
in Cave 444 dated to the high Tang
Dynasty at Mogao Grottoes

图：高雪 Painted by: Gao Xue

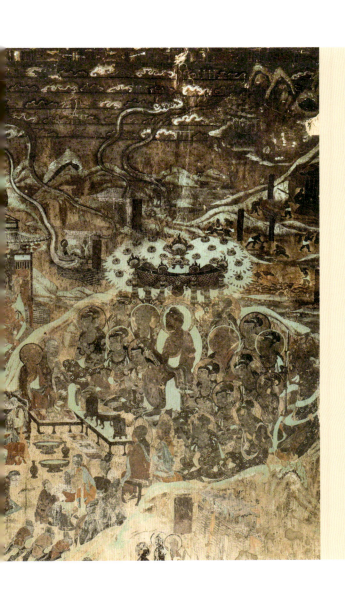

Dunhuang Mogao Grottoes Cave
445 of the High Tang
Dynasty

敦煌莫高窟盛唐

第445窟

　　第445窟是创建于盛唐时期的覆斗顶形窟，经五代、西夏重修。西壁开敞口龛，龛内存彩塑一跌坐佛、二弟子、二菩萨、一天王。龛顶存西夏残画。龛内西壁存婆罗门残画，南、北壁共存六弟子、六头光。龛沿绘卷草及一整二半团花边饰。龛外两侧台上各塑一菩萨。龛下存五代画供器及供养人。南壁绘阿弥陀经变一铺，下西夏绘男供养人数身。北壁绘弥勒经变一铺，下西夏绘女供养人数身。东壁门上绘地藏菩萨，门南绘千佛，门沿存五代壁画。甬道存五代壁画。

　　此窟北壁弥勒经变为盛唐代表作之一。其画面内容非常丰富，包括《佛说观弥勒菩萨上生兜率陀天经》与《佛说弥勒下生成佛经》，前者描绘了弥勒菩萨在兜率天宫修行的场景，后者则表现了弥勒下生成佛的画面，周围绘剃度图，一种七收，树上生衣，女子五百岁出嫁，人活八万四千岁的场景，表现了太平盛世的弥勒世界。壁画中的场景丰富生动，人物众多且身份不一，有着窄袖襦的女眷、着圆领袍衫的男子、着袈裟的僧人，人物面部表情、身体姿态各不相同，将场景氛围烘托得生动逼真，体现出画师在壁画的场景塑造上具有高超的水平。

（文：杨婧嫱）

Cave 445 is a truncated pyramidal ceiling cave built in the high Tang Dynasty, which was repaired in the Five Dynasties and the Western Xia Dynasty. A niche in the west wall contains painted sculptures of one sitting Buddha, two disciples, two Bodhisattvas and one Maharāja-deva. There are Western Xia painting remnant on the top of the niche, and the west niche wall has Brahman painting remnant, and the south and north walls have six disciples and six head lights in total. The niche is decorated with scrolling vine pattern and a whole and two halves round flower pattern decoration. Outside the niche, a painted sculpture Bodhisattva on both sides of the platforms. Below the niche are Five Dynasties offering utensils and donors. On the south wall is painted Amitabha Sutra illustration, and a number of male donor images dated to the Western Xia Dynasty on the lower part. Maitreya Sutra illustration on the north, and a number of female donor images dated to the Western Xia Dynasty on the lower part. Above the east door is painted with Ksitigarbha Bodhisattva, on the south side of the door is painted with Thousand Buddhas, and there are murals of the Five Dynasties along the door and in the corridor.

Maitreya Sutra illustration on the north wall in this cave is one of the representative works of the high Tang Dynasty. The paintings are rich in content, including Maitreyaparipṛcchā Sutra and Maitreyavyākaraṇa Sutra. The Maitreyaparipṛcchā Sutra depicts the scene of Maitreya Bodhisattva practicing in Tusita deva-world, while Maitreyavyākaraṇa Sutra depicts that Maitreya Bodhisattva comes to this world and becomes Buddha, which are surrounded by tonsure, harvesting seven times by one sowing, clothes growing on trees, women getting married at the age of 500, people living 84000 years, showing a peaceful and prosperous Maitreya world. The scenes in the murals are rich and vivid, which have many characters and different identities, like women in narrow sleeves Ru, men in round collar robes and monks in kasaya; they have different facial expressions and body postures, making the whole atmosphere vivid and lively, which reflects the painter's great ability in shaping scenes of mural painting.

(Written by: Yang Jingqiang)

The attendant
Bodhisattva's clothes
on the west side of the north wall in the main
chamber of Cave 445 dated to the high
Tang Dynasty at Mogao Grottoes

胁侍菩萨服饰
莫高窟盛唐第445窟主室
北壁西侧

盛唐第445窟主室北壁西侧的胁侍菩萨，其面相慈祥端庄，眉目含笑。左手轻扶璎珞，右手轻托莲花，身体微微倾向右侧，善跏趺坐姿态，脚踩莲花。

胁侍菩萨头上佩戴华丽的宝冠，冠体中间与左右有三颗宝石镶嵌，冠缯在两侧打成花结，臂钏与手镯造型结构相一致，颈饰与璎珞相连接经胸腹飘垂于身前。菩萨斜披深棕色络腋，络腋上点饰浅绿色细小的四瓣花纹，下身穿绣有淡灰色四瓣花纹的透体罗裙，裙下摆镶饰绿色贴边，腰间系有黑色腰裙，腰带上有珠串装饰。同时，腰部还围裹绿色宽带，并在腿部自然缠绕，其两端垂于两腿之间；肩披丝织络腋，络腋正面为棕色，背面为绿色，绕左右臂自然飘落，与腰部的宽带相呼应，给人以静中有动的视觉效果。

（文：刘元风）

The attendant Bodhisattva on the west side of the north wall in the main chamber of Cave 445 dated to the high Tang Dynasty, He has a kind and dignified face and smiling eyebrows, touching keyūra by left hand and holding a lotus with right hand. His body is slightly lean to right, in sitting posture and steps on lotus carpet.

The attendant Bodhisattva wears a magnificent lotus crown. In the middle of the crown and on the left and right are inlaid with three jade stones. The crown laces are tied in a flower knot on both sides. The armlets and bracelets style are in accordance with each other. The neck ornaments are connected with keyūra and hang in front of the chest and abdomen. The Bodhisattva is draped in dark brown Luoye on the upper body, which is dotted with light green, four-petaled flowers, and long skirt on the lower body, embroidered with light gray, four-petal flower pattern, with green welt at the hem of the skirt, and tied a black waist wrap with a string of beads on the belt. The waist is also wrapped in a green wide band, which is naturally wrapped around the legs and hangs down between the legs. The shoulders are covered with a Luoye, which is brown on the front and green on the back. The Luoye wraps around the left and right arms and falls naturally in response to the wide band around the waist, creating the visual effect of moving in stillness.

(Written by: Liu Yuanfeng)

图: 刘元风　Painted by: Liu Yuanfeng

The attendant
Bodhisattva's clothes
on the east side of the north wall in the main
chamber of Cave 445 dated to the high
Tang Dynasty at Mogao Grottoes

胁侍菩萨服饰
莫高窟盛唐第445窟主室
北壁东侧

　　盛唐第445窟主室北壁东侧的胁侍菩萨有一副温婉可人的面容，眉间画白毫。左手轻托莲花，右手放于膝部，坐姿舒展，脚踩莲花。上身斜披赭红色的络腋。络腋有精致的滚边装饰。下身着浅褐色宽绰的裙子，腰部围裹有绿色的宽带，与肩部披着的绿色和赭红色彩带融为一体。菩萨头束高髻，余发垂肩，佩戴化佛宝冠。冠体左右各有两颗绿宝石镶嵌，冠缯打结贴于耳后，自冠缯延伸下来的白色细带绕臂飘落，左右臂钏均有绿宝石镶嵌，与头冠装饰相协调。自项圈两侧垂下的长璎珞环膝缠绕。

　　从菩萨穿着的裙子可以清楚看出，盛唐以来女性的裙子造型越来越宽且长，呈现出飘然拂动的感觉，与盛唐现实生活中女性的裙子如出一辙，彰显了盛唐社会的开放和自由，特别体现出女性服饰上个性张扬的世俗风尚。

（文：刘元风）

　　The attendant Bodhisattva on the east side of the north wall in the main chamber of Cave 445 dated to the high Tang Dynasty, who has a gentle and pleasant face, with a Urna between His eyebrows. He holds a lotus flower lightly by left hand, rests the right hand on right knee, sits comfortably, steps on the lotus flower carpet. His upper body diagonally wears ocher red Luoye which has exquisite binding decoration. The lower body wears a wide skirt with a green wide band around waist, blending in with the green and ochre ribbons wrapped around Her shoulders. The Bodhisattva ties His hair into a high hair bun, the rest hair hanging down covers His shoulders, and wears a Buddha image crown. The crown has two emeralds on both sides respectively, and the crown laces are tied behind ears. The white ribbons extending from the crown laces fall around arms. The two armlets are inlaid with emeralds to match the crown, and the keyūra hanging from both sides of the collar surround the knees.

　　From the skirts worn by Bodhisattvas we can clearly see that since the high Tang Dynasty, women's skirts had become wider and longer, showing a feeling of fluttering. They are the same as women's skirts in reality during the high Tang Dynasty, highlighting the openness and freedom of the high Tang Dynasty society, especially the secular fashion of individuality in women's clothes.

(Written by: Liu Yuanfeng)

图：刘元风　Painted by: Liu Yuanfeng

The attendant
Bodhisattva's clothes
on the west side of the south wall in the main
chamber of Cave 445 dated to the high Tang
Dynasty at Mogao Grottoes

胁侍菩萨服饰
莫高窟盛唐第445窟主室
南壁西侧

此图为盛唐主室南壁西侧阿弥陀经变西侧底部的胁侍菩萨，有头光，宽额丰颐，弯眉长目，高鼻厚唇，容貌端庄秀美，神态怡然，双手捧青莲，身材修长，姿态典雅，赤脚立于宝座之上。

此身菩萨服饰华美精致，梳高髻，戴宝冠。菩萨斜挎条帛或称络腋衣，从左肩部斜垂至右边肋下。双肩搭饰带有小花纹样的披巾，也作霞帔，"唐代在盛行帔子的同时，还出现了霞帔，上施彩绘，或以五色纱罗制作，或印画各种图纹，又称画帔"。菩萨戴臂钏、手镯，腰部饰有璎珞。下着围腰和长裙，长裙似两层，围腰外裹于长裙之上并在身前打结，结带随裙子自然垂落，增加了飘逸感。此身菩萨的衣饰从色调上看，以蓝绿色为主调，披巾为红绿双面，饰有白色小花，随身形低垂飘拂，衬托身体，整体色调主次分明，轻重相宜。

（文：赵茜、吴波）

This painting shows a attendant Bodhisattva at the bottom of the west side in Amitabha Sutra illustration on the west side of the south wall in Cave 445 dated to the high Tang Dynasty. He has head light, wide forehead and full cheeks, curved eyebrows and long eyes, a high nose and thick lips, with dignified and beautiful appearance; He looks peaceful, and holds a cyan lotus by both hands, with slender and elegant posture, and stands on the stages barefoot.

This Bodhisattva's dress is gorgeous and exquisite, He combs a high hair bun and wears a crown, a silk scarf or so-called Luoye hangs diagonally from the left shoulder to the right rib. The silk shawl with small flower pattern on the shoulders is also known as Xiapei, "Silk scarf was popular in the Tang Dynasty, also with Xiapei, which has painted pattern, or made by five-color gauze, or printed and painted various patterns, also known as Huapei." He wears armlets, bracelets, and His waist is decorated with keyūra. Waist wrap and long skirt on the lower body, the long skirt seems like having two layers, the waist wrap is wrapped on the long skirt and knotted in front of the body. The knot ends fall naturally with the skirt, increasing the sense of elegance. In terms of color, the Bodhisattva's clothes uses blue-green as the main tone, the scarf is red and green two sides, which is decorated with small white flowers, fluttering down with the body shape to set off the body. The overall color is clear in primary and secondary, and well balanced in darkness and lightness.

(Written by: Zhao Xi, Wu Bo)

The shavers' clothes
on the west side of the north wall in the main
chamber of Cave 445 dated to the high Tang
Dynasty at Mogao Grottoes

剃度者服饰
莫高窟盛唐第445窟主室
北壁西侧

盛唐第445窟主室北壁西侧剃度图为《佛说弥勒下生成佛经》中的主要内容之一，此剃度图又是相关几组剃度场景的其中之一。

画面主要表现为宫廷妇女剃度出家的现实场面。其中，法师持剃刀削发（其服饰为上身穿棕色的大袖衫，下着绿色落地长裙，外披土黄色袈裟，袈裟内里为蓝色，脚上穿笏头履）；被剃度者正襟危坐（其服饰为上身穿绿色襦，下着高腰阔裙，裙上有精致的花枝点缀其间，脚穿翘头履，身披白色围布）；侍婢双手轻奉剃度发具（柳条编制的筥笭）跪地承接被剃度者的落发（婢女头梳双丫髻，上身穿圆领袍，腰系黑色带子，并有珠串装饰，脚上穿布履）；另有一比丘尼双手撑起袈裟遮挡（比丘尼上身穿交领偏衫，领子镶有贴边，外穿黄色袈裟）。剃度的人物面部表情各有不同，或认真、或虔诚、或恭敬、或安详，将一幅现实生活中削发为尼的场景刻画得生动鲜活、惟妙惟肖。

（文：刘元风）

The tonsure picture on the west side of the north wall in the main chamber of Cave 445 dated to the high Tang Dynasty is one of the main contents of the Maitreyavyākaraṇa Sutra illustration. This tonsure picture is one of several groups of shaving scenes.

This picture mainly shows the scene of court women getting tonsured. Among them, the master is holding a razor and shaving (she dresses a large-sleeved brown Ru on the upper body, a green long skirt on the lower body, an earth yellow kasaya covers the whole body, the kasaya lining is blue, and board-head shoes on the feet); the person who is being shaved is sitting upright (she wears a green wide-sleeved Ru on upper body, a high waist wide skirt on the lower body, dotted delicate flower branches pattern on the skirt, up-head shoes on her feet and white cloth around body); the maid gently holds the shaving tool (a basket made of wicker) and kneels down to take the falling hair of the shaved person (the maid has Shuangya hair bun, wears a round collar robe on the upper body, ties a black belt around waist, which is decorated with beads, and cloth shoes on her feet); a Bhiksuni holds up a piece of drapery by both hands (the Bhiksuni wears a "V" shaped collar shirt with welt on the collar and a yellow cloak outside). The facial expressions of these characters are different, either serious, pious, or respectful, peaceful, which vividly depicted a scene of women getting tonsured and becoming nuns in real life.

(Written by: Liu Yuanfeng)

图：刘元风

Painted by: Liu Yuanfeng

The shavers' clothes
on the north wall of the main chamber in
Cave 445 dated to the high Tang Dynasty
at Mogao Grottoes

剃度者服饰
莫高窟盛唐第445窟主室
北壁

盛唐第445窟主室北壁的剃度图场面宏大、人物众多，画师通过帷幕等道具将剃度仪式的六个单元有序串联，仪式以儴伝王与王妃为代表分列两厢，被剃度的国王、王妃、太子、大臣等人与执行剃度的比丘、比丘尼，以及佞臣、侍者各司其职，画师不仅将所有人物的身份、性别、职能准确地表达出来，还通过各异的肢体语言与惟妙惟肖的神态传达出不同人物的内心世界。

这一场景的中心是一位神情虔诚、正在接受剃度的老者。他正襟危坐，双手扶在膝上，穿着红色交领半臂上衣，内衬的绿袍下露出白色长裤，脚穿圆形翘头履。为老者剃度的比丘神态平和安详，身着袈裟持刀做剃发状。戴幞头的侍者跪在老者身侧，双手托着盛装老者剃下长发的藤编托盘。后侧的比丘张开手臂、双手展开袈裟，头却望向了女眷剃度的另一个方向，通过肢体语言建立起与其他帷幕单元的关联。

（文：李迎军）

The tonsure scene on the north wall of the main chamber in Cave 445 dated to the high Tang Dynasty has a grand arrangement and many characters. The painter orderly connected the six units of the tonsure ceremony through curtains and other props. The ceremony is divided into two groups, represented by the king and the princess. The shaved king, princess, prince, ministers and others and the Bhiksu and Bhiksuni who perform the shaving, as well as the courtiers and waiters all suit their identities. All the characters' gender and roles are accurately expressed by the painter, and the inner world of different characters are vividly conveyed through different body languages and expressions.

At the center of this scene is an old man who looks pious and undergoing shaving. He sits upright, hands on knees, wearing a red cross collar half sleeves shirt, white trousers under the green inner robe, and round upturned head shoes on feet. The Bhiksu who is shaving the old man looks calm and peaceful, dressed in kasaya and holding a knife to shave. The servant with Fu hat kneels on the side of the old man, holding a rattan tray to catch the old man's long hair by both hands. At the back, the Bhiksu opens his arms and spread the kasaya with both hands, but his head looks at other direction to the female group, which established the connection with other unit through body language.

(Written by: Li Yingjun)

图：李迎军　Painted by: Li Yingjun

The shavers' clothes

on the north wall of the main chamber in
Cave 445 dated to the high Tang Dynasty
at Mogao Grottoes

剃度者服饰

莫高窟盛唐第445窟主室

北壁

这是剃度图画面左侧僧侍王的王妃、女眷们剃度出家的场面，在一个帷幕内由比丘尼为王室女眷剃度。比丘尼身着袈裟，面带微笑，手持剃刀小心翼翼地为女眷剃度。正在接受剃度的女眷穿着红色窄袖襦与绿色长裙，双手虔诚合十端坐在凳子上。身后的侍女梳双髻，着男式圆领襕衫（一侧领子翻下），持盘恭敬伺候。三个人物身份明确、形态各异、个性鲜明、惟妙惟肖。

画面中描绘的"女着男装"是盛唐时期的流行时尚，被称为"丈夫靴衫"或"幞头靴衫"。太平公主曾经穿着紫衫玉带皂罗折上巾在皇家筵上歌舞，《新唐书·车服志》中也记载："宫人从驾……有衣男子衣而靴，如奚、契丹之服。"除了这铺壁画中表现的仕女穿着男士圆领襕衫外，当时还有戴男子的幞头、穿男式乌皮靴等女着男装的穿法。

（文：李迎军）

This painting is the king's princesses shaving and becoming nuns on the left side of the tonsure scene. Behind the curtain, a Bhiksuni shaves the royal woman who is dressed in kasaya and smiling, carefully shaving those women's hair by a razor. The woman who is being shaved wears red narrow sleeved Ru and green long skirt, sitting on a stool with her hands devoutly folded. The maid behind her combs double hair bun and wears a man's round collar shirt (the collar on one side turned down) and serves respectfully with a plate. The three characters have clear identities, different forms, distinct personalities and vivid images.

"Women wearing men's clothes" depicted in the painting was a popular fashion in the high Tang Dynasty, which was called "men's boots and clothes" or "Fu hat, boots and clothes". Princess Taiping once sang and danced at the royal banquet wearing purple clothes, jade belt, black folded headdress. It is also recorded in *Xin Tang Shu · Che Fu Zhi*: "Palace servants... with men's clothes and boots, looking like Xi and Khitan's clothes." In addition to the servants wearing men's clothes in this mural, there are also women wearing men's Fu hat and black leather boots.

(Written by: Li Yingjun)

图": 李迎军　Painted by: Li Yíngjun

The attendant's clothes
on the north wall of the main chamber in
Cave 445 dated to the high Tang Dynasty at
Mogao Grottoes

侍从服饰
莫高窟盛唐第445窟主室
北壁

在第445窟主室北壁，盛唐画师以周密的布局、细腻的表达再现了
"儴佉王率众剃度图"这一场面巨大、人物纷杂的场景，除了剃度的中
心人物儴佉王、王妃、比丘法师、比丘尼法师等人之外，周围的众多侍
臣、侍者、比丘同样千姿百态、神态各异、惟妙惟肖。这组在剃度仪式
上成排侍立的大臣共有五人，他们神情虔诚恭敬，或拱手、或托物，躬
身侍立在剃度团队后边。五大臣均戴进贤冠，穿交领大袖襦，腰中系革
带，下着白裳。五位侍臣中，有三人穿红色襦、二人穿白色襦，五人的
服色按红白色彩间隔的方式排列，五件上襦的领口、衣襟、袖口均有异
色宽缘装饰。

（文：李迎军）

On the north wall of the main chamber in Cave 445, the painter of the
high Tang Dynasty depicted the huge and complex scene of "the king with his
people get tonsured" with careful layout and exquisite expression. In addition
to the main figures such as the king, princess, Bhiksu and Bhiksuni, other
figures like courtiers, waiters and Bhiksu also have various postures, different
expressions and lifelike. This group of five ministers stand in line at the
shaving ceremony, they look pious and respectful, some hold hands together,
some hold objects and bow behind the shaving team. All the five ministers
wear Jin Xian hat, large sleeves Ru with cross collar, leather belt around the
waist and white clothes. Among the five courtiers, three of them wear red Ru
and two wear white Ru. The clothes of the five are arranged in the way of red
and white color alternating. The necklines, trims and cuffs of the five upper
Ru are decorated with wide edges with different colors.

(Written by: Li Yingjun)

The soldier's clothes
on the north wall of the main chamber
in Cave 445 dated to the high Tang
Dynasty at Mogao Grottoes

兵宝服饰
莫高窟盛唐第445窟主室
北壁

北壁的巨型弥勒经变画的下方绘有佛前儴佉王奉献七宝的故事，七宝原为古印度神话中转轮王福力所生之宝，包括：轮宝、象宝、马宝、珠宝、女宝、藏宝、兵宝。其中，兵宝绘一武士，女宝绘一仕女……

壁画中绘于象宝身侧的兵宝手托莲花台，莲上宝珠火光炎炎。他头戴兜鍪，身着两裆甲，腿的下部与脚都被象宝遮挡，绘画整理时根据同时期甲胄造型补充了胫甲与战靴。兵宝头戴的兜鍪由头盔、顿项两个主要部分组成，坚实的半球形头盔用于保护头颅，头盔下边连接的是保护脸、颈、肩部位的顿项。顿项通常用皮革或布匹做顿底，上面钉满甲片以起到防护作用。自头盔垂下的顿项还可以向上翻起形成上折，甚至三折的效果，图中兵宝头戴兜鍪的顿项就是上折的状态。这种顿项上折的兜鍪造型在中晚唐频繁出现，在盛唐的盔甲造型中较少见。

（文：李迎军）

Below the giant Maitreya Sutra illustration on the north wall is the story of the seven treasures offered by the King in front of Buddha. The seven treasures were originally the treasures born from Cākravartirāja blessings in ancient Indian mythology, including wheel treasure, elephant treasure, horse treasure, jewelry treasure, woman treasure, box treasure and soldier treasure. Among them, soldier treasure is painted into a warrior, woman treasure is painted into a lady.

In the mural, the soldier treasure holding a lotus base in hands is painted on the side of the elephant treasure, and the precious jewel on the lotus is burning. He wears helmet and Liangdang armor, the lower part of his legs and feet are blocked by elephant treasure. When doing the painting, his shin armor and boots are added according to the armor design of the same period. The helmet worn by soldier treasure consists of two main parts: helmet and neck armor. The solid hemispherical helmet is used to protect the head, and the neck armor protecting the face, neck and shoulders is connected with the helmet in the lower part. Neck armor was usually made of leather or cloth, which is nailed with armor pieces for protection. The neck armor hanging from the helmet can also be turned up to form an upward folding or even three foldings effect. In the painting, the neck armor of the soldier treasure is in an upward folding shape. This kind of upturned neck armor appeared frequently in the middle and late Tang Dynasty, but it was rare in the high Tang Dynasty.

(Written by: Li Yingjun)

The woman treasure's clothes
on the north wall of the main chamber in Cave 445 dated to the high Tang Dynasty at Mogao Grottoes

女宝服饰
莫高窟盛唐第445窟主室
北壁

在佛前傩伎王奉献七宝图中，女宝绘于说法弥勒及供宝香案下方，她双手虔诚地托着莲花台、宝珠，肩若削成、腰如约素、翩若惊鸿，这"妙入毫巅"的身姿与曹植在《洛神赋》中描绘的神女如出一辙——"扬轻袿之猗靡兮，翳修袖以延伫""践远游之文履，曳雾绡之轻裾"。女宝身着广袖襦、长裙、围裳，装饰在围裳边缘的长飘带称"襳"，衣裙上的燕尾状装饰称"髾"，长长的襳、髾随着走动飘扬飞舞，正是典型的魏晋时期女装"蜚襳垂髾"的形象，甚至这身女宝的整体造型与东晋顾恺之的《列女仁智图》中人物的角度与动势几乎一致。褒衣博带、襳髾飘逸的服饰是魏晋审美精神的体现，在莫高窟盛唐时期的这铺壁画中，凌波微步、飘忽若神的风姿满足了唐人对佛国世界的想象。

（文：李迎军）

In the painting of the seven treasures being offered by the the king in front of Buddha, the woman treasure is painted below the Maitreya Buddha and the table for offering treasures. She holds a lotus base and jewel in her hands. Her shoulders are well shaped, with thin waist, looks graceful. This so beautiful and detailed body is the same as that of the goddess depicted by Cao Zhi in *Luo Shen Fu* (Nymph of the Luo River) — "From time to time, she raises her clothes flying with the wind, covers the light long sleeves, looks into the distance, and stands for a long time." "She wears patterned shoes and misty like trained dress." The woman treasure wears a wide sleeved Ru, long skirt and Weichang. The long streamers decorated on the edge of the Weishang is called "Xian", and the swallow tail decoration on the skirt is called "Shao". The long Xian and Shao flutter and move along with walking, which is the typical image of "flying Xian and draping Shao" in women's clothes in the Wei and Jin Dynasties, even the overall shape and angle of this woman treasure is almost the same as the figures in Gu Kaizhi's *Lie Nv Ren Zhi Tu* in the eastern Jin Dynasty. The wide clothes and long belts, flying Xian and Shao are the embodiment of the aesthetic spirit of the Wei and Jin Dynasties. In this mural of the high Tang Dynasty in Mogao Grottoes, the graceful walking and celestial feeling met the imagination of the Tang people about the Buddhist world.

(Written by: Li Yingjun)

图：李迎军　Painted by: Li Yíngjūn

The Bhiksu's clothes
in the central part of the north wall in the
main chamber of Cave 445 dated to the
high Tang Dynasty at Mogao Grottoes

比丘服饰
莫高窟盛唐第445窟主室
北壁中部

此图为盛唐第445窟主室北壁弥勒经变中跪拜的两位比丘，绘于经变的中部。

比丘（梵文Bhiksu），又称"苾刍"，含有净乞士、破烦恼、出家人、净持戒、能怖魔五义，是出家为佛弟子、受具足戒者男子的统称。图中的两位小弟子均穿袈裟，左边弟子穿红色格纹田相袈裟，内着绿色僧祇支；右边弟子的袈裟为赭红色，在背部还有蓝色布帛搭饰，内着灰色僧祇支。袈裟"佛教之法服。敦煌彩塑、壁画中的佛陀、罗汉、僧侣皆着之。其形制为长布不加裁剪，衣法裹身"。而田相袈裟为袈裟的一种，因"袈裟之竖横割截而不缝缀，似田畔者，名田相衣"。其内，两位小弟子均着僧祇支，即"僧人之覆肩衣、衬衣"。他们虽背对观者，仅见侧面轮廓，但还是能从其肢体语言中感受到他们正在虔诚地倾听。

（文：赵茜、吴波）

This painting shows two kneeling Bhiksu in the middle of Maitreya Sutra illustration on the north wall in the main chamber of Cave 445 dated to the high Tang Dynasty.

Bhiksu is a sanskrit word which contains four meanings: wishing Pure Land, get rid of troubles, tonsured, keeping precepts, and being able to defeat demons. It is a general term for monks as Buddhist disciples and men with sufficient precepts. The two little disciples in the painting are all wearing kasaya. The disciple on the left is wearing a red checks field pattern kasaya with green Sankaksika inside. The kasaya of the little disciple on the right is ocare red, and there are blue cloth and silk decorations on the back, with gray Sankaksika inside. Kasaya is "the Dharma suit which is worn by Buddhas, Arhats and monks in Dunhuang painted sculptures and murals. Its shape is a long piece of cloth without trimming, wrapped around the body." The field pattern kasaya is a kind of kasaya, because "the kasaya is cut horizontally and vertically without stitching, which looks like fields, so named as Tianxiang clothes." Inside, the two little disciples wear Sankaksika, that is "monk's inner clothes or shirts." Although the two little disciples turned their backs to the viewers, we could still feel that they are listening Dharma piously from their body language.

(Written by: Zhao Xi, Wu Bo)

图：吴波

Painted by: Wu Bo

The musician's clothes
on the south wall of the main chamber in
Cave 445 dated to the high Tang Dynasty
at Mogao Grottoes
伎乐天服饰
莫高窟盛唐第445窟主室
南壁

据《祇洹寺图经》记载："次北大院名为佛经行所，南开一门，中有大堂。前二珠柱，帝释所作，昼夜常照""有两部天乐，帝释所施，乐器纯以七宝作之，形小前乐，天诸童子六时常鼓"。这一场景在莫高窟第445窟主室南壁的阿弥陀经变画中有生动展现：画面中主尊佛的左右两侧，有两座大型宝幢，宝幢的平台上东西两边各排列一组六身伎乐天人。东边一组演奏横笛、箜篌、琵琶、排箫、笙、铙，西边一组演奏羯鼓、答腊鼓、鼗鼓、鸡娄鼓、横笛、铙。

本图选取的是东侧乐队中凭栏演奏横笛的伎乐天人。她头梳髻、戴宝冠、上身半裸、戴颈圈与手镯、肩搭披帛、腰束长裙；双手持笛，头歪向一侧，专注地吹奏横笛，身体自然地扭动成"S"形，韵律优美和谐。

（文：李迎军）

According to *Qi Huan Si Tu Jing* (Qi Huan Temple book with illustration), "The north courtyard is called Buddha walking place, with gate facing to south, a lobby with two front columns, which were made by Śakro devānām indrah and illuminated day and night", "There are two groups of heavenly musicians, which were given by Śakro devānām indrah, and the musical instruments are made of seven treasures, small but with great sound, and celestial children playing them all the time". This scene is vividly presented in Amitabha Sutra illustration on the south wall of the main chamber in Cave 445 of Mogao Grottoes: in the painting, there are two large treasure buildings on the left and right sides of the main Buddha. On the platform of the treasure building, a group of six musicians are arranged on the east and west sides respectively. The east group plays horizontal flute, Konghou, Pipa, Panpipe, Sheng and Cymbals, and the west group plays Jie drum, Dala drum, Tao drum, Jilou drum, horizontal flute and Cymbals.

This painting selects the musician who plays a horizontal flute against the railing in the east band. She combs a hair bun, wears a crown; the upper body is half naked, necklace and bracelets, silk scarf on her shoulders and a long skirt on the lower body. She holds a flute with both hands, tilts her head to one side, and focuses on playing the horizontal flute. Her body naturally twists into an "S" shape, looks beautiful and harmonious.

(Written by: Li Yingjun)

图：李迎军 Painted by: Li Yíngjun

　　第446窟是创建于盛唐时期的覆斗顶形窟，经五代重修。主室窟顶残毁，仅残存垂幔及千佛一角。西壁开敞口龛，龛内存彩塑一跌坐佛、二弟子、二菩萨、二天王。龛内西壁浮塑佛光，四周共绘二菩萨、六弟子、六头光。龛沿口内侧绘龟背纹、外侧绘方格纹边饰。龛外南侧、北侧分别绘卢舍那佛和药师佛。南壁绘观无量寿经变一铺，北壁绘弥勒经变一铺，东壁及甬道存五代壁画。

　　此窟几身彩塑虽出现了一定的变色，但服饰结构清晰。彩塑上的服饰图案具有一定典型性，除了有沿袭早期的几何纹外，还有盛唐流行的卷草纹样。服饰上的唐代卷草纹，也称"唐草"，花叶卷曲优美，疏密有度，极具生命力，体现出画工对自然的观察及超高的手绘技巧，烘托出盛唐富丽堂皇、气象万千的艺术风格。

（文：杨婧嫱）

Cave 446 is a truncated pyramidal ceiling cave built in the high Tang Dynasty, which has been repaired in the Five Dynasties. The ceiling of the main chamber was destroyed, only the valance and a corner of Thousand Buddhas remained. A niche in the west wall contains painted sculptures of one sitting Buddha, two disciples, two Bodhisattvas and two Maharāja-devas. Buddha light relief on the west niche wall, surrounded by two Bodhisattvas, six disciples and six head lights. The inner side of the niche edge is painted with turtle back pattern and the outer side is painted with checks pattern decoration. The south and north sides outside the niche are painted with Vairocana Buddha and Bhaisajyaguru Buddha respectively. The south wall is painted with Amitayurdhyana Sutra illustration, on the north wall is painted with Maitreya Sutra illustration. There are murals of Five Dynasties on the east wall and corridor.

Although several painted sculptures' colors in this cave have changed to some extent, their clothing structures are clear. The dress patterns on the painted sculptures are typical, in addition to the geometric patterns in the early stage, there are also scrolling vine pattern popular in the high Tang Dynasty. The scrolling vine pattern of the Tang Dynasty also known as "Tang grass", with beautiful curly flowers and leaves, density and sparseness are balanced and with great vitality, reflecting the painter's observation of nature and great hand painting skills, which sets off the magnificent and colorful artistic style of the high Tang Dynasty.

(Written by: Yang Jingqiang)

The painted sculpture attendant
Bodhisattva's clothes
on the north side of the west niche in the main
chamber of Cave 446 dated to the high Tang
Dynasty at Mogao Grottoes

彩塑胁侍菩萨服饰
莫高窟盛唐第446窟主室
西壁龛内北侧

盛唐第446窟主室西壁龛内北侧彩塑胁侍菩萨，头束高髻，面容端庄华美，秀目朱唇，额上有白毫，头后有火焰纹头光，内饰半团花纹样。菩萨上身袒裸，皮肤光洁如玉，跣足站于莲花台上，左臂贴体下垂，右手持莲叶和莲蕾；下身穿浅褐色多褶形曳地长裙，其多彩的蔓草花纹呈波浪状装饰在裙子的相应部位，颇具流动性的节奏感。腰部系绿色的腰裙且镶饰荷叶形贴边。长长的璎珞自项圈两侧向下垂落并双膝缠绕，由肩部披下的黄色彩带与裙子相映成趣而飘落左右。

值得指出的是，此尊彩塑菩萨在艺术处理上，其形体丰腴优雅，微微隆起的小腹圆润而柔美，映照其母性的光辉和圣洁，散发着盛唐时期彩塑艺术所特有的艺术感染力和无穷魅力。

（文：刘元风）

The painted sculpture attendant Bodhisattva on the north side of the west niche in the main chamber of Cave 446 dated to the high Tang Dynasty. He has a high hair bun, a dignified and beautiful face, clean eyes and red lips, a round Urna on the forehead, a flame pattern halo behind His head which has half round flower pattern. The Bodhisattva stands on the lotus platform with upper body bared, and skin is as smooth as jade. Her left arm lays close to body, holding a lotus leaf and a lotus bud in right hand, wearing a light brown multi-pleated long skirt, the colorful creeper pattern is decorated in the corresponding parts of the skirt, with quite a sense of rhythm of mobility. The waist is tied with a green waist wrap and trimmed with a flounce-shaped welt. The long keyūra hangs down from the sides of the collar and winds around the knees, and yellow ribbons fall down from the shoulders to match with the skirt.

It is worth pointing out that in the artistic treatment of this painted sculpture Bodhisattva, the body shape is plump and elegant, slightly raised lower abdomen, round and soft, reflecting maternal brilliance and holiness, emitting the unique artistic appeal and infinite charm of the painted sculpture art of the high Tang Dynasty.

(Written by: Liu Yuanfeng)

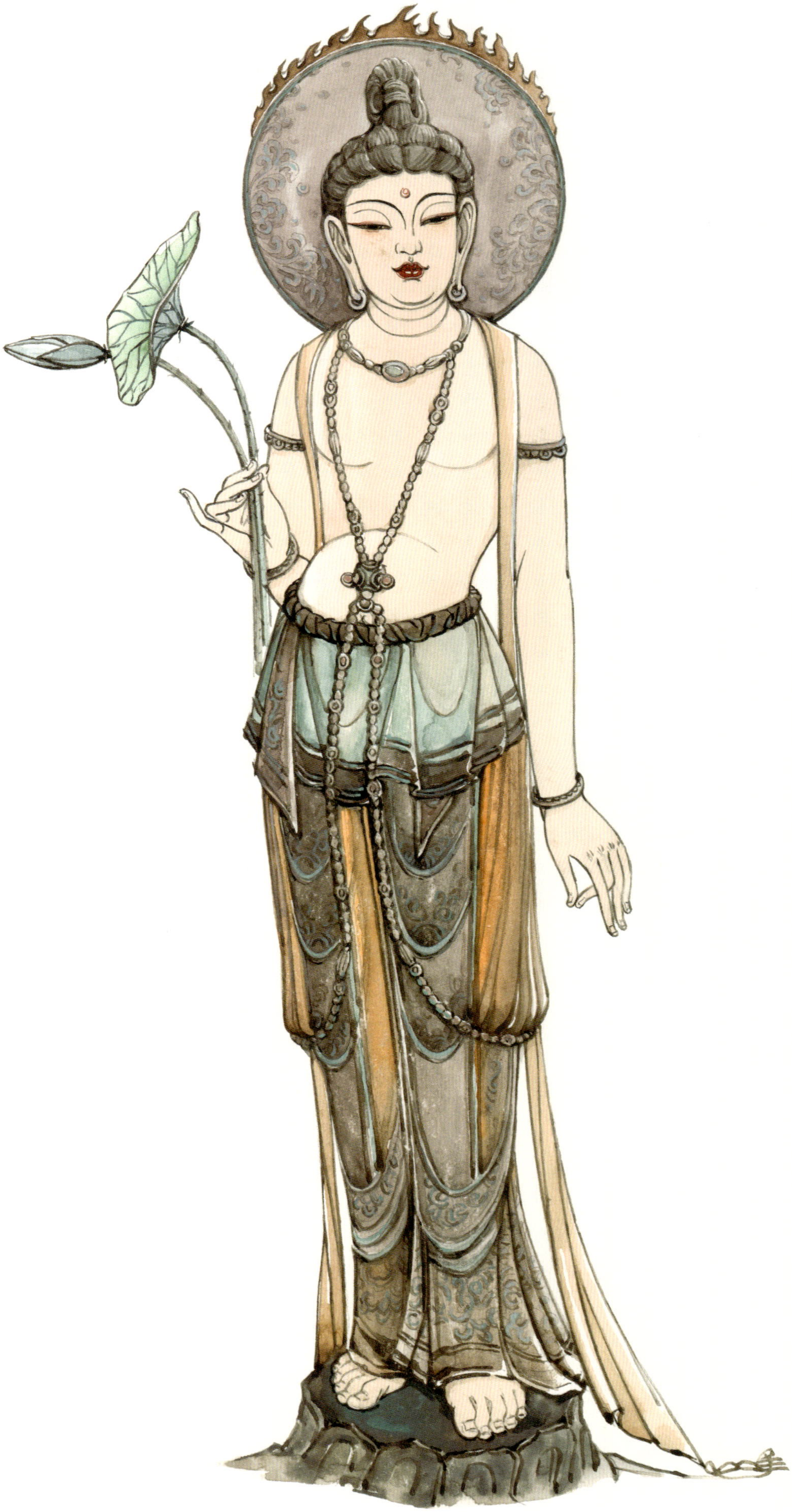

图：刘元风 Painted by: Liu Yuanfeng

The painted sculpture attendant Bodhisattva's skirt pattern

彩塑胁侍菩萨裙子图案

莫高窟盛唐第446窟主室西壁龛内北侧

main chamber of Cave 446 dated to the high Tang Dynasty at Mogao Grottoes on the north side of the west niche in the

这组图案装饰于彩塑胁侍菩萨的裙身正面，单元花型用单片大花瓣做底，内绘多瓣小莲花，花心处以石榴造型点缀，与本窟整窟的装饰主题相呼应，下方两片叶瓣相对而翻卷，竖排构图一整二破，破开的两半相邻托住完整花型，蓝、绿二色交替排列，与背景色冷暖调和，形成亦花亦叶的效果。

这组石榴卷草纹装饰于菩萨的裙边，双枝石榴、单簇卷草茎叶交错，叶片舒展，叶端顺应叶片形态自然翻转，石榴果实写意化的表现为多种形态，有单独和叠压两种关系，饱满的果实外形和写意的籽粒装饰成为唐代石榴图案的重要识别特征，富有丰沛的生命韵律，是唐代对外开放、兼收并蓄、与外来文化交流融合的象征。作为裙饰的边缘装饰，在卷草图案的上下两侧散布着方向各异的小叶卷草，叶端宽阔多裂，叶片后部回卷，填充负形空间，形成独特韵律。

（文：高雪）

This pattern is decorated on the painted sculpture attendant Bodhisattva the front side of the dress. The pattern unit is composed by single large petals as the frame, with many small lotus flowers being painted inside. The flower center is decorated with pomegranate shape, which echoes with the decorative theme of the whole cave. The lower two leaf petals are rolled opposite to each other, and the vertical composition is one whole and two halves. The two halves hold the complete flower shape adjacent to each other. The cyan and green colors are arranged alternately, which is harmonious with the background color, looking like flowers or leaves.

This pomegranate scrolling vine pattern is decorated on the skirt edge of the Bodhisattva. Two pomegranate branches, a single cluster scrolling vine stem and leaves are alternative arranged and stretching. The leaf ends turn naturally in accordance with the leaf shape, the freehand expression of pomegranate fruits are in a variety of forms, with separate and overlapping relations. The full fruit shape and freehand seeds decoration have become important features of pomegranate pattern in the Tang Dynasty, full of life rhythm, which is a symbol of the Tang Dynasty opening to the outside world, inclusiveness and integration with foreign cultures. As skirt edge decoration, small scrolling leaves in different directions are scattered on the upper and lower parts of the scrolling vine pattern, the leaf tips are wide and split, and the base of the leaves are rolled backward to fill the space to form a unique rhythm.

(Written by: Gao Xue)

图··高雪　Painted by: Gao Xue

The painted sculpture
Maharāja-deva's armor pattern
on the south side of the west niche in Cave 446
dated to the high Tang Dynasty at Mogao Grottoes

彩塑天王铠甲图案
莫高窟盛唐第446窟主室
西壁龛内南侧

这身唐代天王铠甲，整身呈蓝绿主色调。上身相对彩绘石榴卷草纹，果实造型饱满、线条流畅，半圆形护腹甲外边缘施金色，其上装饰多个内绘石榴花型的饱满花瓣，并以龟背纹间隔。图案由上至下，分别是胸前横直两条束甲襻交叉纵束，将图案对称分隔，对称的胸甲内绘有两朵饱满的宝相花，束甲襻两侧对称绘有石榴卷草纹。

（文：高雪）

This Tang Dynasty Maharāja-deva's armor has blue-green as the main color. The upper body is painted with pomegranate scrolling vine pattern; the fruits shape are full and the lines are smooth. The outer edge of the semicircular belly armor is painted with gold and decorated with a number of full petals that have pomegranate flower shape inside and separated by turtle back pattern. From top to bottom, the pattern is divided symmetrically by two transverse and vertical cords in front of the chest. Two full Baoxiang flowers are painted on the symmetrical chests, and pomegranate scrolling vine pattern is painted symmetrically on both sides of the cord.

(Written by: Gao Xue)

图'': 高雪　Painted by: Gao Xue

The painted sculpture
Maharāja-deva's battle skirt
and shin armor pattern
on the south side of the west wall in the main
chamber of Cave 446 dated to the high Tang
Dynasty at Mogao Grottoes

彩塑天王甲裙裙
身、胫甲图案
莫高窟盛唐第446窟主室
西壁龛内南侧

　　彩塑天王的甲裙裙身用小甲片规律编制，长条形甲片造型独特，上缘有饱满的下翻云头、内嵌小花。甲片下方左右对称装饰多枝双头的石榴纹，共同构成一幅饱满富丽的天王铠甲服饰图案。袍肚主体以单独花型作适合纹样填充。每一间隔区域由丰富的装饰花纹填充，值唐代经济文化发达之际，装饰风气日盛，宝相花应运而生，装饰于彩塑天王胸甲上，用合瓣、分瓣两种方式丰富了层次；卷草茎叶缠绕，承托石榴纹，结构起伏交织，线条流畅自如，共同构成这幅美观豪华、注重装饰的天王铠甲服饰图案，反映出唐朝国力鼎盛、天下承平的气象。

　　彩塑天王小腿胫甲部位的彩绘图案两侧对称，图上所绘为单侧展开图案，以两侧条带为边，表现在塑像上可围合成前后对应的护腿，单侧以金色条带斜向连接，以此为界分隔出上下两个装饰空间，上下各彩绘一个单独卷草纹，设色与整身彩塑色调相适应。

（文：高雪）

　　The lower body of the Maharāja-deva's armor is compiled by small armor pieces regularly. The strip armor pieces have unique shape. The upper edge of the armor piece has full downward scrolling cloud pattern and embedded with flower pattern. The lower part of the armor piece is symmetrically decorated with pomegranate pattern with multiple branches and double heads, which together form a full and rich pattern of Maharāja-deva's armor. The main body of the robe belly is an independent pattern filled with suitable decorations. Each interval area is filled with rich decorative patterns. At the time of the economic and cultural development heyday of the Tang Dynasty, the decorative atmosphere was booming, and Baoxiang flower pattern came into being. It is decorated on the painted sculpture Maharāja-deva's chest armor, enriching the layers in two ways: combined petals and split petals; the winding stems and leaves of scrolling vine support the pomegranate pattern. The structure is wavy and intertwined, and the lines are smooth and free. Together, they form this beautiful and decorative pattern on Maharāja-deva armor, which reflects the prosperity of the national strength of the Tang Dynasty and the peace of the world.

　　The painted sculpture Maharāja-deva shin armor pattern is symmetrical on both sides. The illustration is one part of the pattern, with strips on both sides as edges, which can be the corresponding front and rear shin armor. One side is diagonally connected by golden strip, which is used as a boundary to separate the upper and lower decorative spaces. A scrolling vine pattern is painted on the upper and lower parts, and the color is suitable for the whole body color.

(Written by: Gao Xue)

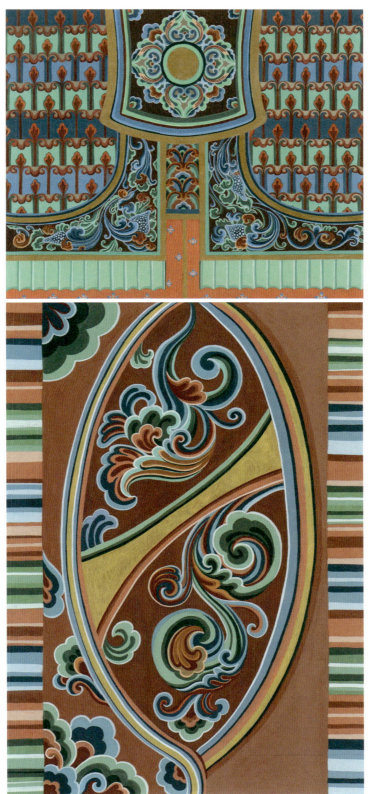

图：高雪　Painted by: Gao Xue

The Buddha's clothes
on the west side of the south wall in the main
chamber of Cave 446 dated to the high Tang
Dynasty at Mogao Grottoes

佛陀服饰
莫高窟盛唐第446窟主室
南壁西侧

此图为盛唐第446窟主室南壁西侧佛陀。

佛陀侧立身，有头光，面目圆润清秀，眼神凝注，紧闭双唇，神情庄静，法相慈和，体态丰圆，赤足立于宝座之上，意境恬淡，身后有菩萨跟随。佛陀作螺髻，"实为佛顶之肉团，高突周圆，其状如髻。……敦煌壁画和塑像中，早期佛像髻状多为波纹状，唐以后则旋于头顶，满塑颗颗卷发，呈海螺状，故名螺髻。"佛陀内着绿色僧祇支，外覆褐色通肩袈裟。袈裟从双肩垂下，并于体前形成一个大"U"形开口至腹部，露出了内穿的僧祇支。从整体上看，因袈裟的宽松以及由此形成的层层衣纹，营造出旷达洒脱、超然于世的仙人气息。

（文：赵茜、吴波）

This painting is the Buddha on the west side of the south wall in the main chamber of Cave 446 dated to the high Tang Dynasty.

The Buddha stands in the side perspective with head light; He has a round and beautiful face, eyes focused, lips closed, looks solemn, quiet, caring; He has a round body, barefoot on the stages, with tranquil artistic conception, and followed by Bodhisattvas behind. The Buddha combs a snail shell shaped hair bun, "Which is actually a meat ball on the top of the head, high and round, and its shape is like a hair bun. In Dunhuang murals and sculptures, the bun shape of early Buddha sculptures mostly have wavy lines, since the Tang Dynasty, usually as a reel on the top of the head, covered with curly hair in the shape of conch, so it is called conch bun." The Buddha has a green Sankaksika inside and a brown both shoulders covered kasaya outside. The kasaya hangs down from both shoulders and forms a large U-shape opening in front of the body to the belly, revealing the inside Sankaksika. On the whole, the loose kasaya and layers of folds create a free and immortal atmosphere.

(Written by: Zhao Xi, Wu Bo)

图: 吴波 Painted by: Wu Bo

The offering
Bodhisattva's clothes
on the west side of the south wall in the
main chamber of Cave 446 dated to the
high Tang Dynasty at Mogao Grottoes

供养菩萨服饰
莫高窟盛唐第446窟主室
南壁西侧

此为盛唐第446窟主室南壁西侧观无量寿经变中的供养菩萨。

菩萨梳高髻，有头光，戴宝冠或称三珠冠，在宝冠的中央及两侧有三颗圆形宝珠；眉眼俊秀，高鼻厚唇，戴手镯、项饰，项饰由大小不同的圆片组成。菩萨双手捧红莲置于胸前，赤足立于宝座之上。菩萨内着络腋，下着围腰和长裙。外穿天衣，天衣颇似宽幅披肩，披覆在菩萨的双肩上，轻薄的带状条帛从左右两肩垂绕两臂。天衣一面为赭红色，另一面为石绿色，围腰为深色，长裙有小散花纹样。菩萨重心稳定，姿态典雅，动静相宜。

（文：赵茜、吴波）

This offering Bodhisattva is located in the west side middle part of Amitayurdhyana Sutra illustration on the south wall of Cave 446 dated to the high Tang Dynasty.

The Bodhisattva combs a high hair bun, with head light and wears a treasure crown or so called three jewels crown. There are three round jewels in the center and on both sides of the crown. He has beautiful eyes and eyebrows, high nose, thick lips, wearing bracelets and necklace. The necklace is composed by discs of different sizes. The Bodhisattva holds the red lotus by both hands in front of chest and stands on the stages barefoot. The upper body wears Luoye inside, and the lower body wears waist wrap and a long skirt, the heavenly clothes outside, which quite like a wide silk shawl, covering the shoulders, and the thin silk ribbon hangs around the two arms from the left and right shoulders. One side of the heavenly clothes is ochre red, the other side is malachite green; the waist wrap is dark color, and the long skirt has small flower clusters. The Bodhisattva stands still, with elegant posture and balanced in movement and static.

(Written by: Zhao Xi, Wu Bo)

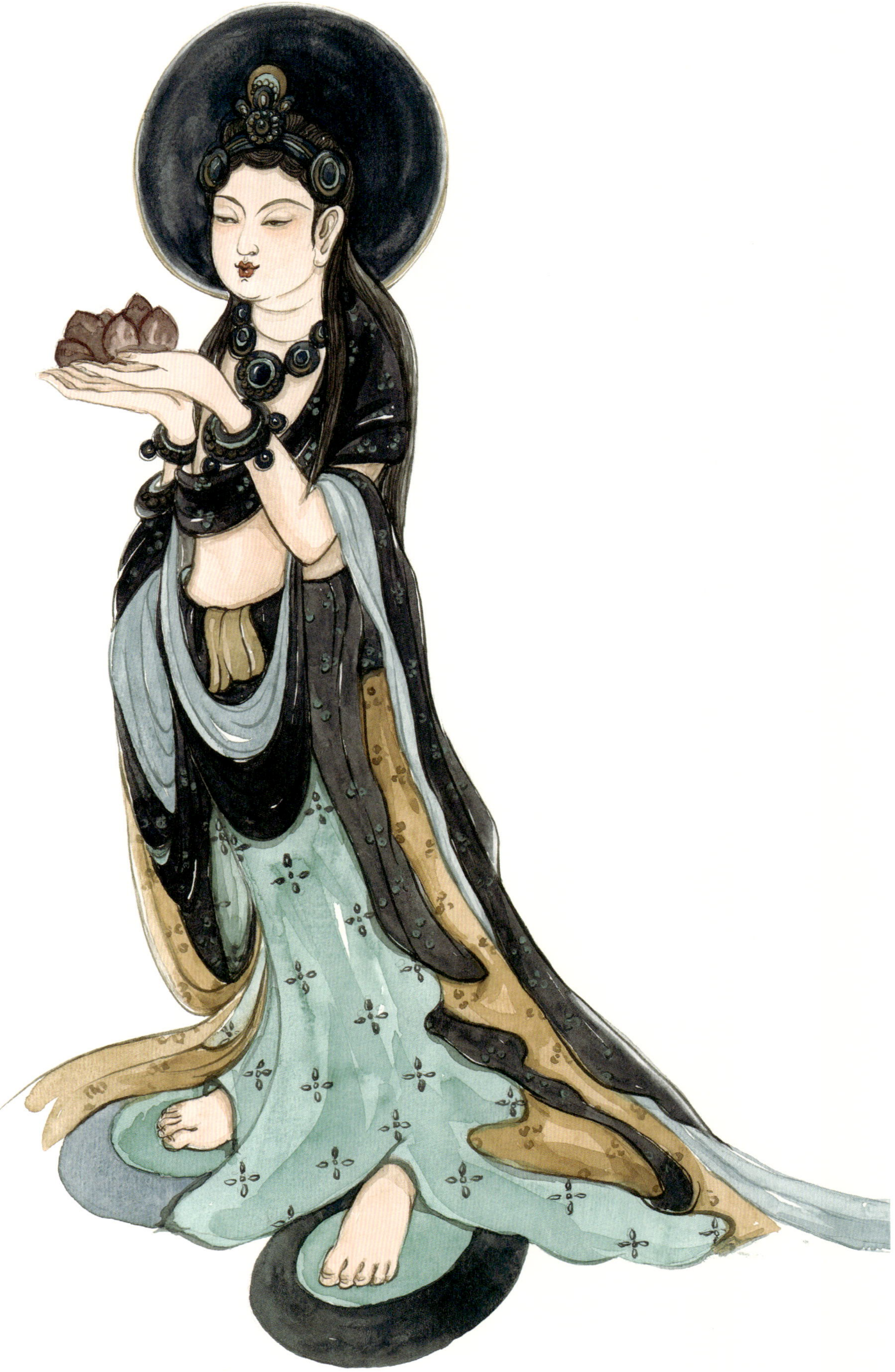

图：吴波 Painted by: Wu Bo

服装复原：楚艳、崔岩、王可

设计助理：常青、杨婧嬙、蓝津津

文字说明：崔岩、楚艳、王可

摄影：杜帅、陈大公

化妆造型：林颖、吴琼、张明星

模特：高丹丹、杨立成、[巴基斯坦] 阿里、黄洪源、王青年、王可

Costume Reproduction: Chu Yan, Cui Yan, Wang Ke

Design Assistant: Chang Qing, Yang Jingqiang, Lan Jinjin

Text: Cui Yan, Chu Yan, Wang Ke

Photo: Du Shuai, Chen Dagong

Make-up: Lin Ying, Wu Qiong, Zhang Mingxing

Models: Gao Dandan, Yang Licheng, (Pakistan)Isa Aitesam,
Huang Hongyuan, Wang Qingnian, Wang Ke

The Artistic
Reappearance of
Dunhuang Costume

敦煌服饰
艺术再现

The artistic reappearance
of the painted sculpture
Bodhisattva's clothes
Cave 194 of the high Tang Dynasty at
Mogao Grottoes

彩塑菩萨服饰艺术
再现
莫高窟盛唐第194窟

菩萨面容圆润丰腴，头挽双鬟髻，神情温婉慈祥。上身穿绿色圆领无袖襦衫，点缀红色和褐色的四簇小团花纹，领缘镶嵌贴边。下着绿底腰裙和长裙，装饰着卷草及团花纹边饰，扇纹裙带自腰部经腹部打花结垂落身前。肩部天衣飘垂并回绕于左肘，饰以可爱自然的花叶纹。整体服饰以绿色为主调，清新雅致，叠穿层次丰富，装饰繁缛，图案轮廓多有朦胧的白色边缘，推测以唐代夹缬工艺制作。菩萨优雅的姿态与华美的衣裙营造出服装的律动美感。

The Bodhisattva's face is round and plump, combed in double rings hair bun, with gentle and kind expression. His upper body is wearing a green round collar sleeveless Ru shirt, dotted with red and brown four petals little round flower pattern, and the collar edge inlaid with welt. The lower body wears a green waist wrap and a long skirt, decorated with scrolling vine and round flower pattern trim, and the fan pattern skirt band falls in front His body from the waist over the belly. The shoulders are covered with long silk scarf and winds around left elbow, which are decorated with lovely and natural flower and leaf pattern. The overall dress is green based, fresh and elegant, with rich layers of overlapping and complex decoration. The outline of the patterns used hazy white edges, which is speculated made by tie-dye technique in the Tang Dynasty. The Bodhisattva's elegant posture and gorgeous dress created a rhythmic beauty of clothing.

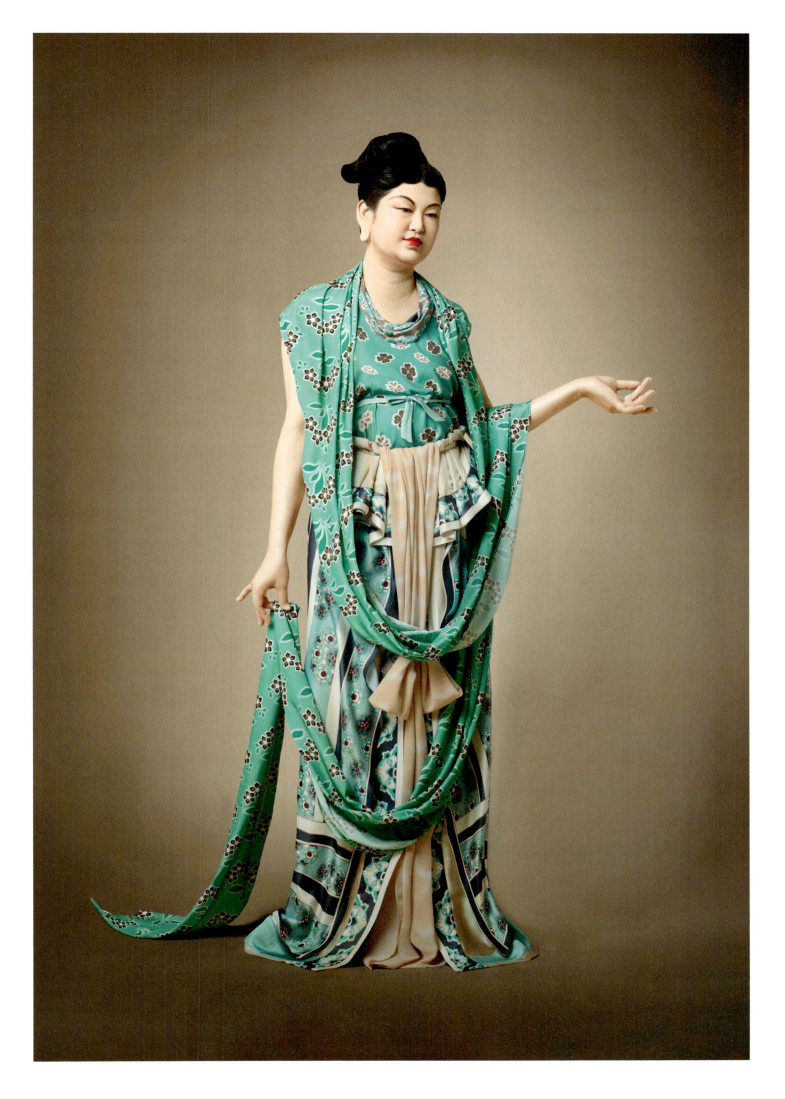

这位异域王子红发梳髻、须髯飘扬、体毛浓密，戴头饰、颈圈、手镯、足钏。其服饰由整块面料缠绕围裹而成，具有明显的东南亚及南亚地区服饰的特征。上衣通肩总覆，下着"敢曼"，面料采用伊卡特传统工艺制作，上身所裹面料图案以沙黄色为地，间以石绿色的"S"形和蓝色的"Z"形纹样；下身服饰图案分别以浅青色和褐色为地，主体纹样为石青色或石绿色的"S"形，呈现出扎经染色织物特有的朦胧美感。

The foreign prince has red hair and combed into a hair bun, long beard and thick body hair, wearing a headdress, neck ring, bracelets and foot bracelets. His clothes is a whole piece of cloth wrapped around the body, which has obvious Southeast Asia and South Asia clothing characteristics. The upper body is covered including two shoulders, the lower body wears "Gan man". The fabric is made by the traditional Ikat technique. The upper body clothes is sand yellow as background, decorated with malachite green "S" shape and blue "Z" shape patterns. The lower body clothes has light cyan and brown backgrounds, and the main pattern is azurite and malachite green "S" shape, showing the unique hazy beauty of tie-dye fabrics.

异域王子服饰艺术再现

莫高窟盛唐第194窟

此身昆仑王子体壮肤黑，头顶蓬松卷发，戴颈圈、臂钏、手镯、足钏，其服饰同样以不加裁剪的面料缠裹而成。上身斜缠披帛，下身缠绕出及膝短裤的样式。伊卡特纹样与前图类似，体现出鲜明的地域特征。

This Kunlun prince is strong and dark, with fluffy curly hair. He wears a neck ring, armlets, bracelets and foot bracelets, the clothes are also untrimmed cloth wrapped around the body. The upper body is diagonally covered with a silk scarf, and the lower body is wrapped with knee length shorts style. The Ikat pattern is similar to the previous figure, reflecting a distinct regional characteristic.

The artistic reappearance of
foreign prince's clothes
Cave 194 of the high Tang Dynasty at Mogao
Grottoes

异域王子服饰艺术
再现
莫高窟盛唐第194窟

此位王子体态丰腴，蓄络腮胡须，气宇轩昂。他头戴镂花皮革制高冠，身着石绿色缺胯圆领袍、面料较为厚重；腰系革带，带上有带銙装饰，体现了游牧民族服饰较为紧身利落、适于骑射的特点。

This prince s plump, bearded and dignified. He wears a high crown made by carved leather and a malachite green round collar robe with thick fabrics. Leather belt is tied at the waist with decoration, which reflects the tight and neat characteristics of nomadic clothes suitable for riding and shooting.

异域王子服饰艺术
再现
莫高窟盛唐第194窟

此王子披发垂于脑后，头戴笼状镂空高冠，身着石青色右衽大袖上衣，领口与袖口均有宽大的边饰，装饰以联珠花纹二方连续图案，下面搭配宽松肥大的浅米色长裙和石绿色围裳，裙前饰有绿褐相间的层叠式蔽膝，足着尖头靴。虽然整体沿袭了汉族传统的上衣下裳式服制，但是人物束辫发和戴高冠等细节透露出明显的异域风情。

The prince's hair hangs at the back of his head. He wears a cage shaped hollow high crown and a large sleeved malachite green right lapel upper clothes, and the collar and cuffs both have wide trims, which are decorated with beads pattern two in a group repeated. The lower body matched with a loose and big light beige skirt and malachite green apron. In front of the apron hanging a green and brown layered knee covering and feet in pointed boots. Although the traditional Han nationality clothes style upper Yi and lower Chang was adopted, the braided hair and high crown revealed an obvious foreign style.

The artistic reappearance
of foreign prince's clothes
Cave 194 of the high Tang Dynasty at
Mogao Grottoes

异域王子服饰艺术
再现
莫高窟盛唐第194窟

此位王子头戴尖顶立檐帽，内穿圆领褐色上襦，外罩交领右衽的窄袖翻领缺胯长袍，翻领处为石绿色内里，与深红色的袍面形成鲜明的色彩对比。其腰间系革带，带銙开孔悬垂皮带，随身吊挂着一柄弯刀，显示出游牧民族特有的生活习惯。

The prince wears a pointed hat with upturned brim, and a brown round collar upper Ru inside. The outer covers a narrow sleeved right lapel cross collar robe with slits. The lapels have malachite green inner lining, which formed a sharp color contrast with the dark red robe. The leather belt is tied around his waist, perforated and suspended leather belts, hanging a machete, showing the special living habit of nomads.

The artistic reappearance
of the Avalokitesvara
Bodhisattva's clothes
Cave 199 of the high Tang Dynasty at
Mogao Grottoes

观世音菩萨服饰艺
术再现

莫高窟盛唐第199窟

这尊观世音菩萨的形象端庄秀美，含情脉脉。因原壁画中人物服饰色彩已大部分变黑，因此在进行复原时参考同时期壁画人物形象进行了合理推测。菩萨头戴火焰形化佛冠，身披璎珞，上身穿绿色右袒式僧祇支，边缘有半团花二方连续纹样装饰，围腰袱，系有精美的嵌红蓝宝石腰带。下着绿色腰裙和深红色散花长裙，裙摆处镶饰红色或蓝色贴边，并配有红色裙带在膝部打花结垂至身前。肩披青色丝质天衣，交互搭于两臂弯后垂下，使整套服饰动感十足，飘飘欲仙。

This Avalokitesvara Bodhisattva image looks dignified, beautiful and caring. Because the most colors of the clothes in the original murals have turned into black, reasonable speculation was made referring to the same period mural images. The Bodhisattva wears a flame shaped Buddha image crown, and keyūra on body, a green right shoulder bared Sankaksika on the upper body, semi round flower pattern two in a group repeated on the trim, waist cloth, and an exquisite belt inlaid with ruby and sapphire. The lower body wears a green waist wrap and a long crimson floral shaped skirt, with red and blue rims at the hem, and matched with red skirt band with a flower knot at the knee hanging in front of the body. He wears a cyan silk scarf on the shoulders, which are held by the crook of the arms then falls down, making the whole set of clothes dynamic and celestial.

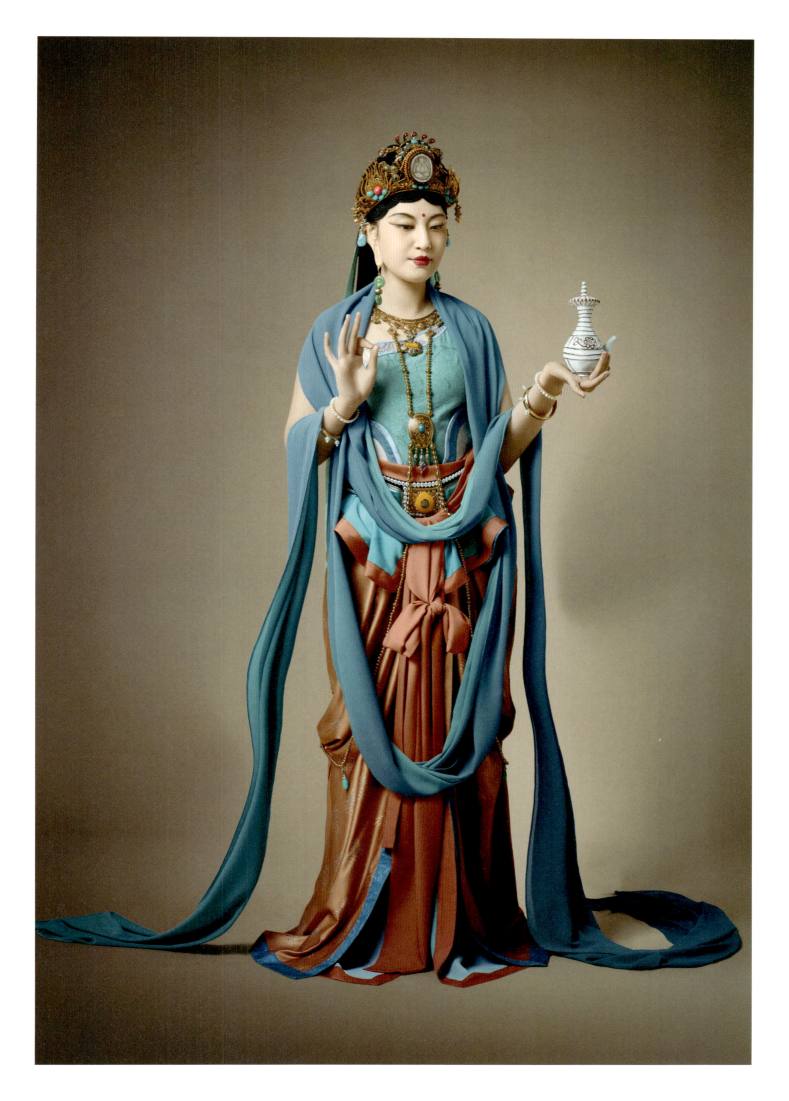